TOWARD A THEOLOGY
OF INVOLVEMENT

Toward
a Theology
of Involvement

The Thought
of
Ernst Troeltsch

by
BENJAMIN A. REIST

Philadelphia
THE WESTMINSTER PRESS

LIBRARY OF CONGRESS CATALOG CARD NO. 66–11919

Acknowledgment is made to the following:

Beacon Press, Inc., for extensive quotations from Troeltsch, *Gesammelte Schriften*, Vols. I–IV, Verlag von J. C. B. Mohr (Paul Siebeck), Tübingen.

Harper & Row, Publishers, Inc., for quotations from Martin E. Marty, *Second Chance for American Protestants* (1963).

The Macmillan Company, for quotations from Max Weber, *The Methodology of the Social Sciences,* tr. and ed. by Edward A. Shils and Henry A. Finch (1949).

J. C. B. Mohr (Paul Siebeck), Tübingen, for permission to translate passages from *Die wissenschaftliche Lage und ihre Anforderungen an die Theologie* and *Die Bedeutung der Geschichtlichkeit Jesu für den Glauben.*

B. G. Teubner, Stuttgart, for quotations from " Protestantisches Christentum und Kirche in der Neuzeit " in *Kultur der Gegenwart,* herausgegeben von Paul Hinneberg (Berlin and Leipzig, 1906).

The World Publishing Company, for quotations from Troeltsch, *Christian Thought* (Meridian, 1957).

Published by The Westminster Press®
Philadelphia, Pennsylvania

PRINTED IN THE UNITED STATES OF AMERICA

To Harriet

Contents

◈ ◈

Preface

◆ ◆

This study had its origins in research for my doctoral dissertation at Princeton Theological Seminary under Prof. Paul L. Lehmann. The dissertation, submitted in 1958, was the initial result of the attempt to deal comprehensively with the thought of Ernst Troeltsch. My interest in Troeltsch's thought did not come to an end with the doctoral work. It has expanded in many ways since then, for it has become increasingly evident that his labors deserve much more prolonged consideration than they have been customarily accorded, particularly in the light of the directions in which theological conversation is now moving. Both for his early inspiration and his continued encouragement over the years, in this and many other respects, I owe incalculable debts of gratitude to Professor Lehmann.

My thanks are due to the American Association of Theological Schools and the Sealantic Fund, and to the Board of Trustees and the Faculty of San Francisco Theological Seminary, which made possible my sabbatic leave during the academic year 1963–1964. The year in Basel, Switzerland, was richly rewarding for its contacts with Karl Barth, as well as for the opportunity to begin work on this manuscript.

I have deliberately avoided dialogue with the works of others in connection with this effort to set out the thought of Ernst Troeltsch. This is not because these are insignificant by any means. However, the problem in the English-speaking world is that the thought of Troeltsch is simply not considered on the broad spectrum across which it moves. Though there have been many incisive treatments of Troeltsch in English, these are all restricted in scope. The only comprehensive discussion we have is R. S. Sleigh's remarkable *The Sufficiency of Christianity* (1923), and even this work has severe limitations. It was written before *Der Historismus und seine Probleme* (Historical Relativism and Its Problems), 1922, could be given close attention. Sleigh was able to note this massive study only in passing, with the result that he could not take into account the final outcome of Troeltsch's labors. The thought of Troeltsch as a whole now demands new attention, and hopefully my efforts are a beginning step in that direction.

Throughout this study the translations of Troeltsch's formulations are entirely my own. I have indicated at many points in the notes my disagreement with those translations of Troeltsch's works which we do have. These disagreements are often severe, and are clearly indicated as such. Accordingly, I wish to pay my respects here to the work of those who have struggled to put Troeltsch's German into English. Particularly, of course, I salute Olive Wyon for the massive undertaking nearly forty years ago of translating *The Social Teachings*. I have been driven to reject radically many of her renderings, but let it be said that my efforts to understand the thought of Ernst Troeltsch had their beginnings with the translation which must have cost her endless hours of scholarly labor.

This work owes more than can be stated to the rich association that it has been my privilege to have with my senior colleague in Systematic Theology, Prof. Arnold B. Come, Dean of the Faculty of San Francisco Theological Seminary. He has willingly listened at length to my attempts to refine such insights into the significance of the thought of Troeltsch as I may have achieved, and he has always encouraged my efforts with his own grasp of the present theological situation. Similar debts of gratitude can only be acknowledged — they can never be repaid — regarding the friendship and scholarly companionship of Profs. Aaron J. Ungersma and Neill Q. Hamilton. Finally, Prof. Martin Anton Schmidt has always been more than willing to interrupt his work in order to help me find my way through the labyrinth of Troeltsch's complicated German. I alone am responsible for the errors of translation that exist; at the same time, there are more than a few fine points that he has enabled me to see.

BENJAMIN A. REIST

San Anselmo, California
August, 1965

1 Introduction

❖ ❖

It will come as no surprise to those who have worked with the thought of Ernst Troeltsch that comprehensive theological analyses of his concerns should make their appearance now. To those who have not pondered him at length it may come as a very questionable enterprise. Why bother returning to Troeltsch now?

There is an obvious initial answer to this question. A full-scale consideration of the thought of this figure is overdue simply on the ground of the basic sensitivity to the history of doctrine that all theology must have. There are good reasons why such treatments are few in number. Most significant of these is the complexity of his writings. He published only two major works, *Die Soziallehren der christlichen Kirchen und Gruppen* (The Social Teachings of the Christian Churches and Groups) in 1912, and *Der Historismus und seine Probleme* (Historical Relativism and Its Problems) in 1922. The remainder of his vast literary output exists in the form of monographs, journal articles, contributions to various encyclopedias, and book reviews. The problem with Troeltsch is that all these must be considered before a penetrating theological analysis of his thought is possible. For the English-speaking theological community this problem is intensified by the fact that the bulk of these writings, including, of course, many of the most significant pieces, neither has been nor will be translated.

There is, however, a much more basic answer to our question. The most cogent theological reasons for a new consideration of Troeltsch's efforts have only recently appeared. Troeltsch died abruptly at the height of his intellectual powers on the first of February, 1923, at the age of fifty-seven. His work had not known its final fruition. Indeed, it is debatable on several grounds whether it ever would have, even had he lived. The theological revolution, which was to challenge so drastically and permanently the intellectual milieu Troeltsch presupposed, was under way and gathering momentum in the year of his death. The reformulation that would have then been necessary if his concerns were to be given their due could probably never have been developed by him, despite his astonishing intellectual equipment.

Such reformulation is now both possible and needed. We hear much these days about the so-called post-Christian era in the midst of which theological effort must now unfold. The idea has been most trenchantly articulated by Dietrich Bonhoeffer in his brief but unforgettable reflections on " the come of age world." [1] The most interesting thing about Troeltsch is that he was one of the first to give serious theological attention to the problem that Bonhoeffer would later struggle to clarify. No one before him, and few since, have given it such massive and penetrating consideration. The most significant thing about Troeltsch is that his efforts to meet this problem both shattered his own theological position and, at the same time, yielded a perspective that is indispensable for understanding both the past and the present efforts of the church to make its gospel clear in and to its time. There are astonishing theological implications in what he saw, and in the way that he saw it. Now, in the light of the constructive developments that have shaped theological reflection in the four decades since his death, we must begin to wrestle with these implications in ways of which Troeltsch himself would never have dreamed. There can be no question of a " return " to Troeltsch, as if nothing had happened in the world of theological reflection since his death. It would be grossly irresponsible, however, especially in the context of the debates that now preoccupy theological exchange, to ignore his work. Notwithstanding the pivotal significance of this figure for the sociology of religion, to assume that this is his only lasting contribution is to do precisely that. For such a conclusion either overlooks or fails to understand that the basic problems with which he was concerned were theological in character, and are capable of solution only on theological ground.

The biographical details of Troeltsch's life have been succinctly sketched by Baron Friedrich von Hügel, his friend and the editor both of the German edition and of the English translation of the lectures that he wrote for delivery in England, and that he completed shortly before his death in 1923. In the introduction to the English translation, von Hügel wrote as follows:

> Ernst Troeltsch's antecedents, environment, and career may be stated in a few words. He sprang from an ancient burgher family, settled for centuries in the Lausitz between Swabia and Bavaria, and more recently at Nürnberg and Augsburg in Bavaria itself. His father was a physician practicing in Augsburg, and there the eldest son, Ernst, was born in 1865. From 1883 to 1888 he studied Protestant Theology at Erlangen, Göttingen, and Berlin, and was most influenced by Albrecht Ritschl. He next

served for some time as an Evangelical (Lutheran) curate in Munich; became Lecturer at Göttingen in 1891, Extraordinary Professor in Bonn University in 1892; and already in 1894 obtained the Ordinary (full) Professorship of Systematic Theology at Heidelberg, where he remained 21 years. There he wrote almost all his abidingly important minor works, and especially his only complete, large, and now standard, book, *The Social Teachings of the Christian Churches and Groups* (1912) ; and whilst there he sat for many years as an elected member in the Baden Upper House.[2]

Baron von Hügel noted that Troeltsch was married in the spring of 1901, and that his only child, Ernst Eberhard, was born in July of 1913. He then continued:

At Easter 1915 he succeeded in Berlin to the Philosophical Chair of Otto Pfleiderer and Edvin Lehmann; and there he lectured on the Philosophy of Religion, Ethics, Philosophy of General Civilization, Introduction to Philosophy, History of Modern Philosophy, and Philosophy of History. From 1919 to 1921 he was a member of the Prussian Landtag and Under-Secretary of State in the Ministry of Public Worship.[3]

As von Hügel went on to note, Troeltsch " just lived to see published the concluding part of the first volume of his second large work," *Der Historismus und seine Probleme* (Historical Relativism and Its Problems) .[4]

The widely scattered and diversified writings of Ernst Troeltsch almost defy any all-encompassing organization. His first published work, the extensive elaboration of his Göttingen dissertation, *Vernunft und Offenbarung bei J. Gerhard und Melanchthon* (Reason and Revelation in [the thought of] Gerhard and Melanchthon) , appeared in 1891. The definitive edition of his celebrated *The Social Teachings* appeared in 1912.[5] During this twenty-one-

year span he had written some forty important monographs and articles, many of which were of substantial
length, plus numerous minor articles and reviews. He first
gave precise formulation to the underlying unity of this
welter of literary activity in the Foreword to *The Social
Teachings*. The integrating principle of his research, he
noted, should be clearly recognizable as the result of his
training under Ritschl, whose concern to grasp and combine both the dogmatic tradition and the modern spiritual
and religious situation had evoked his own twofold interest: the analysis of classical Protestantism (*Altprotes-
tantismus*) and the analysis of the modern world. Troeltsch
regarded this twofold research as intrinsic to " the solution of the systematic task." As he moved on immediately
to delineate it, the systematic task is " to think through
and formulate independently the Christian world of
ideas and life *with unreserved involvement in the modern world*." [6] Thus Troeltsch's endeavors revolved around
three foci: (1) the probing of the past, particularly classical Protestantism, (2) the attempt to grasp as precisely as
possible the profiles of the contemporary, modern world,
and (3) in the light of these insights, and in a way that
continually nourished the passion to broaden and perfect
them, the attempt to think through and articulate what
might be called the theology of involvement.

The most widely known and influential of all
Troeltsch's works is *The Social Teachings,* and it will
probably always be regarded as the high point of his literary activity as a whole. His researches, however, did not
come to an end with this study, and any intensive investigation of his thought will be completely undermined if it
treats as the *terminus ad quem* of his writing what actually
was only the halfway mark. At first glance his move in 1915

from the chair in dogmatics at Heidelberg to a chair in philosophy at Berlin is misleading. This manifests his increasing preoccupation with the second of the three foci we have just noted — a preoccupation that culminated with his second major work, the massive though incomplete *Der Historismus und seine Probleme* (Historical Relativism and Its Problems). However, throughout this period neither the first nor the third of his concerns was completely missing. Above all, any penetrating understanding of the end product of his *theological* thought must reckon with his reflections in Berlin as well as those in Heidelberg. As we shall see, the fact is that the struggle with historical relativism was generated by insight into the whole sweep of the development of Christian thought. It is not too much to say that in this struggle Troeltsch envisioned ultimately, or at least yearned for, a new clarification of what it means to speak religiously for religion in the midst of the modern world. Accordingly, it is possible to consider the whole range of his writings in terms of the threefold concern that is spelled out in the Foreword of *The Social Teachings*.[7]

As one considers Troeltsch's writings as a whole, one is faced with a vast welter of activity in which issues emerge and are confronted, only to generate new problems and lead to new frontiers of investigation. One looks in vain for a completely articulated and interrelated system in this material. In one way or another this is true of any thinker worthy of extended consideration. In the case of Troeltsch, however, the problem is intensified by the fact that his own version of ultimate questions was continually taking shape as his thinking developed simultaneously along each of the three lines we have noted. Furthermore, these questions always defied solution on the only ground Troeltsch was willing to call his own. That he was neither reluctant nor ashamed to indicate this explicitly is the measure of the astonishing integrity that he brought to his tasks. To discern all this we must move through the content of his thought along each of these three lines, and we must do so as comprehensively as possible, with the entire spectrum of his labors before us. The questions that he reached at the far horizon of his thought have yet to be answered. Indeed, one of the most illuminating ways to deal with the issues that now confront Protestant theology in these middle decades of our century is to ponder them in the light of the unanswered problems that Troeltsch has left us.

In considering the thought of Troeltsch, we shall turn first to the second focus of his concerns, since it is from the analysis of the modern world that his methodological reflections were derived (Chapters 2, 3, and 4). When this is clear, we shall be able to discern the principal findings of his analysis of classical Protestantism, and of the Christian tradition at large (Chapter 5). Against the background of each of these we shall then review the development of his theology and chart its collapse (Chapter 6). The legacy of his labors will then be before us (Chapter 7).

2 The Modern Spirit and the Question of Methodology

❖   ❖

The constant factor in Troeltsch's understanding of the modern world may be simply stated: The modern world had its beginning in the Enlightenment, and not in the Protestant Reformation.

This view was succinctly expressed in a late and revealing essay entitled *Meine Bücher* (My Books), which Troeltsch wrote in 1922. He noted that in his first work, the study of the thought of Johann Gerhard and Philip Melanchthon, he had independently arrived at a conclusion that he shared with Wilhelm Dilthey, namely, that the thought of the Reformation is basically medieval in character. This conclusion raised the broader question as to the dating of the rise of the modern intellectual situation as a whole. This situation he defined as " an autonomous and worldly formation and culture," to be sharply distinguished from the " theologically bound " culture of the medieval period. Now, just when was this " autonomous and worldly formation and culture " achieved? For Troeltsch, " The answer to my studies was ' at the time of the Enlightenment.' " [1]

This " answer to my studies " was one that emerged early in his thinking. In 1897 he began his article on *Die Aufklärung* (The Enlightenment) for the third edition of the *Realencyklopädie für protestantische Theologie und Kirche* with a categorical assertion of the point:

> The Enlightenment is the beginning and foundation of the intrinsically modern period of European culture and history, in contrast to the hitherto regnant ecclesiastically and theologically determined culture.[2]

Throughout the whole of his writings Troeltsch never deserted this contention. It informs his understanding of the modern situation. Out of this understanding grew the methodology in terms of which he worked out the massive argument of *The Social Teachings*. We shall treat these in turn.

1. THE MODERN WORLD

Troeltsch's writings contain many delineations of the emergence and nature of the modern world. He was convinced that the movements of thought that gave rise to the spirit of the Enlightenment completely condition modern reflection in all its spheres, including, of course, the theological realm. The decisive early work in this connection was his discussion of " the scientific situation [3] and its claims on theology " (*Die wissenschaftliche Lage und ihre Anforderungen an die Theologie*), which appeared in 1900.

The discussion begins with the assertion of the generally recognized fact of the decline in modern man's interest in traditional Christianity. Troeltsch noted that this is all-pervasive, involving both Catholicism and Protestantism, and actually amounts to an ultimate rejection, calling into question Christianity itself. He argued that the root of this decline is to be found in the " colossal revolution " that has occurred in modern thought. He characterized this as

" a profound change of mood" (*jener tiefe Stimmungs-wechsel*) involving " the fundamental transformation of human knowledge, both in its methods and in its results." [4]

The crucial element in Troeltsch's argument now emerges. The rise of modern thought has radically questioned the conception of the relationship between Christian belief and human knowledge in general which has been in operation for centuries. According to the traditional view these had been regarded as harmoniously related. Human knowledge in general had been understood as the *natural* knowledge of God and morality, in contrast to the " supernaturally communicated and effective revelation of the Church and its Holy Scripture." [5] What was involved was simply the " confrontation of supernatural and natural knowledge as two basically homogeneous dimensions of knowledge " (*zweier prinzipiell gleichartiger Erkenntnismassen*) . [6] Troeltsch observed that it was in terms of this understanding that the vexatious question of the relationship between faith and reason had always been debated. Sometimes revelation was understood in terms of reason, sometimes reason in terms of revelation, the accent falling upon either the contradiction between the two, or their basic agreement. But whatever the case might be, at the root of the whole struggle, whenever and wherever it developed, this fundamental conception was to be found. For it had room both for " the hatred of reason on the part of a Tertullian, an Augustine, an Ockham, and a Luther, and the enthusiasm for reason of an Origen, a Thomas, or a Zwingli." [7]

Now it is precisely this conception of the harmonious and homogeneous relationship between natural and supernatural knowledge that fell before the onslaughts of modern thought. For Troeltsch, this was evident in that modern thought most emphatically rejects the notion that it is another way of knowing God. The proof of the matter is apparent in the fact that for modern thought religion itself is properly a subject for observation and comment, precisely as are all the other phenomena that make up human experience and accordingly come before human scrutiny. The basic change in the scientific situation has challenged once and for all the relationship between faith and knowledge, since the former is now capable of investigation by the latter with no reservations whatsoever. Troeltsch was willing to put the matter that forcefully. " Science," he baldly asserted, " does not produce religion — it comprehends it. It is not a parallel to religion; it is not another way of knowing God." It rather has to do with " the conceptual unification of reality," and religion, just as " countless other sections of reality," is capable of precisely this treatment.[8]

The implications of all this were far-reaching for Troeltsch. From the very outset they were at least twofold. The distinction between natural knowledge and supernatural knowledge must be discarded, because it presupposes an understanding of thought in general that no longer obtains. Any self-understanding on the part of Christianity in any of its forms that is based on this distinction, insofar as there is implied a self-evident connection between faith and knowledge in general, must fall. Troeltsch argued that this is the claim on theology coming from the side of the scientific situation. As he saw it, theology is being challenged to make itself intelligible apart from this distinction and all that it implies. This is the challenge that he took up in the remainder of this discussion, with his plea for the development of a *scientific* theology. It is not an overstatement to say that the whole of his thought from this time forward reflects the position he began to elaborate in this discussion in 1900. Either directly or indirectly, explicitly or implicitly, the view that to think theologically as a modern man presupposes the fact that the distinction between the natural and the supernatural is no longer cogent is to be found on every page he wrote. This was his way of reckoning with the fact that the older apologetic is dead. It is astonishing that to this extent he anticipated so much of the mood of that drastically different theological reflection which would soon assault and overcome the theological temperament of the nineteenth century.

At the same time, Troeltsch was clear that his view had important implications for the other side of the coin. If science does not produce religion, if it is not another way of knowing God, then the scientific investigation of religion (*Religionswissenschaft*) must not be confused with either theology or the philosophy of religion. It was Troeltsch's contention that this was continually happening, and that accordingly the *scientific* character of the scientific investigation of religion was being undermined. He argued this in an extended discussion of " the essence of religion and the scientific study of religion " (" Wesen der Religion und der Religionswissenschaft "), which he contributed to the symposium *Die Kultur der Gegenwart* (The Culture of the Present) in 1906.[9] Here he insisted that the proper subject matter of the scientific investigation of religion lies between the theological and philosophical poles and is phenomenological in character. Its decisive questions have to do with " the essence of religious phenomena, the content of truth and knowledge in these phenomena, and the value and significance of the great historical structures of religion." [10] This is what it means to say, as he puts it in this essay, that the scientific investigation of religion " thus does not bring forth religion, and does not produce the true religion, but analyzes and evaluates the given religiosity." [11]

Such was the manner in which Troeltsch began the task of taking the measure of the modern world and coming to terms with it. As we shall see, this dimension of his thought is always present. It receives vast elaboration as his work unfolds. These elaborations, however, invariably add to the cogency of his early arguments. They never destroy that basic sensitivity to the modern situation that is already before us.

2. THE METHODOLOGY OF " THE SOCIAL TEACHINGS "

Certainly the most impressive and important yield of Troeltsch's understanding of the modern situation is his celebrated portrayal of the history of Christian social thought and the attendant clarification of the nature of Christianity's involvement in the modern world that is its result. In itself this work is enough to assure him an honored place in the history of Christian thought, since he who would understand the history of the Christian ethic and the massive challenge on the social front persistently facing Christianity in all its forms must begin here. It goes without saying that one cannot stop with Troeltsch, but the road beyond him lies through him, and this is so primarily because of what he achieved in this, his best-known work.

This book is complicated and extremely problematical. It has always been subjected to severe criticism for a reason often noted. Roland Bainton's observation, for example, is typical. Speaking of the manner in which Troeltsch wrote *The Social Teachings,* he says:

> The procedure of Troeltsch consisted in an effort to reconstruct the characteristic marks of Christianity in particular epochs and cultures, and then to compare the one manifestation with the other. He made no pretense of an exhaustive acquaintance with the sources. His procedure was rather to take the best dozen or so books for each period and out of these to construct a picture of the dominant characteristics. The method has its obvious limitations. Any work so executed is bound to be subject to the fire of specialists. Yet there is scarcely any other way in which a sweeping synthesis can be achieved. This only must be borne in mind that conclusions reached in such a fashion must ever be regarded as tentative, and a work like that of Troeltsch should be canonized rather for its methodolgy than for its positive conclusions.[12]

Insofar as it refers to Troeltsch's procedure in this work, Bainton's statement may be taken as an accurate reflection of the facts of the case, and it gives ample indication of the broad spectrum of vulnerability to which Troeltsch opened himself with the publication of *The Social Teachings.* However, procedure and methodology are not quite the same things, and the methodology for which Troeltsch is to be canonized is anything but simply the summing up of secondary sources regarding the history of Christian social thought. The real problem is that of *the precise basis of comparison* whereby the characteristic marks of Christianity in one epoch or culture are to be juxtaposed with those of another epoch or culture. Troeltsch found this basis of comparison in what he came to call " the sociological formulation of the question." [13] He introduced it briefly in the Foreword, and spelled out in detail the elements of his idea in the "Introduction and Preliminary Questions of Method" with which the work commences.

In the Foreword of *The Social Teachings,* Troeltsch asserted the inescapably ethical character of the problem of the present for Christianity in all its forms. If, he argued, Christianity is primarily a matter of practice, then it is in the practical sphere that the key issues of the present are to be found, for it is here that the most difficult complications and contradictions arise, and it is here that the precariousness of the involvement of Christianity in the modern world is most apparent. " Particularly as over against the claims of the contemporary social ethic the ethic of the Church is obsolete." [14] This was no hasty assumption for Troeltsch. Two decades of research and reflection lie behind *The Social Teachings.* He was now willing to state concisely the options that indicated what he regarded to be the only real possibilities in the present. The rise of the modern world evokes a new understanding of the Christian frame of reference at large. The question now is that of the relationship between such new understanding and Christianity's ancient form of organization, the church. Can a new understanding be " grafted onto " this ancient organization? If not, what in general are the possibilities for new structural developments within Christianity? [15] This was what Troeltsch sought to clarify by " the sociological formulation of the question."

The argument begun in the Foreword was carried to its full development in the introductory, methodological section. Troeltsch noted that the involvement of the churches and religious groups in the social struggles of the modern scene raised two specific problems. On the one hand there was the question of the *usefulness* of such activity. On the other hand, there was the question of the *basis* of this activity. Troeltsch desisted from discussing the former of these on the ground of his lack of competence. Specialized technical knowledge and skills would be necessary for valid analysis of this question, and Troeltsch made no pretense to be expert in such procedures. The latter problem, however, raises the historical question, since Christianity is primarily a historical phenomenon. This Troeltsch did undertake to discuss since such analysis is the proper concern of theologians and the historians of religion. Given the nature of the question before him, he proposed to do this by utilizing as thoroughly as possible the theoretical insights to which his contemporaries had moved in the still young but rapidly developing field of social science.

The linchpin of the methodology of *The Social Teachings* is the conception of " the social " that Troeltsch appropriated entirely from the social scientists, whom he regarded as having reached a consensus on the meaning of the obviously central category of their discipline.[16] The concept takes its rise from the initial and basic distinction between those relationships, on the one hand, that are decisively political in character and that are consequently ordered by the state, and those relationships, on the other hand, that are not of a political nature but that are nevertheless discernible within the nexus of the observable sociological phenomena at large. The term " social " designates the latter of these.[17] For Troeltsch, this distinction generated a clarity that was twofold. First, to reverse the order in which he presented this, in the light of this distinction the term " society " achieved a precision that overcame the abstract, meaningless aura usually surrounding it. Secondly, the distinction made possible a clear conceptualization of the interaction between the political and the social. Following the lead of his contemporaries,

Troeltsch termed this interaction "the social problem."
This conceptualization enabled him not only to delineate
precisely the problematic of Christian social thought and
action, but also to suggest what was for him the absolutely
necessary method by which alone the dynamic of the historical development of Christianity is to be penetrated and
understood. We shall deal with each of these in turn.

Basic to the distinction between the political and the
social is the precision that the latter is meant to have.
"The Social" refers to nonpolitical, or indirectly political, but nevertheless observable phenomena. Troeltsch
noted with disdain that "society" is something that can be
discussed without qualification only by dilettantes. It was
his contention, of course, that Christian thinkers are all
too often major offenders in this regard. What he was insisting on was the view that the social is that part of the
general sociological context which is empirically discernible. He noted that there is no conception of society which
parallels that of mechanics, for example, in the realm of
natural science, which can subsume all the particular phenomena in question. Society is too historical in character
for that. The conception of society never exhausts the general area connoted by the term. To think that it does is to
conceive an abstraction about which no scientific discussion is possible. Thus he argued, "This means for our case
that 'society' and the 'social,' in the sense of contemporary problems, are only an especially important part,
strongly emphasized by the situation, of the general sociological context, not the context itself." [18] Throughout his
study, his use of these two terms reflects this narrower, and
concrete, conception.

This conception of the social carried with it a delineation of the social problem that is likewise precise and con-

crete. The social problem is simply defined as that of the relation between the political community and the social phenomena. The latter are at root nonpolitical; they are nevertheless significant from the political point of view. The social problem thus eventuates from the political task of controlling and coordinating the social. This was pivotal for Troeltsch. In arguing that only the concrete meaning of the term " society " may be employed, he was asserting that the scientific analysis of Christian social thought has to do with that thought generated by Christianity itself with reference to the social problem as it is thus delineated. He was obviously thus assuming that the relationship between Christianity in any of its forms and social problems is a relationship that takes place in terms of factors not all of which are generated by or under the dominance of Christianity itself. The corollary of this assumption is close at hand: The involvement of Christianity in any of its forms in the realm of social problems is only one of many factors included within this realm.

With the conceptual basis of the methodology of *The Social Teachings* now before us we may set out in four steps the key elements and implications of this methodology itself. In the *first* place, *the sociological formulation of the question* may now be stated in detail. Troeltsch defined *Christian social doctrine* as Christian teaching concerning the most important nonreligious sociological structures. In the language of Christianity itself, this is its doctrine of " its relation to the most powerful formations of the ' world.' " [19] Thus, when one studies the history of Christian thought with an eye toward discerning the emergent Christian understanding of the world and the relationship of Christian structures to it, one is in fact tracing the history of Christian social doctrine. This definition is the formulation upon which *The Social Teachings* takes its rise. Troeltsch did not hesitate to indicate the ultimate problem it envisions. If, he argued, the state and society, in their interrelationship, have always been the dominant forces in the shaping of civilization, then the implication is that the church has had a role to play in this evolution only when and insofar as it has moved in collusion with these forces. Accordingly, the question is: "How can the Church go hand in hand with these key forces in such a way that a unity of culture will emerge?"[20]

From the standpoint of strictly theological reflection one can hardly imagine a more vulnerable question than this one. However, it must always be remembered that in *The Social Teachings* Troeltsch was not attempting to develop a purely theological argument. The cogency of this question is dependent upon the manner in which he proposed to deal with the history of Christian social thought. From this standpoint the question as formulated does not foreclose theological reflection as much as might be thought at first glance. Given the scientific facts regarding the formative and dominant role of the political-social interrelationship, the consequence is that the extent to which Christianity in its manifold forms has had a *cultural* significance is directly related to the extent to which it has brought its own unique faith to bear on the social problem, in Troeltsch's sense of the terms. As we shall see, the final result of his reflections, both in *The Social Teachings* and in his writings as a whole, was an increasing perplexity as to whether *any* "unity of culture" comprised of specifically Christian and modern elements can ever be formed. The ultimate problem yielded by the sociological formulation of the question was for Troeltsch an open one. It still is.

Secondly, the precision demanded by his line of argument forced Troeltsch to embark on a new, completely unprecedented understanding of *the uniqueness of the church.* In the context of a scientific discussion of the history of Christian social thought traditional doctrinal formulations no longer sufficed. The issue was not that these were insignificant. The issue was, rather, that they were not germane to the problems with which he wrestled. How could one clarify the uniqueness that evokes the traditional formulations in such a way that at the same time one could do justice to a scientific understanding of the social problem?

That Christianity involves an all-embracing point of view was completely beyond debate for Troeltsch, both from a theological and from a sociological perspective. Any Christian understanding of the relationship between the individual and the community yields a comprehensive sociological schema, leaving no phase of human relationships untouched. The trouble is that from the viewpoint of social science the operation of this comprehensive schema is only partially visible. As is the case with all other segments of the social, here too the limits of scientific knowledge are sharp. Any attempt at clarifying the universal sociological significance of Christianity must always be based on particular investigations. For neither society nor any of its segments can be dealt with in general.

One can hardly overestimate the significance of this element of the methodology of *The Social Teachings.* It provided Troeltsch with the opening for two decisive insights. On the one hand, seen from the standpoint of the modern delineation of the social problem, the contrast between the church as over against the state and society is simply the contrast between religious forces and economic-social-political forces. As Troeltsch put it, this is the contrast between the sociological circle organized with reference to "the religious idea of the love of God and man" as over against those sociological powers organized around purely worldly goals.[21] On the other hand, there is an overtone in this contrast with which strictly scientific thought cannot reckon. The contrast between religious forces and economic-social-political forces is a wholly different problem from the scientific distinction between the political and the social, even though this contrast is dependent on the concept of the social which the latter distinction yields. This is what gives the "moment of truth"[22] to the continual struggle from the side of dogmatics to formulate the uniqueness of the church.

It was the genius of Troeltsch to be able to deal with this latter insight without doing violence to the line of argument he was so rigorously following. In the light of his point it is entirely possible to contend that the sociological analysis of the church in society is neither to be confused with, nor does it contradict, the church's own understanding of itself. However, Troeltsch's stricture on this point must be carefully observed. The issue at hand must not be obscured by allowing it to fall under the weight of a premodern formulation. One cannot state the uniqueness of the church as over against society in terms of the distinction between the natural and the supernatural. For if by society one means the scientific concept, such terminology is both irrelevant and misleading. The contrast between the church and society cannot be grasped by means of abstractly general concepts.

Thirdly, one of the most valuable insights contained in the methodological section of *The Social Teachings* is the indictment that Troeltsch felt compelled to level at the churches of his day for their characteristic attempts to deal with the social relevance of Christianity. Invariably an obscuring oversimplification is involved:

> Men believe that with the social nature of the Church (that is, its *sociological* nature) they have already solved the social problem (that is, the problems belonging to the life of society and the state). They believe that with the organization of love, a love originating from God and returning to him, they envelop human communities altogether. However, that is out of the question; indeed, any opinion such as this will obscure the understanding of the real historical significance of the gospel and its historical development, and all the repeated utterances about " the social spirit of Christianity " contain this ambiguity for the problems of the present also. They are not necessarily false, but ambiguous and deceiving.[23]

The social problem is not removable! It is intrinsic to humanity. Men cannot live without political structures, and the relation between these and all the innumerable other groupings into which they gather will always be problematical. A theocracy or a monastery will manifest the social problem as surely as the most secular civilization which ever has or ever can come into being.

Accordingly, when Christians talk as though the " social spirit of Christianity " can solve social problems they usually are naïvely ignoring both the nature of such problems and the potentiality of their own faith. For the Christian faith both can and has developed that kind of structural sensitivity which has led and can lead to authentic participation in the political-social interrelationship. When this happens, the relevance of faith to life in the world enjoys powerful illumination. When it does not, that relevance is always vague, remote, and evanescent. The tragedy is that naïve oversimplification of the social problem by

Christians themselves is one of the major causes of their all too often abortive attempts to articulate the social spirit of Christianity. That Troeltsch's insight forces one to see this is reason enough to commend his labors.

Fourthly, in the light of these theoretical assumptions Troeltsch was able to indicate precisely the *specific objectives* giving point and direction to *The Social Teachings.* The initial objective would be the determination of the specific sociological idea implicit in Christianity and understood in terms of its completed form and organization. This objective points directly to a broader one, the consideration of the relationship between the sociological structure of Christianity and society in general, of which it is a part.[24]

Troeltsch saw that the achievement of the second of these objectives would condition and control the realization of the first. This is so because any penetrating analysis of the sociological structures generated by Christianity must understand the emergence of these against the more comprehensive background of the social at large. There is in fact a *mutually reciprocal relationship* between the development of Christianity and its social context. The question of the sociological influence of Christianity is directly tied to the question of the influence of the social context upon Christianity. This brings to the fore the problem of " inner contact and penetration ": Does this ever occur between Christianity and its context in such a way that " an inner uniformity of the entirety of life emerges? " [25] With this reiteration and refinement of the sociological formulation of the question, Troeltsch had put in final form the leading issue with which *The Social Teachings* as a whole is concerned.

The methodological formulations upon which *The So-*

cial Teachings was built, and which we now have before
us in detail, are obviously cut from the same cloth as the
conclusions Troeltsch had articulated in 1900 in his effort
to state the claims of the scientific situation on theology.
By 1912 he had fashioned from those earlier insights the
criteria whereby the characteristic marks of Christianity in
each of the epochs through which it has passed can be
compared. In the light of the sociological formulation of
the question the history of Christian social thought can be
put simply. In terms of its interaction with its social context the Christianity of antiquity did not achieve an " inner uniformity of the whole of life "; the Christianity of
the medieval period did achieve such a uniformity, at least
in theory; in the modern period discord (*Zwiespalt*) between Christianity and its context is once again inescapably clear.[26]

The vigor and sense of urgency with which Troeltsch
argued the case for his methodology is traceable only in
part to the fact that it was grounded in two decades of research and reflection. There is also an unmistakably polemical overtone to the position. His case was controversial
and he knew it. His deep affinity with the social scientists
was such that a sharp rejection of standards long accepted
for the treatment of the history of doctrine was unavoidable. In its simplest terms his demand was that the context
within which Christian thought develops must be given its
due. There is, of course, nothing new in this. No historian
worth his salt would ever debate such a concern. What
was new was the decisively sociological character of
Troeltsch's version of this demand. He was peculiarly sensitive to the earthy, empirical, ethical character of the
substratum of all Christian thought. In his view, the character of the modern world is such that it admits no other

possible treatment of history than one that takes this factor into account at the level of first principles.

Troeltsch was aware of the controversial character of his position from the beginning. The outstanding early indication of this is in his extended, critical review of the second volume of Seeberg's *Lehrbuch der Dogmengeschichte* (Textbook of the History of Doctrine). Seeberg's volume treats the history of doctrine in the medieval and modern periods. It was published in 1899. Troeltsch's review appeared in 1901.[27] He paid high tribute to Seeberg's accomplishment in this work, comparing it favorably with the efforts of Harnack and Loofs. But at the same time he stated profound reservations, amounting to a thoroughgoing rejection of Seeberg's basic point of view. To treat the history of doctrine as simply the matter of tracing the emergence of official church dogma against the background of the general history of ideas can indeed be done with great brilliance, but it assumes the validity of an objective that is no longer defensible.

In arguing against Seeberg, Troeltsch was challenging the entire accepted procedure not only for the history of doctrine but for church history as well. Both of these have come into " doubtful insecurity." " Both have been changed by modern historical and non-dogmatic ways of thought, and these changes cause all presentations to stagger." [28] New historical methods have destroyed once and for all the simple continuity hitherto presupposed by church historians and the historians of dogma. To speak, within the framework of either discipline, of a pure and undefiled primitive period, a blurred and distorted Catholic period, and a time of great restoration in the Protestant period is no longer possible. Modern historical method rejects " any such constant, uniform, and supernatural subject." It has in fact made all things " fluid, mobile, and relative," and, above all, " has placed in the foreground the great cultural and institutional contexts, on which depends the actual, definite sphere of governing religious structures of thought." [29] The trouble with Seeberg's and all such treatments is that the uniformity of presentation is gained at the price of ignoring all this.

For Troeltsch the constructive alternative lay close at hand only if one could see that the real question transcends the confines of the history of doctrine itself. In this review the decisive turn in the argument comes with the distinction Troeltsch pressed between the *importance* and the *function* of dogma. The former is self-evident. But the latter cannot be seen if one ponders dogma alone. For the function of dogma is " to maintain the *doctrina publica* with compulsory indoctrination and thus to preserve the continuity of church teaching." [30] To deal with this, one must take into account not only the dogma in question, but also the doctrines of order (*Ordenslehren*) and the theories of education (*Schultheorien*) implicit within it, as well as the habitually practiced traditions. In the light of this Troeltsch argued that " the historical explication of dogmas leads so deeply into the history of theology and religion that the limitation [of this] to the more or less accidental development of dogma is only a completely arbitrary fixing of objectives." [31] Indeed, if the history of doctrine is not concerned with " a juridical statement of the legally binding *doctrina publica* (and it can be so only in spite of all modern revolt against this) , then the history of the disintegration and decomposition of dogma, as it has been brought about in the last century, must be presented." [32]

It is a long way from this critical review to the methodological formulations that informed *The Social Teachings*. The refinements that were necessary before Troeltsch's case could know its real cogency were almost innumerable. Some of them he never recognized. For example, he never moved beyond the hopelessly limited view that the sole point to dogma is indoctrination of an authoritarian type. As we shall see, this is one of the roots of the ultimate collapse of his theological position. But no single man can see everything, and what he was to become increasingly incisive about, namely, the concrete character of the context of all Christian thought, was already being robustly asserted in the attack on Seeberg in 1901. The real point to *The Social Teachings* will never be grasped until one is aware of the broad assault on all customary church history and all the accepted history of doctrine that generated it. Troeltsch, moreover, was increasingly convinced that the history of Christian social thought is the only penetrating index to the history of Christian thought in general. He says this in countless ways as his writings progress, one of the most memorable of which occurs in an obscure passage in his last great work, the study of historical relativism, *Der Historismus und seine Probleme* (1922). The statement concludes a technical footnote in which he set out and categorized what he regarded to be the most important writings of Max Weber:

> I may on this occasion refer also to my book, The Social Teachings of the Christian Churches and Groups, 1912, which places alongside the great, essentially ideological-dogmatic presentation of Christianity which Harnack has given, an essentially sociological-realistic-ethical [presentation].[33]

Thus Troeltsch was willing to counter the most celebrated student of the history of doctrine of his generation.

As we shall see in the next two chapters, in our analysis of the work which contains this note, this challenge does indeed represent the implication of the methodology of *The Social Teachings*. It does so, however, at the cost of the clear recognition of the broad spectrum of problems such a position necessarily entails.

The critical juxtaposition of the " sociological-realistic-ethical " with the " ideological-dogmatic," with an unequivocal decision in favor of the former — this is the cutting edge of Troeltsch's view that the methodological issue is the crux of the problem confronting Christianity's historical self-understanding. Before the Enlightenment it was not possible to see this; given what has developed since the Enlightenment, it is impossible to ignore it. With the rise of the modern world and its own scientific genius the issue may be avoided only at the price of the complete abdication of intellectual responsibility.

This is what makes Troeltsch's labors still fruitful for a generation that has long since deserted the theological basis upon which he built. One must distinguish between his theological position and the methodology we have been examining in this chapter. To be sure, these are intertwined, and there is much yet to be seen before we can appraise this fully. But enough is before us for a tentative judgment. The fact is that Troeltsch's sensitivity to the modern scene and the method it necessitates for dealing with the history of Christian thought far outruns his grasp of that thought itself and his own place within it. He focused the demands of dealing significantly with the *context* of the development of the Christian tradition, and insisted, rightly so, that this will yield its secrets only if it is approached sociologically. Formal dogmatics all too often stands aloof from such concerns. This is understandable, and correct in its own way, for reflection on the content of the gospel and its meaning for any given time is not simply a matter of reacting to the stimulus of involvement in the world. However, the structural involvement of the church and its doctors has its own decisive role to play in the emergence of new insights into the meaning of the ancient faith.

The strongest point in the methodology of *The Social Teachings* is Troeltsch's insight into the *mutually reciprocal character* of the relationship between Christianity in any of its forms and its context. When Christian thought has had measurable influence and effect upon the life around it, both within and without the confines of the community of belief, it has in turn manifested at the most profound levels of its reflection insights traceable to the experience of such involvement. The issue at hand will be much more evident when we have examined the substance as well as the form of Troeltsch's investigations. Then it will be clear that the history of Christian thought conclusively demonstrates this mutual reciprocity between Christianity and its context. Already, however, this much may be said. To order the consideration of the history of Christian thought sociologically, realistically, and ethically — to order, that is, not simply the consideration of the history of Christian social thought but the consideration of the history of Christian thought in general in this way — is to take the first step in the development of a theology of involvement, and this is the legacy of the thought of Ernst Troeltsch.

3 The Nature of Historical Relativism

◈ ◈

In 1915, Troeltsch left his chair in dogmatics at Heidelberg to take a chair in philosophy at Berlin. Depending on one's point of view this may or may not be misleading. From the standpoint of strict theology it is all too easy to appraise this move hastily. Troeltsch was not the first, nor will he be the last, to be driven by an impasse theologically seen to philosophical struggle of the most tortuous kind. The exact route of his movement is revealing, and the close examination of it is indispensable for any penetrating insight into the significance of his labors. The rich yield of *The Social Teachings* may not be exploited unless one knows where such a treatment leads. Troeltsch knew. It leads irresistibly into the problem of historical relativism. This is the problem which he could neither deny nor solve. But he could scout the terrain, and he did indicate the paths along which he thought solutions might ultimately be found. This, in general, was exactly what he was doing in Berlin, in the chair he would hold until his death in 1923.

Troeltsch's preoccupation with the problem of historical relativism was rooted in the fact that the strongest point in his approach to the history of Christian social thought was also the point of its most acute vulnerability. The demand for concreteness unmasked the unique particularity of every historical phenomenon. Once unmasked, this element of uniqueness, or *individuality,* to use Troeltsch's characteristic term, makes a shambles of any attempt to impose on the raw data of history a simple, overarching rationale. Thus the demand for concreteness that was Troeltsch's forte landed him in the impasse between the necessity and the impossibility of developing a frame of reference for the interpretation of history.

As we have seen, the critical thrust of Troeltsch's view took shape early. The sharply probing review of Seeberg's work, which we have already examined, really centers on the insistence that modern thought has made all historical matters "fluid, mobile and relative." [1] The initial, imposing result of this kind of thinking was *The Social Teachings.* At the same time, the process of moving from critical broadsides such as those contained in this review to the production of *The Social Teachings* also entailed wrestling with the broader implications of dealing with history in the light of modern thought. Here insolubilities began to assert themselves even before this work appeared. The article on "Historiography," which Troeltsch wrote in 1910 for the *Encyclopedia of Religion and Ethics,* clearly indicates his sensitivity to these broader problems and foreshadows the way in which his thinking would develop over the next decade. The same can be said for the article on "Contingency," written in the same year for the same encyclopedia. [2]

Der Historismus und seine Probleme (Historical Relativism and Its Problems) is Troeltsch's second and last major work. [3] It appeared within months of his death. The Foreword is dated September 19, 1922; he died on February 1, 1923. Though incomplete as it stands, the work represents the culmination of his labors at Berlin. As had been the case with *The Social Teachings,* this work too had been in process a number of years before being published in its present form as the third volume of the *Gesammelte Schriften* (Collected Writings) .[4] However, it is not nearly as well known as its mighty predecessor for a number of reasons. For one thing, it takes its rise within the broad context of Neo-Kantianism, and philosophical reflection has now, on a number of fronts, broken beyond the boundaries of this intellectual milieu. For another thing, unlike *The Social Teachings,* it has never won its way into English translation. It probably never will, despite the fact that it contains an enormous amount of incisive analysis and useful information.

Troeltsch began the Foreword to this study by noting that he had been driven to it by a lifetime of reflection. He called attention to the second volume of the *Gesammelte Schriften* (1913)[5] which had been an attempt to bring into view " the history of the rise of the modern spirit." [6] Subsequent reflection, however, had forced him to see that the scope of the collection of those articles and essays comprising the second volume was not extensive enough. The delineation of the rise of the modern spirit is not simply a historical task; it has a philosophical dimension that is irrepressible. To this whole problematic of the philosophy of history Troeltsch turned his attention in what he proposed to be a two volume discussion. The first of these was to deal with the conceptual basis of the problem (*die begriffliche Grundlegung*) , the second, the material explanation of the problem (*die materiale Ausführung*) .[7] Accordingly, the first volume was given the subtitle, " The logical problem of the philosophy of history," and was deliberately confined to an attempt to clarify the

formal problems raised by the emergence of historical relativism. It is all that we have.

The argument that Troeltsch pursued in *Der Historismus* was developed in terms of an exhaustive analysis of
the whole realm of modern thought on the question at
hand. Virtually no one who had wrestled with these problems, or any phase of them, escaped his notice as he attempted to find his way out of the cul-de-sac of historical
relativism. His own constructive thought must be disen-
tangled from his extensive critical summations of the work
of others. We can do this in terms of three broad points:
his articulation of the modern character of the philosophy
of history, which we shall treat in this chapter, and his iso-
lation of the two crucial problems that the rise of historical
relativism has thrust to the fore, which will be before us in
the next chapter.

Der Historismus contains four broad chapters. The first
of these bears the title " The Reawakening of the Philosophy of History." Troeltsch's point of departure in delin-
eating the contemporary crisis in the historical disciplines
involved the distinction between the technical aspects of
these disciplines and the philosophical problems raised by
them. It is in the latter realm, that of " the historical
thought of man in general," that the decisive questions
arise.[8]

Regarding the technical side of historical reflection, or
what he sometimes called " the sphere of empirical historiography," [9] Troeltsch asserted that there has emerged a
disciplined area of investigation containing its own sense
of internal consistency and worthy of being termed " an
approximately exact science." [10] " Here," he insisted, " the
crisis cannot lie." [11] In saying this, it was certainly not the
intention of the author of *The Social Teachings* to mini-

mize the significance of concrete historical investigation. He regarded this as one of the great achievements of modern thought in general, and he was willing to say that its loss would be suicidal.[12] It was his contention, though, that the crisis of modern historical thought lies at a deeper level, that of the basic point of view informing all historical research. When one is considering this crisis, the basic factors are the distinction between the situation of technical historical research (*der technischen-historischen Forschung*) and that of historical-philosophical thought (*des geschichts-philosophischen Denkens*), and the understanding that the former is subordinate to the latter. For the point at which the real perplexity arises has to do with " the general philosophical bases and elements of historical thought in the comprehension of historical value, in terms of which we have to reflect on and construct the coherence of history (*den Zusammenhang der Geschichte*) ." [13] In a memorable phrase Troeltsch spoke of " an enormous yearning after the recapitulation of historical life (*Eine ungeheure Sehnsucht nach Zusammenfassung des Historischen Lebens*) " [14] as one of the characteristic elements of the modern scene.

In this light Troeltsch moved directly to the general statement of the problem of historical relativism. The problematic of the philosophy of history arises out of the tension between history and one's general frame of reference. This relationship is reciprocal in character; one's understanding of history (*Geschichte*) and one's world view (*Weltanschauung*) condition each other.[15] This contention yielded his initial characterization of the basic issue:

> Thus seen, the problem certainly implies a fundamental question of our present intellectual life, nothing less than *the problem of so-called Historicism* generally, i.e.,

the " profits and losses " resulting from the fundamental historicizing of our knowledge and thought for the formation of a personal intellectual life and the creation of the new politico-social conditions of life.[16]

Troeltsch asserted emphatically that " the philosophy of history is a modern creation, a child of the eighteenth century." [17] The crucial issues involved in it are not merely implicit in the history of thought in general. They have, rather, emerged as an intrinsic part of modern man's longing for a comprehensive frame of reference within which to interpret meaningfully the whole of reality. His insight is focused in the claim that this longing is intertwined with the development of modern historical investigation, and that the mutually penetrating combination of these two elements yields the concerns of the philosophy of history. Consistent with the most constant dimension of his thought, he traced this to the break with the medieval, ecclesiastically dominated world, which coincides with the rise of the modern temperament with its propensity to challenge and sift its entire legacy from the past.

> It [the philosophy of history] is more a matter of world-view (*Weltanschauung*) than of historical investigation (*Geschichtsforschung*), and both of these first draw closer together in the moment when reflection needs the essential intellectual goals of historical knowledge and when history longs for a fundamental arrangement in philosophical thought. The need arose from both sides at the same moment and on the same ground. The cultural consciousness demanded settlement with the more and more well known and clearly growing change of the great periods of culture, and history (*Geschichte*) demanded an answer to the question concerning unity, goal, and meaning, as soon as it extended itself over sufficiently manifold spheres. But both resulted from the break with the remains of the middle ages and the Church, along

with the agility of a thinking middle class which saw a new time lying before it and which must come to terms with the old era.[18]

Such an assertion of course raised the question of all premodern attempts to deal with the interpretation of history. Troeltsch was not naïvely contending that modern thought has a monopoly on the puzzle of history. His point was, rather, that given the route along which modern thought has developed, the only admissible solution to this puzzle must be found *within* history itself. On this ground he measured and found wanting the classical premodern efforts to render history intelligible. The philosophers of ancient Greece had obviously dealt with history, but for them " the dark finiteness is just the world of accidents, and any individual uniqueness (*Individuell-Einmaliges*) generally has no significance for the eternal essence, but on the contrary receives [its significance] solely from it." [19] Given his meaning of the terms, the conclusion for Troeltsch was categorical: " Under these presuppositions it requires in fact no philosophy of history."[20]

Sharply to be distinguished from the Greek view is the treatment history received at the hands of Christian thought. " It is no longer knowledge of the timeless-substantials (*Zeitlos-Substanziellen*), but faith in a historical revelation (*eine historische Offenbarung*) and in the attainment of the perfect final goal in the Kingdom of God at the end, which transforms the earthly world into an eternal one." [21] Now this, argued Troeltsch, involved " an enormous change," and in its positive appraisal of history Christianity in fact ascribed to history " a powerful significance " for man's struggle toward a comprehensive world view. But again, given his meaning of the terms, the conclusion was unavoidable:

But after all this history is nevertheless no history and these fundamental thoughts about history [are] no philosophy of history. . . . And as these events are not actually history, so is its theory not philosophy, but faith in doctrine supported by authority and revelation, *which also in its turn has to do with the agitation and finiteness (Beweglichkeit und Endlichkeit) of human life only externally and formally.*[22]

Clearly, this passage is extremely important for the theological appraisal of the work of Troeltsch. His sweeping denial of the historical character of revelation is surely subject to radical critique from a number of points of view, given the manifold development of theology since his day. At the moment, though, we must reserve judgment in this connection until we have the whole spectrum of his theology before us.[23] What is important at this point is the parallel that, Troeltsch argued, exists between the Greek philosophical heritage and the maturest flowering of pre-modern Christian thought. What he says regarding the latter coincides with his appraisal of the former. No external, formal superimposition of an overarching rationale can make sense of " the agitation and finiteness of human life," given the modern, irrepressible sensitivity to the full and devastating range of that fluctuation.

In thus rejecting the attempts of the past, Troeltsch brought his argument to the point where he enthusiastically took up his own challenge. He located the real impulse for the development of the philosophy of history, as he understood it, with Rousseau.[24] German philosophy of history, " stimulated by Rousseau," begins with Kant.[25] Troeltsch formulated the basic insight to be drawn from Kant in a way that suggests the ultimate yield of his own reflections: " History is the kingdom of freedom as over

against nature and it has laws of development in which nature and freedom are bound up with each other." [26] This
implies the direction his argument takes, since from this
point forward *Der Historismus* entails his attempt to do
justice to empirical historical research while at the same
time insisting that on its own ground such empirical investigation cannot solve the problem of relativism it inexorably generates. Despite his formal rejection of the
solutions of the problem of history offered by the ancient
Greeks and traditional Christianity, and notwithstanding
the fact that his most extensive historical treatise, *The
Social Teachings,* was shaped by his affinity with the social
scientists, Troeltsch was never willing to conclude that the
problematic discovered by empirical historical research
can be deciphered on the level of the facts alone. He was
convinced that what he called the " bitter opposition " between the philosophy of history and empirical historical
research both can and must be overcome.[27]

The constructive strand of Troeltsch's discussion begins
with an incisive, almost brilliant, attempt to show empirically that the philosophy of history is both possible and
necessary. This occurs in section 3 of the first chapter, entitled " The formal logic of history " — a section that is the
real nerve center of the chapter, and, for that matter, of
Der Historismus as a whole. Here he tried his hand at elaborating the distinction on which his understanding of the
philosophy of history is most dependent. Stated in its
sharpest form, this is the distinction between " pure natural science as mathematical-mechanical-physical-chemical
theory on the one hand, and pure history as investigation
and presentation of the spiritual *(seelischen)* movements,
creations and contexts of humanity on the other." [28] Such,
of course, is the hallmark of the Neo-Kantian approach to

the problem of history, within which Troeltsch's discussion is generally to be understood,[29] and in the light of which the double dedication of *Der Historismus* to Wilhelm Dilthey and Wilhelm Windelband becomes intelligible.[30]

In Troeltsch's view the categories and concepts that are necessary for and evident in historical investigation offer an incontrovertible case for the distinction between the natural sciences and the historical sciences. He discussed ten of these, the mere enumeration of which is illuminating. In sequence, he treated: (1) the " category of individual totality," (2) the " concept of originality and uniqueness," (3) the " necessity of the narrow choice " intrinsic to any notion of " essential or characteristic features " invariably present in historical discussion, (4) the concept of " representation," (5) the " indication of a value or meaningfulness " necessarily implicit in the delineation of the essential or characteristic marks of any given individual-totality, (6) the " tension between the general and the particular, between the collective spirit and the individual spirits," (7) the " concepts of the unconscious," (8) the " element of the creative " and the closely related " decisive role of the new," (9) the question of " freedom in the sense of the arbitrary," and (10) the concept of the " accidental." [31] These ten categories are directly involved in what Troeltsch called " the constitution of the historical subject matter." [32] At the conclusion of their presentation he explicitly stated that the first is the pivotal one.[33] It is given the most extended treatment, by comparison with the rest, and in fact it so permeates what is said under the subsequent nine headings that we may treat it as an axiom from which nine corollaries are drawn.

The discussion of these ten concepts and categories centers on the concept of *individuality*. When he had worked this out, Troeltsch moved directly to a similarly extended discussion of the concept of *development* (*Entwicklung*). This covered three broad points in terms of which he placed the concept of *development* alongside that of *individuality* as a second " basic concept (*Grundbegriff*) ." [34]

His treatment of the formal logic of history thus revolves around the two foci suggested by these two concepts. We shall deal with them in turn.

The concluding remark that Troeltsch made after presenting the ten categories and concepts just noted epitomizes his concern throughout his discussion of the first basic concept:

> The concept of individuality and the sense of totality is decisive, referring to a forcing of the historical material by means of the obvious unity of life. . . . But this is solely and quite self-evidently a work of comprehensive abstraction.[35]

This concern was twofold. The situation of the historian himself dominates and shapes all that he sees, and his subject matter is rooted in the very nature and fluctuation of humanity. These conspire in such a way that the historical sciences manifest throughout a decisively different contour from anything observed in the realm of the natural sciences. His point of departure in introducing this first concept was to explore what it means to say that " History generally has no simple basic elements analogous to the elements of natural science." [36] In dealing with history, one is rather confronted with magnitudes that have already coalesced. As he put it, these are quantities " in which an abundance of psychic elemental occurrences together with known natural conditions are always already massed in a unity of life or totality." [37] Everything turns on the fact that these clusters do not arise from " an adding

together of elemental occurrences " but from " the evident
unity and fusion of these in greater or lesser historically
significant totalities of life *(Lebensganzen)* ." [38]

By " psychic elemental occurrences " Troeltsch pointed
to the specifically human character of history, which shares
with " natural conditions " in constituting the clusters of
phenomena with which the historian must deal. He put
the matter this way purposely (his more characteristic
word for the human dimension of history was *geistig,* or
" spiritual " in the nontheological sense) . He did so because at the outset of his discussion of the concept of individual-totality he wanted both to resist any psychologizing of history and, at the same time, to draw his decisive
analogy from that discipline. He insisted that " though
psychic occurrences shape its most important material, the
basis of historical logic does not lie simply in psychology,
but in the already evident conglomeration of such occurrences lying before us." [39] At the same time it is also clear
that the individual, whether one is pondering a given human being or a specific historical occurrence, is only understandable against the background of the totalities of which
he or it is a part. Accordingly, just as the individual himself
must be understood in the light of the family, race, class,
etc., " so the proper subjects of scientific history have become less and less the biographical particular individuals,
but rather the collective-individuals, [that is] peoples,
states, classes, estates, cultural eras, cultural trends, religious communities, complexes of events of all kinds such as
wars, revolutions, and so forth." [40]

With the concept thus delineated, Troeltsch proceeded
to explore, fully though briefly, the overtones of his formulation. For example, he touched on the epistemological
problem, to which he gave extensive consideration later in

Der Historismus. Here he simply noted the unavoidability
of the problem, focused in the fact that the situation of
the observer is intrinsically related to the historical individuals within his purview. " Here is certainly a point
where no longer pure logic, but the personal life situation
of the historically thinking man decides and conversely
determines logic from its point of view." [41] Again, under
the heading of the concept of originality and uniqueness
he insisted that a *causal* interpretation of history is insuffi-
cient. Here he spoke of " the intrinsic charm *(Zauber)* and
content of historical life, the inner freedom and independence from mere conditions and environments, anteced-
ents and influences " [42] which depend on that meaning and
sense of development which is the sole domain of the historian.

Throughout the presentation of what we have called the
nine corollaries the points made are similar to the two we
have just noted. On the whole the discussion is quite repeti-
tive. For our purposes, however, one of these points should
be noted particularly. In discussing the concept of *representation (Vertretung)* , Troeltsch insisted flatly that " historical presentation . . . remains extraordinarily sym-
bolic." [43] His example goes a long way toward explaining
what the art of writing history entailed for him.

> He who denotes Caesar's politics as a military dictator-
> ship founded in democracy, which tends toward heredi-
> tary, oriental divine kingship, has not used concepts of
> type nor concepts of law, but concepts of representation,
> which awaken thousands of vivid details in the imagina-
> tion and only through these details explain the occur-
> rence.[44]

Now it was Troeltsch's point that what he called " the
supplementary imagination of the reader " is presupposed

in such a presentation. He argued further that the decisive question is in the open only when one sees that such " representations and symbolizations " are not simply forced out of " causal contexts " but are rather rooted finally in " the peculiar manner of historical movement " and disclose " the trans-individual (*überindividuelle*) combinations and powerful impulse of historical trends." [45] This led him to offer a second illustration, much closer to his real concerns than the one regarding Caesar, and illuminating in a striking way when one ponders the strength of *The Social Teachings:*

> The total history of the Reformation and local and biographical particular investigations, for example, differ exactly because of the causal elements in the latter and the symbolic elements in the former.[46]

When Troeltsch wrote history he was always working on the broad canvas. This is why *The Social Teachings* will always outrage the specialists, but it is also the reason behind both the astonishing perspective that this work yields and the acute sensitivity Troeltsch himself came to have for the problem of historical relativism. For the concept of individual-totality gathers together both the concrete particularity and the vacillating humanity that constitute the phenomena forming historical subject matter, and the crucial significance of the standpoint of the observer of history in the perception and interpretation of these phenomena. The question is, Did this suggest for Troeltsch a way out of the impasse of historical relativism?

The analysis of the formal logic of history was only at its midpoint with the treatment of this first basic concept. Following directly from it came the somewhat more succinct but equally searching discussion of the concept of *development* (*Entwicklung*). For Troeltsch this second basic concept was already implicit in the first [47] since no *static* totality is conceivable. Movement is the essence of the individual-totality — this would be a fair way to epitomize his point.

> There are the so-called historical ideas, e.g., Christianity, the Renaissance, Capitalism, Feudalism, etc. It is beyond any question that they can only result throughout from the merge of a totality as becoming and [a totality] presenting itself in its development. Where such cannot be shown there is no historical understanding.[48]

But precisely here the tangled problem emerges. For the movement in question is decidedly not one that can be trapped by causal analysis alone. To grasp this is " the essence of the historical sense." Troeltsch's way of putting this should be noted in full, since it is the real basis of his consistent rejection of the spirit of natural science where history is concerned.

> However therein lies the important logical result, that the continual becoming of historical things, insofar as it is in truth continual, cannot be purely causally presented in a ranging together of definable particular events, but that the particular events are fused (*verschmolzen*) into a developing unity (*Werde-Einheit*), in which the particular events are interweaving and dissolving into each other and thereby continually producing just this developing unity. This may be described logically only with great difficulty, but to see and feel it is the essence of the historical sense.[49]

With the two formulations just noted, we have before us the basic elements of Troeltsch's concern regarding the concept of development. As we shall see, he extended the point much farther in the subsequent argument of *Der*

Historismus. At this point he was content simply to set out the broad, critical implications of his view. Thus, he differentiated his concept of development from the concepts of *progress* and *evolution*. The concept of progress is, in his view, " a secularization of Christian eschatology," and must not be confused with the concept of development, which has to do with " historical movement and fluidity." [50] The concept of evolution, on the other hand, is decisively colored by the natural-scientific idea of causality and is accordingly also to be resisted.[51] The concluding phase of this treatment of the concept of development entailed a " glimpse " of " the abstract-historical sciences," which invariably depend upon the forming of the *laws* and *types* necessary for historical analysis.[52] In this context Troeltsch indicated the figures on whom his views were most dependent, notably Dilthey, Simmel, and particularly Max Weber.[53]

Such then was Troeltsch's sketch of the formal logic of history. The reassertion of the " moving drama " [54] that history is — the insistence, that is, on the *human* character of the stuff of history — this breaks the bonds of historical relativism. Troeltsch proclaimed this triumphantly:

> We are delivered from wretched historicism, which for the greatest part . . . was a misunderstanding assimilation of history by the particular elements, general laws, sequence formations, and necessities of natural science.[55]

What he called " the curse of naturalistic determinism," which he compared immediately with " the religious idea of predestination," has been solved in favor of an " elaborating abstraction " that allows room for history to be what it is.

> We are given back life, and do not suffocate in its con-
> fusions, but can develop into scientific rules and prin-
> ciples of formation the axioms of its order and arrange-
> ment, which we instinctively use and which are given with
> life itself, without thereby losing life itself again.[56]

If only this could settle the matter! Troeltsch knew that
it could not. He could and did characterize what he had
thus far worked out as " a great gain," but he went on immediately to say, " However it is impossible that this can
be the last word." [57] Thus he began the section on " The
Material Philosophy of History." In this and the succeeding two sections rounding out the initial chapter of *Der
Historismus* — sections on " The Real Relationship of Nature and History " [58] and " Naturalism and Historicism " [59]
— he explored the decisive and unavoidable defects of any
attempt to dispose of the question of historical relativism
on the ground of formal logic alone. This is crucial, both
because it exemplifies the most unforgettable thing about
Troeltsch and because it sets the stage for the real wrestling
with historicism yet to unfold in the work at hand. He was
one of those figures who periodically renew the theological
world with an extreme sensitivity to the limits of their own
position. To this was added the ability to define these
limits with increasing precision. It is not too much to say
that he would have mounted his assault on historical relativism simply on the ground we have just charted could
he have done so. Furthermore, it is probably true that he
had at one time thought such would suffice.[60] But no one
was quite so persuaded as he had come to be, in the light
of the labors of a lifetime, that this would be to surrender
without firing a shot.

We have already stated that Troeltsch's analysis can be
regarded as an attempt to show empirically that the philos-

ophy of history is both possible and necessary.[61] This judgment would have to be sharply qualified, almost distorted
completely, if what we have been noting were the only
decisive elements of his argument. Moreover, this is true
despite the fact that such an appraisal could claim a real
basis in the concrete character of the concepts of individual-totality and development as these emerge at his hand.
There is far deeper reason, however, for our claim. In a
word, formal logic is not enough because of the involvement of the thinker. The spectator is never a scientist!
" There is," argued Troeltsch, " no purely contemplative
science either in nature or in history, either in motif or in
result. . . . So there is also no purely contemplative history which does not flow into the understanding of the
present and the future." [62] The conclusion for Troeltsch
was inescapable: " If however this is so, then, in a scientific
and logical sense, the material philosophy of history must
grow out of the formal." [63] That is, if the concrete involvement of the historian is not taken equally into account the
discussion of the two basic concepts of the formal logic of
history is completely undermined.

This assertion brings into view the final element of the
foundation upon which Troeltsch constructed the broader
argument of *Der Historismus* as a whole. In its treatment
we begin to see emerging the themes and concerns that
dominate succeeding chapters and that cannot be fully
analyzed without the entire range of *Der Historismus* at
our disposal. One point remains, however, in Troeltsch's
delineation of the modern character of the philosophy of
history, and we must give attention to it before going on.
In the light of his insistence that what we are calling the
involvement of the historian himself must be taken into
account Troeltsch refined his derivation of the problem

of historical relativism itself.

The last section of this initial chapter, entitled " Naturalism and Historicism," begins with the statement of " the final formulation of the problem engaging us ":

> It is the problem of *the significance and essence of historicism generally,* in which this word is to be fully detached from its wretched secondary meaning (*Nebensinn*) and is to be understood in the sense of the fundamental historicizing (*Historisierung*) of all our thought about man, his culture and his values.[64]

The initial phase of *Der Historismus* is thus the clarification of the claim that the involvement of man fundamentally conditions his historical reflection. This is the real meaning of historical relativism. It is not to be confused with the confining notion of deterministic causality, as we have seen Troeltsch argue again and again. Once this confusion is purged the way is cleared for the real struggle — the struggle with the length, breadth, height, and depth of the human involvement in the human enterprise of trying to make sense out of the past. On *this* ground, with the distortion removed once and for all, Troeltsch both could and did see the profound parallel between naturalism and historicism. Both are intrinsically modern, " the two great scientific creations of the modern world," and " the two principal tendencies of modern science." [65] And though he never wearied of contrasting the modern world with all phases of the premodern world — the former rejecting all forms of ontological and metaphysical speculation on the philosophical side and doctrinal prejudgment on the theological side, which he regarded as the hallmarks of premodern, Western civilization — he likewise never relaxed the intensity of his claim that neither naturalism nor historicism can be plumbed without philosophical struggle of the highest order. Before the last word can be spoken, the epistemological, the metaphysical, even the metalogical must have its say.[66] As regards history, however, the limits of this struggle are clear:

> One knows the norms of the shape of life (*Lebensgestaltung*) no longer in church dogma, or in its descendant, rationalistic dogma; there remains only history as the source and the philosophy of history as the solution.[67]

The bulk of *Der Historismus* remains yet to be considered, but the key to this consideration lies in this initial chapter and the refinement of the delineation of historical relativism with which it culminates. To live in the modern world and to think as a modern man is to know " the fundamental historicizing" of all one's thought concerning the shape and meaning of life.

4 The Problems of Historical Relativism

❖ ❖

Historical relativism as Troeltsch understood it cannot be avoided. But can it be mastered? Troeltsch's contention was that there are two broad clusters of problems emerging from the carefully refined delineation of historical relativism that must be controlled before this question can be answered affirmatively. He devoted two lengthy and major chapters of the work to each of these in turn. As we shall see, the first set of problems is basically ethical in character and pivots on the concept of *individuality*. The second is epistemological in thrust and is yielded by the concept of *development*.

1. THE ETHICAL PROBLEM

The second chapter of *Der Historismus* carries the following title: "Concerning Standards for the Judgment of Historical Matters and their Relationship to a Present Cultural Ideal." Its initial object is the clarification of the real task of the material philosophy of history.

Troeltsch commenced this chapter with the assertion that no philosophy of history can be valid that is simply a systematic arrangement of the course of the past or a " teleological construction of the gradual achievement of goals." [1] This is so because in the modern context the phi-

losophy of history must find its sole ground in " the determined and thoroughgoing realism of modern history,"
which has its dynamic in " the critically secured facts of
tradition " and " the individual meaning and character of
every historical creation." [2] In the light of this he could put
the initial question and its answer succinctly:

> But what remains then as the task of the material phi-
> losophy of history? Primarily nothing other than the pro-
> duction of a standard, an ideal, an idea of the actual pres-
> ent — seen on the whole as a total situation and a result
> of thousands of years — for creating a new unity of cul-
> ture.[3]

To be sure, this task will have teleological overtones. But
this teleology must be earthy, devoid of abstraction, having no trace of " the objectively constructable course of
the world, seen from the final eternal purpose." It must be
rooted solely in the significance of the actual present for
the movement from the past to the future.[4]

It is precisely here, as Troeltsch rightly saw, that the
ethical character of the *material* philosophy of history asserts itself. However categorically he argued that to be
worthy of the name the philosophy of history must be
grounded in the *facts* of history, he always insisted that
such reflection has a *normative* and *directive* purpose.
Troeltsch was constitutionally incapable of neutrality regarding the movement of history from this point forward.
For him, the task of the material philosophy of history is
decidedly *practical* and, in this sense, *ethical* in character.
" Its significance is essentially practical, ethical, if one will
understand with the Greeks the word ' ethic ' in this broad
sense, or cultural-philosophical." [5] The reason for this is
clear: " Such a proper and present synthesis of culture cannot be created without a broad over-view of history and

without questioning its prevailing values and forms." [6]
Along this line, and only this line, lies the sole possibility
of mastering historical relativism. [7]

Thus Troeltsch asserted that the ethical is the doorway
to the mastering of historicism. There can be no turning
back. The "historicizing of all our thought about man,
his culture and his values" [8] is here to stay. The only way
to deal with it is to become totally involved in it, with an
eye toward the possibility of giving it fresh content and
new direction. The ethical concern dominates Troeltsch's
thought as a whole. Here, however, this concern receives
forceful and unforgettable illumination. The recognition
of the relativity of all things always seems to bring in its
van the ennervation of the ethical sensitivity. Not so for
Troeltsch! On the contrary, this thrusts the ethical to the
fore with a new and awesome task. The standards for the
appraisal of history have an unmistakably ethical cutting
edge. Not to see this, or to ignore it once having perceived
it is to leave history to the mists and reduce the involvement in the present to caprice. Just because all our thought
about man, his culture, and his values has been historicized
once and for all the interpretation of history is a partisan
affair. (This is reason enough for insisting that *The Social
Teachings* will never be grasped in its fullest magnificence
and pathos unless one knows what Troeltsch was up to ten
years later in the production of *Der Historismus*.)

It is also here that Troeltsch summoned into operation
the concept of *individuality*. He called upon it for the solution of the most intractable problem obstructing the way
toward the authentic interpretation of history. It is one
thing to demand that the philosophy of history be
grounded in the facts of history, but how does one avoid
the error of oversimplification that always attends what he

called " the dogmatizing of one or more moments of the past "? [9] Here the real importance of his reflections regarding the formal logic of history, which we have examined at length, comes into view. For, as he puts it now, in this context, the significance of the formal logic of history lies in the search for " the decisive point of historical thought and perception " within " the logical understanding of empirical-historical investigation " in terms of which this problem may be solved.[10] This search is ended with the formulation of the concept of individuality: " The decisive point is above all the *individuality* of historical forms and the objectivity aspired to in the entire investigation, to measure each form above all only in its particular will and content." [11]

The groundwork of the second chapter of *Der Historismus* is now before us. With these points cleared Troeltsch proceeded into the major phase of the chapter, entailing an extended consideration of what he called " Different attempts to unite the historical-individual and the generally valid," [12] which he introduced with a searching review of his concept of individuality.[13] Kant, Hegel, Nietzsche, Simmel, Bergson, Rickert, and Max Weber are among the figures with whom he dealt, and his discussion included analyses of Positivism and Marxism. This survey confirmed his judgment regarding the primary significance of the concept of individuality and led him into the clarification of the decisive implications of its use. These are in essence twofold, and the formulation of this represents a major step in the argument of *Der Historismus*.

In the first place, he stated more forcefully what had already been suggested at the outset of the chapter. The standard of judgment which it is the business of the material philosophy of history to produce is necessarily dependent upon a *synthesis of culture*. This is why *both* the individuality *and* the ethical character of all such standards must be taken into account. For both the concrete involvement of the historian and his inescapable orientation toward the future are intermingled in the standards whereby he appraises history.

> Every formation of a standard in relation to historical matters thus arises out of the particular living context (*Lebenszusammenhang*), and is at the same time the critique and the improvement of this. As every calculation of motion in the natural sciences is dependent on the position of the reckoner, so also in history is every standard indelibly determined by the position out of which it arises. In fact it arises continually in living connection with the shaping of the future (*Zukunftsgestaltung*).[14]

In short, there is no way of dealing with history apart from at least an emerging notion of how things *ought* to go from here.

Secondly, and here we encounter for the first time one of Troeltsch's most important and complicated conceptions, he contended that any synthesis of culture is necessarily a priori in character. In so doing he had only *one* concern, the clear recognition of the *spontaneous* and *novel* overtones of all historical creativity. In *Der Historismus*, the *concept of apriority* becomes Troeltsch's major instrument for the harnessing of this, at once the most uncontrollable and exciting element of historical reflection.

> It [a synthesis of culture] is an a priori, that is, spontaneous, creation, insofar as it actually brings forth the new out of inner depths and accredits itself only by means of its inner self-certainty (*Selbstgewissheit*) and its will determining power (*den Willen bestimmende Macht*).

However it is not a creation out of nothing and it is not a construction out of reason, but a transformation and continuation, which is at the same time the inspiration of a new soul and a new spirit.[15]

Troeltsch was emphatic in insisting that what he terms his " presupposed sense of apriority " [16] is completely limited to the phenomenon of the spontaneity of the historian himself. This entailed the assertion of both the factual and the novel elements of this involvement. Moreover, it carried him directly to the underlining of the dissimilarity between his conception of apriority and that of Kant.

> [Apriority] signifies nothing other than the autonomy of such formations of standards, ultimately conveyed by the fullest sense of its meaning, and the inexplicability [of such formations] by mere presuppositions and antecedents, with which they indeed stand in continuity, but over against which they are nevertheless something new. . . . Such apriority is a simple fact of life, it is to be recognized as a decision of the will. But without such a recognition of the will there is no valid apriority at all. This is, to be sure, something other than the Kantian apriority.[17]

When Troeltsch referred to this apriority as a " simple fact of life " this is precisely what he meant. Happily, he saved those who would interpret him the trouble of differentiating his view from Kant's. It was inevitable that he do so. As we have seen throughout, his struggle with historical relativism was empirical in tone. This is why he included in his elaboration of this concept the insistence that it is directly related to the objectivity that he sought to secure as the leading characteristic of his enterprise.

> The objectivity of such autonomous and to that extent apriori formed standards thus lies, if one turns especially to history, in two well founded factors, *first* in a most at-

tentive and most unbiased immersion in the facts, in the whole context of action (*Wirkungszusammenhang*), to which we belong, *and then* in the evolution of an ideal of this cultural sphere out of the factual life, which understands itself in the setting of an ascending and spiritual total context of life (*Gesamtzusammenhang des Lebens*), but which must in all crises take hold of this context anew and bring it forth again.[18]

Thus the apriority of that synthesis of culture intrinsic to the task of the historian is closely linked to the concreteness of his spontaneity. The understanding of this serves to facilitate the recognition of the objectivity of his involvement. But more than that, when one recognizes the *concrete* character of *this* spontaneity and sees that the *novelty* which marks all authentic historical reflection is both normative and directive in its aspirations, one has found the locus of the ethical character of such reflection. For Troeltsch the concept of apriority had no other function. The passage just noted is both a choice and a characteristic indication of the fact that for him the first set of problems that a clear recognition of the contours of historical relativism discloses is *ethical* in its nature.

2. The Epistemological Problem

It was a simple step from the line of argument we have been examining to the second of the major problems generated by historicism. Troeltsch discussed this in the very extensive third chapter of his study under the title " Concerning the Historical Concept of Development and Universal History." The title itself suggests why the considerations now before him find their focus in the epistemological question. The matter may be simply stated: We have seen Troeltsch argue that the standards

for the appraisal of the significance of historical occurrences depend upon a synthesis of culture. Now he proceeded to deal with the inescapable implications of this
contention. Such a cultural synthesis necessarily involves a
conception of historical development that itself presupposes a comprehensive view of the whole sweep of history
(*Universalgeschichte*). This raises ultimate issues of an
epistemological nature.

Troeltsch began with the distinction between the concept of development operative in empirical historical research and that which emerges at the hand of philosophical
reflection. He accepted as self-evident the fact that it is at
the point of its concept of development that empirical historical research feels the irresistible urge to broaden its
horizon and thus include more sweeping vistas. What is
not self-evident is the question of both the possibility and
the complexity of this movement from the particular to the
universal.

> It is of course something entirely different if it [the con-
> cept of development] is explored and presented histori-
> cally-developmentally (*entwicklungsgeschichtlich*) in the
> understanding of an empirical investigation of a particu-
> lar, defined context, or if it happens philosophically-his-
> torically (*geschichtsphilosophisch*) in the sense of uni-
> versal history. . . . This circumstance, again, includes the
> question as regards the relation between the two concepts
> of development, the particular and the universal.[19]

In saying this, Troeltsch grounded the discussion now
before him in the basic problem he had been addressing
from the outset of *Der Historismus.* " It is in truth nothing
other than the question engaging us throughout as regards
the relation of empirical history and the philosophical-
historical idea, and as regards the possibility of advancing

from the first to the second." [20] However, he had more in mind than simply the age-old tension between the particular and the universal. What is decisive is the " difference in range " of these two types of concepts of development, and *this* difference comes into the open when one notes the relations of each to their systems of value. Thus, the empirical historian has to do solely with a *factual* meaning and value. Whether he knows it or not, this stems from the historical forms that are part of his own position and it shapes the forces that he discerns in a given context. On the other hand, the philosopher of history is concerned with a *generally valid* system of value, whether he conceives this in either an absolutistic or a relativistic fashion.[21]

This brought the far horizon of the problem into view. Troeltsch's contention was that one cannot stop at the point of the conflict between value systems, however closely the concept of development is tied to the concept of value. As he noted, and rightly so, the fact is that different systems of value can yield identical concepts of development, and, conversely, any given concept of development can be the basis for varying systems of value. Accordingly, the decisive issue is the epistemological one. " In general, the characteristics of systems lie very much more in logical-epistemological-metaphysical elements than in concepts of value." [22]

In this light Troeltsch emphasized once again the importance of the concept of development for the understanding of where modern thought has driven historical reflection, designating this concept as " the center of modern historical relativism as a whole." [23] Seen against the background of his clear recognition of its unavoidable epistemological overtones, his attempt to bridge the gap between " empirical historical logic " and " the material philosophy of history " [24] is fascinating, but it is also self-defeating. Even at the pinnacle of *Der Historismus*, Troeltsch never seemed able to perceive that his argument in fact pointed to *pluralism* as the necessary concomitant of historical relativism. The very formulation of the decisive question at this point of his discussion shows that he thought the problem at hand could be solved on its own terms:

> How does one proceed from the empirical use of a specifically historical, logically secured concept of development to a universal idea of growth (*Werdegedanken*) , in which at the same time our own creative tendency is regulated and objectively substantiated? [25]

As he had done in the second chapter, Troeltsch now proceeded into a comprehensive review of the movement of modern thought, structuring the discussion in terms of the problem crystallized in the question just noted. Here, however, the presentation was much more extensive (over sixty percent of *Der Historismus* is given over to the third chapter alone) . The review began with a presentation and critique of the theory of Windelband and Rickert. It then moved on to include " The Hegelian dialectic," " The ' organology ' of the German historical school," " The Marxist dialectic," " The historical dynamic of positivism," " The idea of development of historical realism," and, finally, " The historian of postspeculative realism." The discussion included detailed consideration of such figures as Hegel, Ranke, Schelling, Schopenhauer, Marx, Sombart, Max Weber, Comte, Mill, Spencer, Lotze, Nietzsche, Dilthey, Simmel, Croce, and Bergson, to mention only some of them.[26]

The point to this exhaustive survey was the confirmation and clarification of the thesis that the question of the concept of development lies at the heart of the problematic of historical relativism. With the mass of evidence compiled, Troeltsch formulated this in the concluding section of the chapter " History and Epistemology " (*Historie und Erkenntnistheorie*). He argued that the survey enables one to see " a particular and special form and significance of the concept of development," [27] one that ties the findings of the most painstaking labor involved in the writing of *Der Historismus* to the point of departure of the study as a whole.

> The result of all this is thus primarily this special place and special significance of a specifically historical concept of development itself. It is founded, firstly, in the essence of the human spirit (*in dem Wesen des menschlichen Geistes*). . . . . It is founded, secondly, in the capability of this same spirit (*in der Fähigkeit desselben Geistes*).[28]

The *essence* and *capability* of the human spirit, conceived as the dwelling place and power of the concept of development — against the background of this formulation Troeltsch took the measure of the labors of others, and sought to appraise the usefulness of their thoughts for the attempt to master historical relativism. Of the host of judgments that now unfold, and thus round out the chapter, two will suffice by way of illustration.

The point to which the argument had now progressed provided Troeltsch with yet another opportunity to distinguish between historical investigation and the natural sciences. For the latter, he now remarked, the problem is only that of discerning the relationships between particular elements or occurrences and of formulating the laws governing these relationships. The methodology for such inquiry excludes at the outset that generalization which is necessary for historical investigation.[29] Now, argued

Troeltsch, Hegel saw this clearly, but his dialectic is so completely confined to the realm of purely theoretical thought that it does violence to the concrete character of historical occurrences. Accordingly, " Hegel's thought is only the most acute and clear indication of the problem, but not its solution." [30] Indeed, Troeltsch insisted further, any general conception of evolution arising on the basis of Hegel's thought is not a concept of development so much as it is a concept of change. Pure logic alone is not enough for the movement from a concept of change to a concept of development. This movement must also involve " metaphysical and religious interpretations." [31]

Comment on this last point is obviously in order. Certainly a critique of Hegel on the ground that he has too much logic and not enough " metaphysical and religious interpretation " has its comical side, especially for one not at home in the complexities of Troeltsch's thought. By now, however, his point should be readily apparent. Just as he had rejected the abstraction of a Kantian a priori only to claim the concept for reformulation and new utilization, so here he rejected that kind of metaphysical and religious interpretation of history which must result if it is derived from Hegel's thought. This reiterates once again what we have seen so often, namely, that for Troeltsch only that metaphysic which is rooted in the raw factuality of concrete historical events can be of any use in the struggle to master " the fundamental historicizing of all our thought about man, his culture and his values." [32] More than that, the point before us intimates a similar refinement in his attitude toward the *religious* element in any authentic attempt to transcend the confines of a mere concept of change and arrive at a real concept of development. But this touches on much broader problems in Troeltsch's thought; before we can do justice to them we must have his theological writings at our command.

As a second example of the appraisals with which Troeltsch rounded out his third chapter we may note his reflections on what might be called the standard procedure followed by the outstanding historians of his day. Here he found a possible solution to the problem of the concept of development in the close conformity betweeen *knowledge* and the *form of presentation* characterizing what he called " the practice of the historian." [33] He noted that this has been highly refined by historians working such diverse fields as the history of the state, economics, art, religion, science, and society. Moreover, in actual practice different means of approach obtain in each of these realms, and invariably they reflect the greatest familiarity with the subject matter in question.[34] Precisely at this point the epistemological problem asserts itself, a fact typified for Troeltsch by the dispute between " those who look at life " and " those who think in terms of form " (*der Streit der Lebens-Anschauer und der Form-Denker*).[35] Lest one conclude too quickly that Troeltsch's heart was with the former, let it be recalled again that he dedicated *Der Historismus* to *both* Dilthey *and* Windelband. In his view the basic question is whether the logical means of approach utilized in these investigations are simply pragmatic arrangements of facts, perhaps even transcendentally constructed results of thought, or whether these approaches in fact disclose the actual coherence of reality.[36] The question, that is, transcends the limits of logic alone.

> This however is no purely logical problem and it is also not to be answered on the ground of logic. In truth it is an epistemological problem and is to be decided only on this basis.[37]

These two illustrations, drawn from the broad survey that forms the substance of the third chapter of *Der Historismus,* indicate how Troeltsch put this material to work against the background of his argument as a whole. That argument is now before us in its entirety. We may proceed to its summation.

As we have seen, Troeltsch worked out both the second and the third chapters of *Der Historismus* in the light of the clarification of the formal logic of history and the refinement of the delineation of historical relativism that had been the burden of the initial chapter of the work. With that discussion in mind we may now draw together the analyses of these two central chapters of *Der Historismus* into a unity as follows: The standard of judgment that the material philosophy of history must yield presupposes a contemporary synthesis of culture. This must be rooted in the spontaneity of the historian himself and invariably turns on an ethical hinge. One cannot, however, synthesize the present without engaging the question as to how history should now unfold. Hence the ethical character of the historian's involvement drives inexorably toward the broad sweep of history as a whole. Here the concept of development assumes universal proportions, but for this to be valid the epistemological question must be faced. One cannot conceive the development of history as a whole without, implicitly at least, advancing a theory of knowledge. The epistemological question, then, follows closely on the heels of the ethical concern, and both of these must be controlled if " the fundamental historicizing of all our thought about man, his culture and his values " [38] is to be mastered.

The need for what Troeltsch called " a unity and correlation of meaning " (*Sinneinheit und Sinnbeziehung*) [39] now looms up as the heart of the full range of problems on the way toward the only solution of historical relativism that modern thought can countenance. With this as the sharpest focusing of the target, Troeltsch sought to abide by the stricture he had formulated at the close of the introductory chapter of *Der Historismus*. Since " one knows the norms of the shape of life no longer in church dogma, or in its descendant, rationalistic dogma," and since " there remains only history as the source and the philosophy of history as the solution," [40] his argument could now only culminate as it does:

> This [i.e., the struggle toward a unity and correlation of meaning] results then in a universal history, which is organized on the basis of the idea of a contemporary synthesis of culture, and a contemporary synthesis of culture which is gotten from the urge toward development (*Entwicklungstrieb*) of our historical context of life. Today the philosophy of history exists in this correlation.[41]

The synthesis of culture, with its unavoidable ethical coloration and universal history, with its irresistible urge toward and dependence upon epistemological clarity, thus stand in creative tension. This tension yields the problematic of the philosophy of history. More than that, it points the way toward the mastering of historical relativism.

3. The Conclusion of " Der Historismus "

Der Historismus is an incomplete study, as we have already noted.[42] By design, Troeltsch did not attempt a real conclusion — this was to follow in a second volume. However, inadvertently perhaps, he was moving in the direction of one in the final chapter of the work. The shortest of the four chapters comprising the volume, it is deliberately transitional in character, as Troeltsch himself explicitly indicated.[43] Notwithstanding this, the process of transition in the direction of the proposed second volume entailed a decisive, twofold extension of the argument that we have now examined at length. We are fortunate that Troeltsch worked this out by way of bringing the first volume to a close, since this twofold extension is of major significance for the interpretation of his thought as a whole.

The title of the chapter, " Concerning the Structure of European Cultural History *(Kulturgeschichte)* ," suggests rather obviously the first element of this extension. To put it in a single sentence, no man knows enough to deal with universal history. In spite of the formal connection, then, between the concept of development and universal history, which Troeltsch took such pains to elaborate in the third chapter of *Der Historismus*, the first thing that had to take place before this insight could be applied was the delimitation of universal history to manageable proportions. " There is for us only a world history of Europe *(eine Weltgeschichte des Europäertums)* . The old idea of world history must accept new and more moderate form." [44] Though he stated the reason behind this with characteristic elaboration it can be epitomized succinctly and in his own words: " In truth we know only ourselves and understand only our own being and for that reason only our own development." [45]

The implications of this turn in Troeltsch's argument are immense. The two foci of his position are occupied by the concept of individuality with its attendant ethical problem, on the one hand, and the concept of development with its unavoidable epistemological thrust, on the other. What takes place in the closing chapter of *Der Historismus* is an overriding preoccupation with the former of these, and an implied, though not developed, inductive solution along these lines of the epistemological problem raised by the universal import of the concept of development. In a word, then, the concept of individuality begins to dominate, even overwhelm, the concept of development.

The concern underlying the assertion that " for us there is only a universal history of European culture " is the insistence that " one must make it clear that there are different possibilities of humanity." [46] The nicest example of this occurs in the remark made regarding the world of Islam (and as we shall see later, this is not the only point at which the stubborn fact of the world of Islam gnawed at the foundations of Troeltsch's certainty) : " Hence Islam has a universal history for itself . . . and it does not belong to the universal history of Europe. *There is no common cultural synthesis for both worlds.*" [47]

The point before us receives a much more conclusive indication when the second element of the discussion in this final chapter is brought into play. This has to do with what Troeltsch called " The problem of an objective periodizing," the title given to the third section of the chapter.[48] Recalling that this transitional chapter is concerned with the *structure* of European cultural history, we can see immediately what he meant by this awkward terminology. He introduced the problem with emphasis and precision:

> The question for the solution of our problem is not at all directly that concerning universal historical development itself, but that concerning its *obviously developing structure of the great strata of our cultural sphere.* . . . The point is easy to define. It lies *in the periodizing of universal history.* . . . In such periodizing lies the particularly philosophical element of universal history.[49]

Of course, this question touches directly on the problem of where to locate the origin of the modern world, and in introducing it Troeltsch pointed to this problem with all the conviction of the settled conclusion he had reached on this matter.[50] Obviously, though, the question of discerning and delimiting the formative and decisive periods into which history falls runs much deeper than this problem alone. It raises again the entire methodological issue to which he had first given full articulation in *The Social Teachings*. His position receives forceful and illuminating reiteration in this closing phase of *Der Historismus* with the insistence that *objectivity* must be the prevailing characteristic of a valid periodizing of history.

The refinement of the question both indicates his position and shapes this presentation of it:

> More correctly put the question is, whether in connection with periodizing one ought to take as a basis the great sociological, constant forms of life, which may well be involved spiritually (*geistig*) , but which, so long as they continue, in their turn define and form the spiritual (*geistige*) life, and decide possibilities and directions of action, or whether one ought to go out from the ultimate and deepest spiritual (*geistigen*) attitudes of the periods, which also surely simultaneously underlie the sociological form at all events and exhibit the driving powers of unity.[51]

At the one extreme suggested by this formulation Troeltsch placed Hegel, " the grandest representative " of the second tendency,[52] and, at the other, Max Weber and Werner Sombart.[53] The rejection of Hegel's solution as " purely ideological " [54] expresses in unequivocal form Troeltsch's critique of all options falling short of that kind of approach typified by Weber and Sombart. This is to be expected. What is of decisive significance is his formulation of the reason why Weber and Sombart, whose work in this respect he regarded as mutually complementary, are to be regarded as exemplary. In a word, it is because their approach carries a built-in guarantee of objectivity. Thus, in summing up his delineation of the full spectrum of reflection on this problem, running from Hegel, on the one hand, to Weber and Sombart, on the other, Troeltsch added his voice to the argument advanced by the latter:

> The theories go from purely ideological periodizing to political-ideological [periodizing], from there to purely sociological-institutional [periodizing], and from there finally to the searching for the ultimate ideological substrata (*Untergründe*) of the sociologically constant forms themselves (*der soziologischen Dauerformen selbst*), which except in naturally confining, geographic and anthropological particulars are always established by means of the deepest predispositions, and tendencies of the will.[55]

He then epitomized the position that he always found most congenial in terms of *externality* and *objectivity*. To emphasize the former is to guarantee the latter, because the clear discerning of the periods of history depends upon the insight that such do not simply follow out of a theory of development, but, rather, unfold, or " pile up," to use Troeltsch's vivid term, in close connection with the concrete fashion in which historical development actually takes place.

> We do not inquire for the periods, insofar as they follow out of the development, but for the structure (*Aufbau*), insofar as it piles itself up out of the results of the great periods. . . . Exactly the externality (*Aeusserlichkeit*) of this means of periodizing guarantees its objectivity.[56]

The issue, then, is *structural* in character, for the attempt to chart the movement of history in terms of structure is the only way in which the concrete externality of the periods of history can effect the objectivity with which these periods are construed. This is why the sociologists, and not the ideologists, must inform the methodology of the material philosophy of history.

> In fact, a really objective periodizing is only possible when derived from the socio-economic, political, and legal sub-structure.[57]

This, to be sure, is not all there is to say. " The ground lies still deeper," Troeltsch continued.[58] What one gains from paying close attention to the substructure disclosed by historical probing with socioeconomic, political, and legal tools is only a clue to the ever-present mystery of the blend of the spiritual with the earthy. But it is the only clue worth taking seriously. For however much one struggles to be clear about the creative independence, even autonomy, of this spiritual element, the fact is that the shaping of its effect is always traceable to the earthy, that is, the structural, factor.

> Certainly it is so, that the elementary life needs of nourishment, of sexual life, of companionship, of the external order of life and peace in great things as in small, in the case of individuals as in the case of historical life groups (*Gruppenleben*), define the form of life and therewith so to say the cadres also of the spiritual life (*die Kadres . . . des geistigen Lebens*).[59]

This strong emphasis upon the structural side of history fits compactly with the delimitation of the scope of investigation to the " universal history of European culture " noted above.[60] Indeed, it suggests that the basic reason why the noted remark with reference to the world of Islam — " There is no common cultural synthesis for both worlds " [61] — is both inevitable and indicative of the real end product of Troeltsch's labors. In approaching the detailed consideration of *Der Historismus,* we stated that Troeltsch actually succeeded only in scouting the terrain of the problem of historical relativism. We are now in a position to state this with precision. When the concept of development is sociologically ordered — and here we use the term " sociologically " comprehensively, to embrace the whole range of the socioeconomic, political, and legal substructure of cultural history — it itself becomes a *function* of the concept of individuality.

This is precisely how the matter ultimately worked itself out for Troeltsch, though we must look beyond the incomplete study in *Der Historismus* for the full demonstration of this fact. What is before us is a volume that remarkably merits its subtitle — " The Logical Problem of the Philosophy of History "! For what emerges as its end product is not a series of questions but a singular perplexity. Both the ethical and the epistemological implications of Troeltsch's assault on historical relativism pale in significance when compared with the striking overtones of this concluding chapter. For each of these in turn had focused the results of the careful refinement of a serious attempt to break the confines of historicism from within its own presuppositions. They yield, in the very initial phases of their application, an overwhelming confirmation of exactly the impasse Troeltsch had sought to break through. To put the issue in terms of his categories, when the concept of development deteriorates into a function of the concept of individuality, " the fundamental historicizing of all our thought about man, his culture and his values " [62] has indeed been clarified, but by no means has it been overcome — it has been furthered.

The real question is whether Troeltsch himself, or anyone for that matter, could solve the problem of historical relativism on the only ground he would admit, history itself. The most important lesson to learn from his particular attempt is that he could not. The implication is that no one can. In the opening paragraph of this final chapter he spoke of the circular relationship (*Zirkelverhältnis*) between the two principal themes of his discourse.[63] As we have seen, he failed to maintain this circle. The emerging conclusion, animating the entire discussion, may not be relaxed. The social sciences must inform historical investigation if one is proposing to deal with *real* history. Accordingly, the only way to avoid an unreal and therefore false concept of development is to move *from* individuality *to* development. What Troeltsch tried to maintain as a reciprocal relationship is in fact a one-way street. This is why the significance of this final chapter can hardly be overstated. The inexorable trend of the argument as a whole becomes unmistakably clear in it. Already the process of inducing a concept of development from the operation of the concept of individuality is in jeopardy. It is necessarily doomed to failure, for the transmutation of the circle into an arrow has irrevocably begun: *development* has been subsumed under *individuality*.[64]

To see this is to begin to grasp the pathos of Troeltsch's thought. Whereas he continually struggled to keep free the role of the intellectual creativity of man and thus successfully resisted the deterministic tendency of the social sciences, at the same time he could never desert the concreteness of history as this unfolds when historians are sensitive to the earthy, structural character of even the most epoch-transcending cultural and spiritual achievements. Although it is clear that the work at hand does represent a monumental and successful effort to block determinism, the "fundamental historicizing" of the present has been clarified but not contained.

When one becomes infected with Troeltsch's way of relating the concrete individuality of each historical occurrence to the intrinsic sweep of development that animates history itself, one is no longer sure that historical relativism should be contained. In effect this is to conclude that the decisive significance of Troeltsch's argument is its implicit confirmation of pluralism as the necessary concomitant of historicism. To be sure, this never reaches even partial articulation in the present treatise, primarily because Troeltsch was still fighting a losing battle against exactly this implication, and secondarily because any formulation of the matter would be in order only at the conclusion of the anticipated second volume. One cannot help wondering, however, whether the particular elements of the strictly philosophical base upon which he was working would ever have been able to support the weight of such a conclusion. Pluralism is certainly tenable on philosophical grounds, but does Troeltsch's version of Neo-Kantian reflection represent such a ground? This question admits only a tentative negative answer — though by no means a hesitant one — for want of evidence we can never have.

Precisely at this juncture the *theological* dimension of Troeltsch's struggle with historical relativism demands attention. We have scrupulously avoided extended reference to it throughout this analysis for the simple reason that it nowhere contributes materially to the argument at hand. However, though it rarely receives explicit formulation it is nevertheless subtly present throughout the whole range of this argument, both in the sense that it provides the broad background against which the study unfolds, and, more significantly, in the sense that it points to the conscious *terminus ad quem* of Troeltsch's intellectual labors as a whole.

The most significant indication of the presence of a theological dimension in the argument of *Der Historismus* occurs in the remarks that bring the lengthy third chapter of the study to a close.[65] We have already noted the culmination of this chapter in Troeltsch's conclusion that the contemporary locus of the philosophy of history exists in the correlation between *universal history* organized on the basis of a contemporary synthesis of culture, and the *contemporary synthesis of culture* itself, generated by the irresistible urge toward development that is empirically observable in the concrete present situation. Moreover, we have insisted that this conclusion must be understood strictly within the context of the restriction formulated at the close of the first chapter, namely, that the norms of the shape of life may only be derived from history itself by means of the philosophy of history, and that they may no longer be drawn from church dogma or from the rationalistic dogma that supersedes it.[66] Exactly because the restriction rules the conclusion so completely, the deeply theological coloration of Troeltsch's own interpretation of this conclusion is striking. For this to be seen, the passage in question must be noted in detail:

Such philosophy of history demands a constructive condensation of the given and a subsidy of faith in a self-revealing divine idea in the given (*einen Zuschuss des Glaubens an eine im Gegebenen sich offenbarende göttliche Idee*), which still essentially and basically distinguishes all universal history, in spite of almost imperceptible changes, from the empirical investigation of developments (*der empirischen Entwicklungsforschung*). Therefore universal history is a part of history and the philosophy of history (*der Geschichte und der Geschichtsphiloso-phie*) and not of the purely exact empirical investiga-tion. It is illusionless critical investigation of facts and most careful historical-developmental construction; then in spite of all the horror and sacrilege of reality it retains the knowledge of the real for the presupposition of all truth; it will not be poetry and it will not be an apriori system. But at the same time it must also be actuated by an impulse of ethical incentive, and religious faith in the content of the ideas permeating the real (*einem Antrieb ethischen Entschlusses und religiösen Glaubens an die im Wirklichen durchdringenden Ideengehalte*) , or it is alto-gether impossible.[67]

Clearly, this points beyond the limits of the argument we have been examining. One does not say this because of the reference to the transcendent which this passage con-tains. We have seen Troeltsch argue this on nontheological grounds countless times. Nor does one make this claim merely because of the presence of theological terminology in the passage. If anything, the presence of the theological dimension in this formulation is both extremely restrained and hopelessly vague. It is, rather, in the light of the way that the argument turns in the final chapter of *Der His-torismus* that the real significance of this passage becomes apparent. What is philosophically tenuous may well be the-ologically necessary and illuminating. Moreover, the strug-gle with historical relativism may both clarify, and be clarified by, reflection of a specifically theological kind. What does it mean to intimate that " a subsidy of faith in a self-revealing divine idea in the given " is one of the ele-ments that distinguishes the search for a grasp of universal history from merely empirical investigation? What could it mean, that is, for one already committed to the view that history itself must be the only source of " the norms of the shape of life "? [68] Again, what is the meaning of the claim that " religious faith in the content of the ideas permeating the real " must be taken along with " an impulse of ethical incentive " in accounting for the sheer possibility of the philosophy of history? What could it mean, that is, for one already convinced that such a faith may only contribute to, and not dominate, that philosophy of history which must unfold the solution of " the norms of the shape of life "?

These questions are unavoidable if the passage before us is not to be ignored, and they crystallize the fact that Troeltsch's argument as a whole was driving him to the very frontier of his own theology. Unfinished business of a theological sort remained before the program begun with *Der Historismus* could reach a final conclusion. Troeltsch himself seemed at least partially aware of this. In *Meine Bücher* (My Books), written during the same year that he brought out *Der Historismus*, he characterized the projected second volume as one that would be " the summing up of all my studies " and that " would go far beyond the original religious beginning point of my work." [69] In what sense would the second volume go beyond this " original religious beginning point "? In the sense that the religious dimension would utterly disappear, or in the sense that it would be vastly expanded? Surely the latter, as is clear from the way Troeltsch continued to reflect:

> If my life and strength remain, I would then gladly return finally to the religious (*zum Religiösen*) and bring my philosophy of religion to its conclusion. This is my first love, for even in the cultural synthesis to be drawn in the contemporary situation by the philosophy of history, the religious remains in the center. Without this there is no naïveté and freshness. [70]

From the struggle with historical relativism *to* the conclusion of his philosophy of religion — this then was the line along which Troeltsch proposed to bring the intellectual labors of his lifetime to their culmination. This was actually the route along which he had always been moving, which is why the full range of his thought must be examined in close connection with the argument in *Der Historismus*. The formal implication is self-evident. This argument had been generated by a probing of the history of Christianity and its present situation which had already taken place. The tools for this probing had been supplied by the social scientists. To ponder the argument now before us in the light of the broader context of Troeltsch's investigations at large is to see that it represents the exhaustive refinement of the methodology that informed his first major work, *The Social Teachings*.

To leave the matter at the formal level, however, would be to overlook the most significant implication of the relationship between the argument of *Der Historismus* and the remainder of Troeltsch's thought. For the most decisive aspect of this relationship is substantive in character. We can only speculate as to how he would have proceeded with the material treatment of historicism. But in a striking sense — and far more significantly than might be expected — something of this is already present in the very context that had driven him to the study in the first place, namely, the probing of the history of Christianity and its present involvement in the modern world. In the case of *this* treatment the *objective periodizing* for which we have seen him contend [71] had already been developed. More than that, he had come to firm conclusions regarding the route along which the involvement of Christianity in the modern world must unfold. Here something closely approximating what in *Der Historismus* is termed the contemporary cultural synthesis had already begun to emerge. In this realm, where it had both the freedom and the necessity to develop, the theological dimension of his reflections took shape.

In turning, then, to Troeltsch's thought regarding the history of Christianity and its involvement in the modern world and to the development and ultimate issue of his theology we are turning to matters that are of a piece with the argument that we have examined throughout these two chapters. Though ruthlessly transmuted, the history of Christianity and dogmatics nevertheless remains the decisive foci of the only substantive treatment of historical relativism he was destined to achieve. Furthermore, though the ultimate issue of his theological reflection was disastrous, it was so because of the persistence of an unavoidable question. It is still unavoidable, *and unanswered,* even for a theological generation that has moved far beyond the horizons that circumscribed Troeltsch's attempt. What is the content of a theology that knows that " the fundamental historicizing of all our thought about man, his culture and his values " [72] can be clarified but not contained? To ask this is to accept the risks of the legacy of Ernst Troeltsch. It is to know both the fascination and the terror of the theology of involvement.

5 The End of Christendom

❖ ❖

Over all Troeltsch's investigations of the history of Christianity there stands a foreboding sense of urgency regarding its involvement in the present situation. His sensitivity to the character of the modern world is the root of his tortuous sifting of the methodological question and its implications, as we have seen. It is also the dominant factor in the increasing clarity with which he sketched and refined his principal substantive conclusions regarding the historical development of Christianity and its contemporary involvement. His response to the publishers' request that he prepare a preface for the English translation of one of his most incisive monographs begins on this note.

> In the aim which guided my studies, two main interests may be distinguished. The first is that of gaining an insight into the intellectual and religious situation of the present day, from which the significance and the possibilities of development possessed by Christianity might be deduced. That has led me to engage in historical investigations regarding the spirit of the modern world, for this can only be understood in the light of its relation to the earlier epochs of Christian civilization in Europe. As Adolf Harnack has described the genesis and the disintegration of Christian dogma, so I should like to examine the present situation and its significance for the fate of Christianity in the modern world.[1]

We must always be aware of this contemporary orientation of Troeltsch's historical investigations. It offers the
only possible way of dealing constructively with his findings. If ever there has been a historian who must be read
critically, Ernst Troeltsch is that man. His material discussions of history — both of the modern temperament and
of Christianity from its origins to the present — invariably
present the reader with an irritating blend of the precise
and the inaccurate. The inaccuracy of his treatments is
patently clear. He was given to broad, sweeping generalizations which rarely, if ever, find support in primary sources.[2]
As we have noted before, his way of writing history will
always outrage the specialists. One always finds Troeltsch
disappointing on what one knows the most about! However, the point to these generalizations is never that of the
specialists. The point is, rather, the attempt to work out
a treatment of the historical dimension of both the modern
spirit and the involvement of Christianity in the new and
singular strangeness of the modern world. As we have seen,
this attempt was informed by the sociological formulation
of historical method. Here Troeltsch was disciplined and
precise to an astonishing degree. The irony of his efforts
is that the element of inaccuracy often eclipses the element
of precision, and thus his work remains peculiarly vulnerable to those who, for any reason, would dismiss his conclusions. When one reads him in the light of his attempts
to clarify the formal problems confronting modern reflection, he cannot be disposed of so easily since the precision
of his findings transcends the limits of his inaccuracies.
The generalizations never disappear from his work — they
are always present and, more frequently than not, aggravat-
ing. But they are the provocative vehicles of an insight that
becomes more precise with each articulation, which may

be stated quite simply, and with which contemporary theology is only reluctantly coming to terms: Christendom is gone, once and for all.

We can see what it means to set this out as Troeltsch's principal finding by examining three decisive points: his distinction between classical and modern Protestantism, his understanding of the typological distinction between church and sect and his use of this distinction, and his portrayal of what might as well be termed the present impasse.

1. THE TWO PROTESTANTISMS

We have examined in some detail Troeltsch's argument that the modern world has its real beginning in the Enlightenment.[3] This is not only important for the understanding of the modern spirit. It is also decisive for any penetrating insight into the total development of Protestant Christianity. For if the Enlightenment is the real matrix from which the modern world emerges, then it is completely erroneous to treat the work of the Reformers from the standpoint of modern developments. This is to read into their time factors that were simply not present and to overlook factors that were decisive. Moreover, failure to grasp this inevitably leads one to misconstrue the nature of the modern involvement of Protestantism. Troeltsch argued emphatically that both the origins of Protestantism and the nature of its modern involvement can be properly understood only in the light of the medieval character of the work of the Reformers and of the structural results of this work which took shape long before the modern world came into being. He was convinced that the difference between the medieval and the modern contexts is so vast that a profound transmutation within Protestantism took place during the transition from the

By way of clarifying what it means to say that the ethic of classical Protestantism and that of medieval Catholicism must be seen in terms of their common context, Troeltsch proceeded to sketch one of the most incisive and celebrated findings of his investigations as a whole. This is his understanding of the role of natural law (the *lex naturae*) in the history of the Christian ethic. He noted that the achievement of a comprehensive cultural ethic by historic Christianity was no easy thing, given the relatively simple character of its original form. The difficulties of relating the ethic involved in the Christian faith to the complexities of the political and governmental order were addressed by ancient Christianity in terms of its identification of the Stoic conception of the *lex naturae* with the Christian moral law. This had occurred in a fashion precisely analogous to the utilization of the concept of the *logos* by ancient Christian thought as a means of explaining the revelation of God in Christ.[14] Now it was the genius of the medieval Catholic Church to utilize this tool for the exploitation of the opportunity that had arisen. What in the context of ancient Christianity had been applicable only in the sphere of private life was now extended to include the state, law, society, and the economic system as well. This led to the incorporation within Christian thought of the Aristotelian and other rational conceptions of the state and the economic order, a process that was possible on the ground of the " identity of the Lex naturae and the Lex Christi " whereby such conceptions were " legitimized at least indirectly as Christian." [15] The basis of Troeltsch's understanding of classical Protestantism is now before us. Its ethic also represented what he called a " completed cultural idea " because it too presupposed the very foundation on which medieval Catholicism had built.

Now the Protestant ethic retains this whole design. It clings to the ideal of a Christian culture guarded by the Church, and it is able also, on its side, to produce the fulfillment of the Christian ethic along with this-worldly conceptions of culture (*innerweltlichen Kulturgedanken*) only by means of the self-evidently retained equation of *Lex naturae* and *Lex Christi*.[16]

That classical Protestantism also entailed a " completed cultural idea " points to the real ambiguities both in distinguishing between it and medieval Catholicism and in dealing with its relationship to the rise of the modern world. These are separate problems, and they invariably tend to be confused. The false lead is to move too quickly from a derivation of incipiently modern elements in the thought of the Reformers to the difference between classical Protestantism and medieval Catholicism, with the inevitable result of overemphasis and distortion. Drastic differences there were, to be sure, and embryonically modern ideas are intertwined with these differences. But as far as premodern Protestantism is concerned these unfold in a way that is parallel to as well as antithetical to medieval Catholicism. For Troeltsch, what sounds like a simple and obvious aphorism was something to be taken with the utmost seriousness. The devastating upheaval within the well-ordered structure of medieval Catholicism brought about by the rise of Protestantism was rooted solely in " the positive religious ideas of the Reformation itself." [17] By this he meant to focus the question where it should be pondered — in the fact that Protestantism in its original form succeeded only in developing a rival medieval Christianity. This is the great refrain that reverberates almost antiphonally throughout his treatment of this matter. Thus he could insist that in terms of its immediate result the Reformation must be construed as a " powerful, two-centuries long, late flowering of the middle ages." [18] He could argue that this is so because the Reformers and Protestantism in general launched an attack on medieval Christianity *from within,* and not *from without,* involving the *reformation,* not the *abolition* of the medieval church.[19] Or again, in what is his most incisive way of putting it, he could say that Protestantism really emerged as a new answer to an old question:

> The most important thing is that Protestantism — considered from the standpoint of the history of religion and the history of dogma — and especially its beginning point, Luther's reform of the Church, is first of all only a reconstruction of Catholicism, a continuation of the Catholic formulation of the question, to which there comes a new answer.[20]

The purpose of this strong emphasis upon the medieval character of classical Protestantism was the precise orientation of the analysis both of its challenge to medieval Catholicism and of the elements within it that may properly be said to have had a role in the rise of the modern world. Troeltsch intended no minimizing of either of these, and he could formulate both with as much polemics and insight as anyone else. Of course there are potentially modern ideas — or better, ideas that will find a later significance only dimly foreseeable in their original form — within Protestantism from the very beginning. But before these can have their real effect they must be disengaged from the framework within which, necessarily, they first came to light.

> Now to be sure throughout all of this " the New " (*das Neue*) must not be overlooked — that which Protestantism brought and by means of which it became at least to some extent the creator of the modern world. But these

new [elements] need throughout and first of all the dissolution of their close connection with the Reformation's supernatural ideas of the Church, authority, and culture, in order really to operate as " the New " in principle.[21]

Thus he spoke of " the dissolution of the concept of the sacraments " as the " central religious idea of Protestantism." [22] He saw in this dissolution a transmutation that made of the two accepted sacraments themselves " only special forms of presentation of the Word." [23] Moving beyond such traditional terminology, he noted that " religion and wonder are drawn into the sphere of the intelligible and the psychologically understandable," and he observed that this " cuts the heart out of the Catholic system " in the sense that what is now needed is " only the preacher of ideas which anyone can find for himself in the Scripture." [24] In all of this Troeltsch saw " ideas of the most enormous significance," and he formulated this significance in terms that demonstrate the relationship of the work of the Reformers to the modern context, even though this way of putting it is clearly limited by his own theological persuasion:

> It is the inner, personal, and spiritual [character] of religion; the autonomy, freedom, and wholeness of the morality arising out of surrender to God; it is the immanence and presence of God in his world and the consecration of all the natural as a divinely willed component of his creation; the overcoming of the evil will purely through the knowledge of the divine determination of holiness and grace.[25]

On the other hand, however, Troeltsch formulated with equal vigor the substantial side of his contention that classical Protestantism was a medieval phenomenon. However radically a new answer might be forthcoming from its labors, Protestantism was still decisively preoccupied with an old question.

> However the Reformers have indissolubly combined these fully modern thoughts with two completely anti-modern ideas: first, with the binding of the redeeming knowledge of God to an absolutely objective supernatural authority, and an ecclesiastical establishment handling this authority [which is] of no less supernatural character; secondly, with the most highly intensified doctrine of original sin, which isolates the Christian from the non-Christian, depreciates the presence of God in the creation and in the natural good, and permanently fixes the whole picture of the world in the myth of the originally perfect, painless, immortal world which then chooses in exchange for freedom [to be] lost and sorrowful.[26]

Here it is even more obvious that Troeltsch's formulation suffers the limits of his own theological position. How obsolete (his word is *unmodernen*) are the Reformers' doctrines of the church and of original sin? Granted the medieval pattern of their doctrines of the church, are these doctrines completely subsumed under the term " supernatural "? Again, is it the Reformers' doctrines of original sin or the development of this doctrine at the hands of Protestant orthodoxy that removes God from his creation and the natural good? May this indictment be made good even against Protestant orthodoxy? Is there no possibility of finding useful lines of inquiry and reflection suggested by premodern Protestantism for a generation of Protestant theology completely at home within the ambiguities of the modern world? In short, may not even the primary concerns of the Reformers and their immediate successors be reformulated profitably in the midst of the modern context? Theology since Troeltsch's day must surely find him vulnerable on issues such as these. But in so doing it must phrase its questions in ways that corroborate, rather than obliterate, his point, and thus suggest the lingering and haunting possibility that his perceptions transcend his limits. For what did it take to yield these ways of formulating the questions? Precisely what Troeltsch claimed, namely, the external pressures of new developments, the rise of the modern world.

With the arrival of the modern world everything was changed. The authoritarian culture of an ecclesiastically dominated age gave way before a ferment defined by *autonomy* and *individualism,* with the added characteristics of historical relativism, the " this-worldliness (*Innerweltlichkeit*) of the aims of life," and a spirit of optimism marked by self-confidence and a belief in progress.[27] In the face of this Protestantism underwent profound alteration. Gone was the context in which its " completed cultural ideal "[28] had emerged and operated. Gone was its own rival way of comprehending the whole of reality within its structural achievements. Gone was its initiative in addressing and dominating its milieu. With the disappearance of this presupposed context the deep-seated changes in the continuing nature of Protestantism had set in and taken effect long before their causes were recognized, let alone confronted. Indeed, they were not really recognized until Troeltsch's pioneering attempt to read the history of Christianity sociologically, and we are still trying to find out what it means to confront them!

These were the factors to which Troeltsch was most sensitive in his insistence that it is necessary " for any genuinely historical consideration and especially for our formulation of the question *to distinguish well between classical and modern Protestantism.*"[29] The heart of the matter for him was the fact and the effect of this shift in the context, and the full impact of this shift becomes apparent when its sociological and political dimensions are taken into account. We may paraphrase his understanding of the situation as follows: As over against classical Protestantism, modern Protestantism, from the end of the seventeenth century on, had to come to terms with a new context — one dominated by the nonsectarian, religiously indifferent state. In this context Protestantism transferred in principle the whole activity of religious organization and the formation of religious communities to the realm of voluntarism and personal conviction. It did so under the influence of the basic acknowledgement of both the possibility and the fact of different religious convictions and communities existing side by side. It acknowledged at the same time, in an even stronger sense, the fact of a completely emancipated secular life existing alongside itself — a life that it did not attempt to dominate either directly or indirectly through the intervention of the state.[30]

The decisive implication of this distinction between classical and modern Protestantism is before us in this delineation. On the far side of the Enlightenment there is no such thing as " a fully emancipated secular life (*ein völlig emanzipiertes weltliches Leben*) "[31]; on this side of the Enlightenment it is not only present, its presence is undisturbed. Troeltsch's point revolves around this central contention. Protestantism's acquiescence in the emergence alongside itself of a realm it did not touch marks the end of its "completed cultural ideal." For this acquiescence presages the disappearance of that central ingredient of medieval Christianity that Protestantism too had presupposed, namely, the equation of the natural law with the law of God. The collapse of Protestantism's mastery of its context took with it the foundation on which this mastery had been built.

> In connection with this it [Protestantism] forgot, even to the point of complete lack of understanding, its old doctrine making possible and promoting this dominance, the identity of the *Lex Dei* and the *Lex naturae*.[32]

The disappearance of this basic equation symbolizes the fact that in the transition from the medieval to the modern world Protestantism lost its entrée into the ongoing development of civilization and culture. The contrast between classical Protestantism and modern Protestantism is thus not simply that between a Protestantism which had a completed cultural ideal and one which did not. It is, rather, the contrast between a Protestantism that had attempted to master its context and one that, without realizing it, had abandoned this attempt completely. This is not to say that Protestant Christianity was hence forth totally excluded from the ongoing development of civilization and culture. It is, rather, to say that in the modern context its relationship to this development came to be paradoxical — shot full of an ambiguity rooted in the fact that change was now shaped by new forces, only some of which had any recognizably Protestant characteristics. The urgency of knowing as precisely as possible just what the relationship between Protestantism and the rise of the modern world is derives from this. Troeltsch could say, without hesitation and in the face of all that we have watched him observe, that there can be " no doubt " regarding the presence of Protestantism in the " production of the modern world." [33] The paradoxical character of its involvement will yield its secret, however, only if one seeks the *indirect, unconscious,* even *unwilling* points of contact at which Protestantism can be meaningfully said to have exerted a measurable force upon the emergence of the modern world. These will invariably be found in " accidental side-effects " or in " influences generated against its will." [34] They will not be discerned in the " general rebirth or rebuilding of the totality of life." [35] Moreover, when the matter is put this way, a fact of the utmost significance asserts itself. In order to discern this indirect impact of " Protestantism proper (*eigentlichen Protestantismus*) " one must consider that in the effects it did produce it was intertwined with " humanistic criticism," " the Baptist sectarian ideal," and " mystical subjectivism." [36]

The illumination of the tangential character of Protestantism's relationship to the rise of the modern world was the catalyst that sped the process yielding the sharp distinction between classical and modern Protestantism. The distinction itself was one of the central and decisive elements of Troeltsch's pondering of " the present situation and its significance for the fate of Christianity in the modern world." [37] In terms of this distinction alone he both could and did penetrate deeply into this broader concern. He did this in two ways, the most *cogent* of which concerns the political point, the most *problematical,* the theological point.

Regarding the political question Troeltsch argued unshakable conclusions. " Protestantism did not create the secular state, the modern idea of the state, and an independent ethic of politics." [38] At best it may be said to have prepared the way for this. In general terms, it did so by effectively challenging the dominance of the hierarchy over the political order and by according to the political calling the status of a direct service of God. More particularly it prepared the way by virtue of the involvement of Calvinism in the decisive, explosive, and far-reaching events of the English revolution at the time of Cromwell. But here one encounters the complicated question of " Protestantism proper," to use the term noted above, in combination with other influences. This is the problem of the fusion of " radicalized Calvinism " with " revived Baptist and Spiritualist movements." [89] Even this is *indirect* influence, which may be said only to have been a part of the process leading to the emergence of the modern state. What, then, does this imply regarding " the fate of Christianity in the modern world "? At the very least, the force of Troeltsch's argument indicates that this question is not rhetorical! Indeed, it is placed in a new, revealing, and complicating light. Since what has come to pass on the political front is not the child of Protestantism, the element of control has passed from its hands. To be sure, this is far too limited a basis upon which to build a negative conclusion regarding Christianity's potentiality for survival in the modern world. One thing, however, is clear: The easy assumption of a straight line from the Reformers to the modern world has been shattered and with it has gone the comfort of an easy prediction of the future.

A similar judgment is also the outcome of the highly problematical theological point that Troeltsch raised in this connection. He was willing not only to admit but to argue forcefully that there is one element in the modern spirit that is the result of the " independent, central, completely unique and direct influence of Protestantism." This is in " the religious sphere." [40] The point is both a *restricted* and a *tentative* one. It is restricted in the sense that sharp limits must be imposed upon it.

> Protestantism is after all primarily a religious power, and only in the second and third place a cultural power in the narrower sense of the word.[41]

More significant than that, and indeed the concomitant of it, is the tentativeness that must be acknowledged and asserted. To believe, as Troeltsch did, that in the religious sphere Protestantism is directly influential on the modern spirit is to assume that there is " a religious spirit peculiar to the modern world." [42] He was fully aware of the controversial character of this question. In the face of it he could only assert his conviction that " without religious foundation, without metaphysics and ethics, an undivided and strong spirit of culture is impossible." [43] Furthermore, he could see both in the role of an extended form of classical Protestantism in Anglo-Saxon life and in the close inner connection between Protestantism and German idealism as " leading forces " in " the religious life of the modern world " the factual basis for the claim that " the religion of the modern world is essentially determined by Protestantism and that herein lies its strongest historical significance." [44] But in all this he was really pointing to the relationship between a transmuted Protestantism and an emerging religious spirit. No one was more aware than Troeltsch himself that this juxtaposition involves new problems and new tasks " the solution of which is not even remotely visible." [45]

The reason for commencing our treatment of the substance of Troeltsch's historical investigations with the distinction between the two Protestantisms is now before us. The implications of the distinction itself are more important than the unwieldy character of the categories by means of which he developed it. One cannot really speak of either of the two Protestantisms in the singular without continual need for clarification (e.g., the contrast between Lutheranism and Calvinism regarding the political point) .[46] This need was already being given serious attention with the progressive publication of the parts of *The Social Teachings* during the very years that saw the publication of the two treatises with which we have been concerned in this section.[47] Moreover, the decisive insights to be drawn regarding " the fate of Christianity in the modern world " do not gain full expression if one is considering only Protestantism and the transition from the medieval world to the modern. This too was in the process of solution with the work on *The Social Teachings* and the broader canvas it provided. Even so, the distinction alone, problematical though it is, provides a leverage which moves more than might be thought at first glance. The insight to be formulated was one that Troeltsch himself was not yet willing to admit when he first began to press his case. For if he is right in the thrust of his argument, then it could — indeed, it must — be said that Protestantism is involved in the modern world as a disenfranchised alien seeking for a home in a strange, new land with no possibility of return to familiar and comfortable surroundings.

2. CHURCH AND SECT

The tangential character of the relationship between Protestantism and the rise of the modern world is only one part of a broad picture. What can be said regarding Troeltsch's substantive historical conclusions is in fact cogent only against the backdrop of the whole sweep of the history of Christian social thought. Thus, in order to clarify what it means to say that the relationship between Protestantism and the rise of the modern world was tangential the hopelessly generalized character of the argument we have just examined must be overcome. This is why Troeltsch's basic articulation of the point at hand will always be found in *The Social Teachings* rather than in the more concise statements with which we have been concerned in the preceding section. This emergent perspective is both illuminated and extended by the decisive matter that must now be treated — namely, the celebrated typological distinction between *church* and *sect,* which Troeltsch took over from Max Weber and developed in terms of his own concerns.

Weber's contribution to Troeltsch's thought at this point was both formal and substantial. One must add that it was also profound. As has been often noted, the relationship between Troeltsch and Weber was an extremely close one.[48] It is undoubtedly true to say that it was from Weber primarily that Troeltsch gained his insights into the emerging discipline of sociology — insights which, as we have seen at length, shaped the very center of his own creativity.

To understand Troeltsch's version of the significance of the distinction between church and sect one must know what Weber meant by an *ideal type.* Without getting lost in the fascinating question of dealing comprehensively with the astonishing breadth of Weber's thought and literary productivity, we can come to terms with this by looking briefly at his essay *" Objectivity " in Social Science and Social Policy,* first published in 1904.[49]

For Weber the relationship between the social sciences and the historical disciplines was always very close. " If one wishes to call those disciplines which treat the events of human life with respect to their cultural significance ' cultural sciences,' then social science in our sense belongs in that category." [50] The investigations in which he was involved could well be characterized as those seeking to unfold " the general cultural significance of the social-economic structure of the human community." [51] This concern animated the emergence of social science as Weber understood it.

> It is not the "actual" interconnections of "things" but the *conceptual* interconnections of *problems* which define the scope of the various sciences. A new "science" emerges where new problems are pursued by new methods and truths are thereby discovered which open up significant new points of view.[52]

Clearly, this delineation of the specific sphere (Weber's word is *Arbeitsgebiet* [53]) of the social sciences turns on the question of the conceptual formation of problems with which such disciplines are concerned. This was the immediate context within which he fashioned the device of the *ideal type* as one of the key analytical tools for the operation of social science. Virtually all the implications of his concept are suggested by the following formulation:

> It [the ideal-type] is a conceptual construct (*Gedankenbild*) which is neither historical reality nor even the "true" reality. It is even less fitted to serve as a schema under which a real situation or action is to be subsumed as one *instance*. It has the significance of a purely ideal *limiting* concept with which the real situation or action is *compared* and surveyed for the explication of certain of its significant components. Such concepts are constructs in terms of which we formulate relationships by the application of the category of objective possibility. By means of this category, the adequacy of our imagination, oriented and disciplined by reality, is *judged*.[54]

The overtones of this conception may be briefly indicated: (1) As the passage explicitly states, an ideal type is *not* identical with historical reality. It is, rather, a limiting concept whereby reflections on given historical phenomena may be oriented and disciplined by reality itself. (2) In the face of this a second implication — the counterpoint of the first — must be emphasized immediately. Whereas an ideal type is not identical with historical reality, it is not divorced from it. Weber did not understand the use of ideal types to involve vague generalizations. On the contrary, precisely the particularity of the cultural phenomena under consideration is what his conception of typological analysis was designed to disclose. As he put it at one point, " The goal of ideal-typical concept-construction is always to make clearly explicit not the class or average character but rather the unique individual character of cultural phenomena." [55]

Alongside these two points a second pair of implications must be noted. (3) An ideal type is " ideal " solely in the sense that it is a deliberately abstract and synthetic " construct," which arises out of empirical data " through the conceptual heightening of certain elements of reality." It serves the purpose of explicating at the level of pragmatic illustration the particular features of a given relationship.[56] (4) At the same time, whereas this " conceptual heightening of certain elements of reality " is both deliberate and can be " indispensable for certain heuristic as well as expository purposes," [57] Weber held it to be self-evident that the construction of ideal types has no ethical overtones whatsoever. The controlling factors throughout must be understood under the rubrics of the " objectively possible " and what could be termed the " sociologically adequate," not the rubrics of the ethically imperative.[58]

In the light of these four points the central significance of Weber's conception of the ideal type becomes clear. An ideal type is a device designed solely for the purpose of organizing the data of research in such a way that one can meaningfully and precisely reflect upon both the causal relationships and the unique elements it discloses. This focuses properly the explicitly Kantian coloration of Weber's conception. " If," he argued, " one perceives the implications of the fundamental ideas of modern episte- mology which ultimately derives from Kant; namely, that concepts are primarily analytical instruments for the intel- lectual mastery of empirical data and can be only that, the fact that precise genetic concepts are necessarily ideal types will not cause him to desist from constructing them." [59] Weber thus sought to recognize productively the gap be- tween empirical data and the concepts used both to dis- cover and to analyze them, allowing for the full acknowl- edgment of and reckoning with the vantage point of the observer: " Concepts are not ends but are means to the end of understanding phenomena which are significant from concrete individual viewpoints." [60]

That all this would be useful to Troeltsch may have been immediately apparent to him in the terms that we have been noting. However that may be, any doubt in this regard would have certainly disappeared with the fact that Weber illustrated both the inevitability and the necessity of ideal type construction with the distinction between church and sect.

> The ideal-type is an attempt to analyze historically unique configurations or their individual components by means of genetic concepts. Let us take for instance the concepts " church " and " sect." They may be broken down purely classificatorily into complexes of characteris- tics whereby not only the distinction between them but also the content of the concept must constantly remain fluid. If however I wish to formulate the concept of " sect " genetically, e.g., with reference to certain impor- tant cultural significances which the " sectarian spirit "

has had for modern culture, certain characteristics of both become *essential* because they stand in an adequate causal relationship to those influences. However, the concepts thereupon become ideal-typical in the sense that they appear in full conceptual integrity either not at all or only in individual instances. Here as elsewhere every concept which is not purely classificatory diverges from reality.[61]

Thus, exactly at the point where the genetic question is raised — in this case this would be exemplified by the question of the significance of the sectarian spirit for the rise of modern culture — the distinction between church and sect loses its purely classificatory significance. This is not to say that it necessarily loses its precision. It is, rather, to note that precision now serves ends other than those of mere classification.

Ideal type construction is always rooted in the present concerns — or better, the living involvements — of the one who constructs them. In the immediate context of the formulation just before us Weber stated this in a memorable way: " Social science in our sense is concerned with practical *significance.*" The point is, now, that the real problem has to do with setting out this significance as precisely as possible. Thus, Weber continues, " This significance however can very often be brought unambiguously to mind only by relating the empirical data to an ideal limiting case." This led him to the scathing insight so characteristic of those absolutely convinced of the cogency of their own argument: The issue is not whether one operates in this fashion; it is only whether one does so in a disciplined, scientific manner.

If the historian (in the widest sense of the word) rejects an attempt to construct such ideal types as a " theoretical construction," i.e., as useless or dispensable for his concrete heuristic purposes, the inevitable consequence is either that he consciously or unconsciously uses other similar concepts without formulating them verbally and elaborating them logically or that he remains in the realm of the vaguely " felt." [62]

Troeltsch took over from Weber the whole conception of ideal type analysis, and not merely the distinction between church and sect. Failure to grasp this will invariably lead to a completely mistaken apprehension of the significance of his own extension of Weber's initial forays into the question. Those critiques of *Troeltsch's* point that worry interminably about the usefulness of his distinction for purposes of classification — whether they do so with an eye toward rejecting his point entirely or improving his distinction — overlook the basic purpose of ideal type analysis. That purpose is not classification but clarification. The precision for which Weber pressed is directly related to the *practical significance* of the given analysis. To be sure, ideal type distinctions are not ordered by ethical preferences but by what we have seen him call " objective possibility." Nevertheless, when the point to the analysis is the clarification of the present, as was surely the case with Troeltsch's appropriation of Weber's suggestion, the ethical problems of the present emerge in forms that are agonizing simply because they are objectively oriented. To see this correctly, however, it must be understood that one does not seek to force historical data into propagandistic use in favor of the church type as over against the sect type, or vice versa. The point is, rather, to clarify the process by which the past has yielded and shaped the problematic of the present.

That Troeltsch did in fact deal with the distinction between church and sect in a way that met Weber's specifications is evident in the high regard that Weber had for

Troeltsch's work. Furthermore, Troeltsch himself was scrupulously clear in attributing the source of the point to Weber. When the distinction first came up for prolonged discussion in *The Social Teachings,* he explicitly acknowledged his indebtedness in superlative terms.[63] Weber, on the other hand, was equally explicit — more than that, he was complimentary in a way that exceeds any explanation merely on the ground of the close personal relationship between them. From his standpoint in 1920, the year of his death, the sum of the matter for Weber was that Troeltsch had " taken over and treated thoroughly " the conception of the sect which he, Weber, had initially devised.[64]

However, the use to which Troeltsch put the ideal type distinction between church and sect extends beyond the limits of Weber's researches, vast though these were. Furthermore, they differed regarding the heart of the distinction. For Weber, the distinction turns on the *voluntarism* of the sect. In Troeltsch's view the heart of the distinction has to do with the question of the attitude toward and the relationship to the world.

A succinct formulation of this from Weber's point of view occurs when, in the well-known *The Protestant Ethic and the Spirit of Capitalism,* he took up the discussion of " The Baptist Sects," proposing to treat " the Baptists, Mennonites, and above all, the Quakers." [65]

> The feature of all these communities, which is both historically and in principle most important, but whose influence on the development of culture can only be made quite clear in a somewhat different connection, is something with which we are already familiar, the believer's Church. This means that the religious community, the visible Church in the language of the Reformation Churches, was no longer looked upon as a sort of trust

foundation for supernatural ends, an institution, necessarily including both the just and the unjust, whether for
increasing the glory of God (Calvinistic) or as a medium
for bringing the means of salvation to men (Catholic and
Lutheran), but solely as a community of personal believ-
ers of the reborn, and only these. In other words, not as a
Church but as a sect.[66]

In the note that Weber appended here he underlined
the point that for him the key to the whole conception of
the sect was the voluntarism that epitomizes the believer's
church. The sect is not to be understood primarily in terms
of its lack of relationship to the state, nor even in terms of
the fact that membership in the believing community depends upon a " contract of admission " between the con-
gregation and the catechumen. The central element is,
rather, the voluntary character of the existence of the sectarian community. The decisive clue to the distinction between church and sect is thus the fact that for the sect
compulsion plays no role at the level of organization.[67]

Troeltsch both could and did share this emphasis. But it
cannot be said that this was the decisive element for him.
The " conceptual heightening of certain elements of reality," [68] which we have seen to be so significant a factor in
ideal type analysis, took shape for him in a different fashion. This was a point that he never tired of attempting to
make clear. Whereas his debt to Weber was immense, his
own creativity was also at work in the use of the tools that
he borrowed from Weber. As he put it on one occasion,
it is " completely misleading " to regard Weber and himself as involved in a " common scientific business." Such a
view fails to note the difference in intention and goal
between an " economic-historical formulation of the question (wirtschaftsgeschichtlichen Fragestellung) " and " in-

vestigations in the realm of the history of religion (*religionsgeschichtliche Untersuchungen*) ." [69] Thus, Troeltsch insisted without equivocation that his work involved a much broader scope than Weber's. Indeed, what was for Weber " the central theme " was for him significant only as a " single phenomenon " within the broad panorama.[70]

The element of reality conceptually heightened by Troeltsch in putting into operation the distinction between church and sect for his own purposes was the sharp contrast between two widely divergent attitudes toward the world. This is of the utmost significance in understanding what Troeltsch uncovered in *his* use of what Weber had shown him. He was in fact looking at the entire spectrum of the history of Christian social thought, and with this subject matter to organize the question of the relationship to the context far transcended, though it did not exclude, the matter of compulsion versus voluntarism in the structuring of the church as over against that of the sect. More than that, this wider range of concern forced Troeltsch to place alongside church and sect a *third* type, that of mysticism. The clue to why this is so is to be found precisely at the point where Troeltsch's thought moved beyond Weber's and incorporated a broader set of criteria. Revolving as they do around the matter of the relationship to the context, rather than simply the question of voluntarism versus coercion, Troeltsch's criteria were related to a range of data that the distinction between church and sect does not exhaust. As we shall see, the most striking thing is that what for Weber was fascinating enough as a genetic problem with a limited scope was for Troeltsch a massive, and ultimately unnerving, problem of *involvement*.

The threefold ideal type distinction that Troeltsch utilized in ordering the data as his history of Christian social thought unfolds may be stated concisely. The church type is distinguished by a *positive* relationship to the world; the sect type, by a *negative* relationship; the mystic type, by the *absence* of both concern and potency in the face of the question of its relationship to the world. This is patent in the summarizing juxtaposition of the three types in the conclusion of *The Social Teachings:*

> *The Church* is the holy institution and the institution of grace, endowed with the result of the work of redemption, which can absorb the masses and adapt itself to the world, since, up to a certain point, it can neglect subjective holiness in exchange for the objective treasures of grace and redemption. *The Sect* is the free union of stronger and more conscious Christians, who join together as the truly reborn, separate themselves from the world, remain limited to a small circle, emphasize the law instead of grace and in their circle set up love as the Christian order of life with greater or lesser radicalism, all of which is the preparation for and the expectation of the coming Kingdom of God. *Mysticism* is the intensification and the making immediate of the world of ideas solidified in cult and doctrine into a purely personal and inner possession of the heart (*Gemütsbesitz*) , whereby only fluid and completely personally limited group formations can assemble, and in which the remaining cult, dogma and connection with history tend to become so fluid that they disappear.[71]

In introducing this passage, Troeltsch claimed that these three types had been implicit in Christianty from the very beginning. This makes sense as a concluding generalization. The interesting thing is, however, that the typological distinctions just summarized are neither clarified nor utilized, either in part or as a whole, until the subject matter of the analysis of Christendom in the medieval period evokes it. The significance of this should be self-evident. It is the negative corroboration of the fact that the heart of the matter for Troeltsch was the question of the relationship between Christianity in any of its forms and its context. Implicitly, of course, this problem is present in Christianity from its origins forward. But it does not become *explicit* until positive recognition of and involvement in the context of the world becomes self-consciously decisive for Christianity. The emergence of just this recognition and involvement is *the* formative factor in the development of medieval Christianity.[72] As this unfolds — and it is a process centuries long — the proliferation always implict within the dynamic of the Christian gospel takes shape *explicitly* in terms of the problem of the relationship between the structures of Christianity and the context of the world.

Thus, in the passage before us the decisive phrase describing the *church* type is that " it can absorb the masses and adapt itself to the world "; all the other elements of the description are in fact either the roots of or the results of this basic, positive attitude toward the context. Moreover, both the *sect* type and the *mystic* type are understandable in contradistinction to this decisive and formative element of the church type. Accordingly, the *sect* type characteristically consists of those who " separate themselves from the world "; and once again, the other elements of the description of this type are related to this basic point as corollaries to an axiom. Finally, the *mystic* type — at once the most elusive and most portentous of the three — is locatable in terms of *individualism* and *fluidity,* with vexatiously little or no direct concern for the context. The decisive point regarding this third type probably suggests itself already: Its major significance for the history of

Christian social thought becomes clear only with reference to the present and the impasse with which Christianity is confronted in the modern world.

Troeltsch's movement beyond Weber regarding the ideal type distinction between church and sect was thus intimately related to the specific goal of his broad argument as a whole. The yield of this movement was rich indeed. With the tools supplied by Weber's clarification of ideal type analysis Troeltsch was able to set out with precision the central elements of the history of Christian social thought. In the process, the conclusions emerging from his insight into what we have called his distinction between "The Two Protestantisms" were simultaneously rendered more comprehensive and more cogent.

The central thesis of the entire first chapter of *The Social Teachings* can be briefly epitomized. The chapter is entitled "The Foundations in the Ancient Church." The Biblical material is treated in this chapter under two headings: "The Gospel" [73] and "Paul." [74] In the concluding phases of the second of these sections Troeltsch formulated a broad conclusion equally applicable to both and anticipating the direction of his subsequent argument.

> It seems a matter of fact that social consequences of two very different kinds lie within it [i.e., early Christianity]: either the idealistic anarchy and love-communism, which with radical indifference or antipathy toward the other orders of the world embodies the love-idea in small circles, or the socially conservative development of an attitude accommodating itself to God's order and will as over against the world, with the strong independence of a community ordered according to its own particular inner concerns, which in connection with its increasing size cannot ignore the orders of the world, but as far as possible must make use of them for its own ends. [75]

In Troeltsch's view, ancient Christianity as a whole was characterized by this "intermingling of conservative and radical elements." He was convinced that he could account for this. Commenting by way of suggesting the future prospects as of the close of the period that produced the New Testament, he noted that for the Christianity of antiquity "an inner connection and continuity between the general political-economic-social conditions and the values of the personal-religious life is neither sought nor found." This is the all-comprehending fact that subsumes the broad spectrum of possibilities. Thus, "the radicalism of its ideology" could take the form of "conviction and will," and proceed "from within," or it could take the form of "law and demand," and be externalized. Accordingly, it "partly abandons itself to the substructures of the spiritual-ethic world," and "it partly rejects them flatly." In either case, however, the end result is the same: It "tolerates and thereby conserves" these very structures, regarding them as "divine institutions or arrangements in the sinful world." [76]

Now the single point that it is the function of the opening chapter of *The Social Teachings* to substantiate is this: As regards its relationship to its context, the Christianity of antiquity was conservative through and through. In Troeltsch's meaning of the terms,[77] it had no social doctrine. That is, it had no doctrine of the world qua world. The precondition for the development of such was not yet present. No inner contact with the substructures of the spiritual and ethical world developed because the complexities of the situation precluded the possibility of this taking place. As Troeltsch observed in the concluding phases of the chapter, there was, on the one hand, "the long-established estrangement from the world (*Welt-*

fremdheit)." [78] Along with this there was, on the other hand, the fact that the church grew up within, but never overcame, and never really sought to overcome, the empire, so that throughout the ancient period Christianity existed in the midst of what Troeltsch called " the parallelism of two independent social structures, the universal empire and the universal Church." [79] Under the impact of these two decisive factors the Christianity of antiquity " never produced, never wished to produce, and never could have wished to produce a uniform Christian culture." [80]

As over against the two extremes — radical and conservative — there was a third possible social consequence implicit within Christianity. This would be the result of the effort " to shape the social orders positively, as the foundations (*Unterlagen*) and prior forms (*Vorformen*) of the attainment of the highest religious-ethical goal." [81] The realization of this third possibility is the decisive fact differentiating the Christianity of antiquity from that of the medieval period. The second chapter of *The Social Teachings*, entitled " Medieval Catholicism," has the function of making this clear.[82]

At several points we have had occasion to allude to Troeltsch's basic observation in this connection.[83] This must now be summarized more comprehensively. As the sole social organism to survive the collapse of the Roman Empire in the west, the ancient Catholic Church was drawn into a civilizing activity it had never known before, having no choice but to fill the void. The resulting process was long, complicated, and richly varied. It included the movement from the territorial church to the imposing development of the Papacy into the decisive and regnant institution that henceforth would be synonymous with the

very term " Catholicism." It carried with it a broad refinement and extension of the Christian understanding of
natural law, to the point where this would be necessarily
self-evident as one of the bases of the homogenizing intermingling of theology and thought in general, so intrinsic
to medieval reflection in all its varied expressions. It provided the context for a gigantic figure like Thomas
Aquinas — the context within which that very *uniform
Christian culture,* so notably missing from the Christianity
of antiquity and so definitively present as the marking
characteristic of the Christendom of the medieval scene,
would be both conceivable and inexorably necessary.

All these factors contributed to and were part of the
realization of that third possibility which was forever beyond the horizon of the ancient Catholic Church. " The
middle ages . . . witnessed the extension of the Church
to an all embracing, combining and mediating social whole,
which embraced the sociological circle of religion itself and
also the political-social formations." [84] As Troeltsch put it
in introducing the section on " The Medieval Social Philosophy According to the Principles of Thomism," this
yielded " the concept of the Corpus Christianum," that is,
" the concept of the Church extended over its natural preliminary stages *(ihre natürlichen Vorstufen)* ." [85]

Such a realization could not take place when " Christianity was able to construct its ideal state, the Church, on
a purely religious basis." [86] The point is that in the medieval context Christianity in its major structural expression did not develop " on a purely religious basis." Precisely because of this the tendency toward a *radical* social
consequence, always present within Christianity, now became irrepressible. It was the genius of medieval Catholicism to contain this, most characteristically in the monastic

orders. Even so, an increasingly unwieldy proliferation must mark any authentic portrayal of the unfolding of medieval Christianity. In order to render this complexity manageable Troeltsch began to build on the ideal type distinction between church and sect.

The concluding section of the chapter on medieval Catholicism thus begins with a broad and detailed delineation of this contrast. Of the host of illuminating observations which here emerge and clarify the basic distinction already before us [87] the following five points will suffice.

1. As an integral part of the presentation Troeltsch formulated explicitly why he had waited until this point to bring the distinction into play. The dualism of these two sociological types had indeed been present from the beginning. The prevailing situation throughout the ancient period, however, had been one fluctuating between church type and sect type. The opposition between " Augustine's sacramental-hierarchical conception of the Church and that of the Donatists " represents an " abrupt surfacing " of the problem. " But this opposition died out with African Christianity, and its decisive coming to prominence succeeded the perfecting of the concept of the Church in the Gregorian Church reform." [88] Given the development of medieval Catholicism from this point forward, the matter now becomes intrinsic to " the clearer understanding of the *subsequent* development " of Christianity.[89]

2. Troeltsch emphasized the fact that the sect type is " an independent sociological type of the Christian idea." In so doing he was insisting that " the term ' Sect ' does not signify a value judgment with regard to the dwarfing of the Church (*ein Werturteil über Verkümmerungen des Kirchlichen*) ." [90] Nothing can be quite so misleading as a failure to grasp this. The sect is not an embryonic church.

Though one cannot escape the inference that in a sense the sects are parasitic in that they characteristically take their rise from calling into question the church type's relationship with the world, the fact remains that refusal to be positively related to the world can find ground for its stand in the gospel as well as the opposite point of view can. Again, though one can hardly avoid noting that in time most, if not all, sects become churches — that is, that only with great difficulty can separation from the world be permanently maintained — the fact is that such a process entails a basic transmutation *from* sect type *to* church type. Both of these inferences are valid implications of Troeltsch's understanding of the contrast itself, but neither of them may be taken to suggest that the sect is only an incompleted variation of the church. Such a view drastically distorts the genuine insight at hand. " They [the sects] are in fact something other than the Church and the Churches." [91]

3. Similarly, a decisive clarification regarding the church type must be underlined. To be related positively to the world will always yield what looks like submissive accommodation. If the matter is left there, however, both the strength and the purpose of the church type's relationship to the world will be overlooked. " The Church is in fact not a simple defection (*Abfall*) from the gospel." [92] No attempt to implement the gospel in a continuing world ever is! This is why Troeltsch's characteristic term in this connection is not " accommodation " but " compromise." The concept of compromise is so centrally important for the thought of Troeltsch that we will give detailed consideration to it in the next chapter. The point here is to listen to him insist that just as oversimplification of the sect type must be ruled out, so must distortion of the

church type be rigorously resisted, lest the distinction between the two yield a premature value judgment in either direction.

> With its unconditioned universalism, it [the church type] nevertheless contains the basic impulse of the preaching of the gospel; only this had left all particular questions of possibility and realization to the miraculous coming of the kingdom, whereas a Church working in the continuing world (*Weltdauer*) organizes and orders itself here, and in so doing must contract its compromises.[93]

4. Only in the light of these refinements will the twofold value judgment that Troeltsch was driven to assert be intelligible in the controlled sense that he had in mind. On the one hand, it must be noted that both types are authentic results of the attempt to implement the gospel.

> The main point is that both types are the consequences of the gospel and only together do they exhaust the range of its sociological results.[94]

On the other hand, one must at the same time insist that the shape and direction of the ongoing development of Christianity is the direct derivative of the operation of the church type. This is so virtually by definition. It is the church type, with its compulsion toward a positive relation with the world, that has been, and throughout the medieval period will continue to be, the bearer of the Christian tradition. The sect type may contribute decisively to this, and such was precisely the case with the long-range development of one form of Protestantism. But this will only be so where and when sectarian concerns have been assimilated in some sense by the church type.

> The main direction of Christian development, of course, follows the Church type, in connection with its in-

stinct for the assertion of a universal, all-controlling ideal, [and] in connection with the need to control the great masses and for that reason to master the world and culture.[95]

5. Finally, we come to the crucial matter of *compulsion versus voluntarism* as an elemental part of the distinction. We have noted at length that Troeltsch's understanding of the distinction between church and sect transcended Weber's in this connection. It did so, however, in an inclusive fashion. Moreover, within the framework of the broad contrast between a positive and a negative articulation of the relationship between the structures of Christianity and the world, Troeltsch's insight in this matter proved to be even more portentous than Weber's. For Troeltsch too, then, this point obtains; it does so in terms of the contrast between an objective and comprehensive institution as over against a voluntary community.

> The essence of the Church is its objective institutional character. . . . The main thing is that every individual be placed under the possibility of the influence of this healing power; therefore the Church is forced toward the control of society, and the compulsory subjugation (*Zwangsunterwerfung*) of every member of society under its sphere of influence. . . . As over against this institutional principle of the objective organism, however, the Sect is the *community of the voluntary*.[96]

In the light of these five points it is clear that the introduction of the distinction between church and sect at this point of *The Social Teachings* represented more than just the groundwork for the concluding section of the chapter on medieval Catholicism. It also prepared the way for the third of the three chapters of the work, simply entitled " Protestantism." Troeltsch's point of departure in this chapter was to insist that the rise of the Reformation cannot be explained in a deterministic fashion.[97]

> Now it is to be emphasized here that in spite of every foundation in an inner change of the total situation spanning a century Luther's religious idea nevertheless had a highly personal originality, and, above all, that it clearly proceeded out of *the inner movement of religious thought itself.*[98]

How did this inner movement of religious thought find structural expression? As a church, not as a sect.

The broad thesis of the third and final chapter of *The Social Teachings* may be stated in a sentence. What begins with Luther, finds expression in Lutheranism, and yields its most important variation in Calvinism, is a vast and new extension of the church type. Both the discussion up to this point and the controlling problem that shapes the chapter as a whole anticipates this. " Our question is this . . . : In what did that change of the Christian idea consist, what are the new religious ideas and what are their sociological results? " [99] Troeltsch moved unerringly in the clarification of this thesis, and though the argument is extensive and detailed, the steps by which this clarification unfolds are not difficult to discern.

The comprehensive point emerges early — in the presentation of Luther — and it is this: With Luther " a reform of the Catholic concept of the Church " took place, one " which had no other objective support than the Biblical word of Christ." This sole objective support of the Word now comes to supplant " the concept of the episcopate and its culminating recapitulation (*Zusammenfassung*) in the Papacy " as the " sociological point of connection, in terms of which it is valid to reconstruct the Church." [100] Now it was Troeltsch's contention that this indicates an inescapable conclusion: " Luther and the Reformers, like Catholicism, comprehended the Christian idea in the schema of the concept of the Church." [101] The point to observing that for Luther Christianity is essentially understandable in terms of " grace as the basis of the certainty of salvation " is that one so thinking " is predestined for the Church type." [102] This led Troeltsch to one of his most incisive formulations:

> Consequently the Church type controlled the whole of Reformation thought and its ultimate root lies in the religious originality (*Eigenart*) of the Reformation itself. Only as a Reformer of the Church was Luther able to work his great effect on world history. Only [on the basis of] the thought of supernatural universality was he also led to universal and institutional results; without this Luther would have been only a founder of a sect or order, or a lonely man like Sebastian Franck.[103]

To put the matter this way is to lay bare the secret of Luther's influence — and not only his alone, but also that of the Reformation at large which he initiated. A new point of reference now orders the structuring of the church, but it is the fact that *the church* is restructured that is decisive. This explains not only why Luther had the influence he did, but also why what begins with him is not a displacement of but a new articulation of the very *Corpus Christianum* which it had been the genius of medieval Catholicism to evolve. With Luther, then, and accordingly with Lutheranism and Calvinism, " all the essential sociological effects " of the church type are to be observed.[104] Accordingly, Troeltsch unfolded his treatment of the rich diversity connoted by the very terms " Luther," " Lutheranism," and " Calvinism " with an eye toward the passion for " uniformity, unity, and the general control of the

Church," [105] and the resulting fact of compulsion, which all this entails. Moreover, he did so with the purpose of exploring fully the development of a new variation on the theme of the positive relationship with the world. Just as had been the case with the discussion of medieval Catholicism, so now with that of Luther, Lutheranism, and Calvinism the " basic completing concepts (*ergänzenden Grundbegriffs*) of natural law " are given close attention.[106]

The presentation of Protestantism in *The Social Teachings* turns on the contention that from the standpoint of the history of Christian social thought Calvinism, not Lutheranism, comes to the center of the stage.

> The extension of the reformation of the Church throughout the West, and from there to the New World, fell to Calvinism, which today must be regarded as the real main force of Protestantism.[107]

Why did Troeltsch assert this? The answering of this question touches the central phase of his argument as a whole.

The substance of this sweeping statement was developed in many ways, the most illuminating, most basic, and most succinct of which was formulated with reference to the problem of asceticism. The sharp distinction that Troeltsch drew between Lutheranism and Calvinism in this connection unfolds against the background of the more general contrast between Catholicism and Protestantism at large in terms of this same issue. Looking back to the subject matter of the opening chapter of *The Social Teachings,* he noted that asceticism first entered the scene " with the adjustment to a continuing sinful and lost world and the postponement of the Kingdom of God into the life to come." From the very outset this asceticism had " a double meaning," entailing both a " metaphysical condemnation

of the world" and a "rational discipline of the sensual."
The crucial point is that these two factors could either exist
in combination, or separately.[108] In the light of Troeltsch's
labors it becomes clear that both Catholicism and Protestantism, in its two major forms, succeeded in controlling
this restless force. Across this spectrum one is observing
variations of the church type. If asceticism is not controlled, an almost inexorable movement toward renunciation of the world and withdrawal from it will set in.

Catholicism achieved this control in terms exactly analogous to and indicative of that basic dualism characterizing its entire relationship to the world.

> It [Catholicism] had solved the problem in its doctrine
> of the two-staged character of the moral and had placed
> asceticism in its full meaning next to and higher than the
> life of the world. . . . It was and is an asceticism next to
> and higher than the forms of the average life of the
> world, essentially cultivated in the cloisters and the re-
> ligious brotherhoods, and in the clergy.[109]

For Protestantism, on the other hand, the only viable asceticism is one that permeates just exactly the forms of
the average life of the world. Accordingly, the Catholic
notion of the two-staged character of the moral was completely rejected. In making this point Troeltsch characterized Protestant asceticism as this-worldly asceticism (in-
nerweltliche Askese), and once again he followed the lead
of Max Weber from whom he took over the term. His own
formulation is memorable:

> To be unbound spiritually by the things of the world,
> to overcome the world in the world: this was its
> ideal. . . . To this extent Protestantism also maintained
> asceticism, but [it did so only] as a this-worldly as-
> ceticism.[110]

This-worldly asceticism is the common characteristic of both Lutheranism and Calvinism. The significant point is that within this context they diverge drastically. Troeltsch formulated this divergence in terms of the two tendencies noted above — namely, the metaphysical depreciation of the sinful world, on the one hand, and the methodical disciplining of life, on the other.[111] Lutheran asceticism, even though fundamentally this-worldly asceticism, took shape primarily around the former, which Troeltsch flatly stated to be its " ascetic mood." [112] As he understood it, this accounts for the fact that in Lutheranism the joy and certainty of justification was accompanied by an attitude that consistently tended to leave the world as it is.[113] Calvinistic asceticism, on the other hand, emphasized the latter, and, if Troeltsch was correct, in its preoccupation with the structured disciplining of life it broke a new trail to the future.

> Thence [from Calvinism] there now follows a this-worldly asceticism which systematically and to the greatest extent acknowledges all worldly means, but it reduces [these] to means only, without any particular value in themselves, in order by this use of every means to produce the holy community.[114]

This leads directly to a formulation that is worthy of Calvin himself and that epitomizes Troeltsch's entire presentation of the asceticism Calvinism developed.

> There follows an active political interest, but not for the sake of the state; a diligent, profitable labor, but not for the sake of wealth; a keen social organization, but not for the sake of earthly happiness; an uninterruptible work which disciplines life (*eine unausgesetzte, die Sinnlichkeit disziplinierende Arbeit*), but not for the sake of the object of this work. The glorification of God, the

gathering of the holy community, the gaining of the blessedness which with election is set as the goal: this is the sole purpose of this ethic, under which all of its formal characteristics are subordinated.[115]

To maintain, as we have, that if Troeltsch was correct all this must be construed as a new road to the future obviously must entail more than simply these different forms of this-worldly asceticism. The distinction between Lutheranism and Calvinism in this connection is even more suggestive in its portent than it is in its immediate confines, for it discloses a far-reaching dimension of this contrast that is to be discerned throughout the whole range of the historical significance of the work of the Reformers. At two points in particular this must be noted.

The first of these involves the broad question of the *Corpus Christianum*. This is, to use Troeltsch's own decisive phrases, the question of the " undivided society " — the question of " Christian culture, Christian society, and the compulsory unity of faith " — the question of the " distinct but not disconnected operation of the spiritual and the worldly authority." [116] Both Lutheranism and Calvinism pressed toward the realization of the *Corpus Christianum*. Each had a clear vision of how it ought to unfold, since each took the form of a church and not a sect. In the case of Calvinism, however, the structure of the church was infinitely more comprehensive and potent, especially when considered from the standpoint of this question. Calvinism yielded an understanding of the church which made it the *partner* of secular authority, not the *beneficiary* of it.

In Lutheranism it [the *Corpus Christianum*] is the voluntary charitable service of authority, which on the basis of natural law is directed toward justice, the public peace, and order, for the sake of the purely spiritual holy institu-

tion. This institution *must be equipped* with its legal organs by the state and *must be supported* in the efficacy of
its spirit. In Calvinism it [the *Corpus Christianum*] is the
dutiful ordering together of the government, which by
reason and the Bible apprehends its Christian duty and
its duty on the basis of natural law, with *the independent
Church, which is capable of action in its own right,* which
has at its disposal specific divine-legal organs for the
Christianizing of society, but which works together with
the state in common obligation to the Word of God.[117]

In this contrast regarding the understanding of the *Corpus Christianum* a striking factor emerges. It would be a
mistake to put the matter causally, though one is tempted
to do so. The fact simply is that along with all this there
goes an astonishing degree of flexibility — astonishing because of the remarkable creativity that Calvinism was able
to muster in the face of unanticipated circumstances. This,
then, is the second point we must consider here, and we
must do so in some detail. As far as the history of Christian
social thought is concerned, Calvinism's most significant
development took place in situations neither identical with
nor parallel to its original setting in Geneva. In the process its version of the church type proved able to contribute
to, learn from, and in a sense become conflated with the
sects.

Relatively early in his presentation of Calvinism,
Troeltsch called attention to the close approximation between it and the sect type.[118] The point is intrinsic to his
reflections on Calvinism's " social ideal of the holy community." [119] Basic to this articulation is his observation
that in Calvinism the church is " not merely the holy institution of the presentation of the objective means of salvation." [120] There is also closely connected with this that
idea of community which is rooted in " the ethical task of

the confirmation and effecting of election." [121] He focused
the issue sharply with reference to the Lord's Supper:

> In Calvinism there comes forward a series of impor-
> tant features which are common to its own and to the
> Baptist ideal of the community. Above all is the adapting
> of excommunication [in combination with] the conceiving
> of the Lord's Supper as the meeting of worthy and believ-
> ing Christians, from which the unfaithful are to be kept
> away. . . . Thus, beyond the objective assurance of the
> saving forgiveness of sins, this will become also the official
> review and purification of the community. The latter is a
> complete deviation from the Lutheran standpoint. The
> celebration of the Lord's Supper becomes the central
> point of the community. . . . Whereas Lutheranism
> handed over excommunication and the control of moral-
> ity to the government, the Calvinistic community exe-
> cuted it itself.[122]

Destiny made much of this propensity. Calvinism, with
its emphasis upon the holy community, yielded a version
of the church type that was not irrevocably incompatible
with sectarian developments. Moreover, with its conviction that election must be worked out in terms of the unfolding of events, so that these must be construed positively, the shifting of circumstances must be exploited,
not damned. Add to this that kind of this-worldly asceticism which compels the church to strive to participate,
actively and *independently,* with the secular in the Christianizing of society. The result is the possibility that destiny
chose — the fusion of Calvinistic church type thought with
developing sectarian views in the emergence of what
Troeltsch, like Weber, termed *ascetic Protestantism.*[123]

It is with reference to this *extension* of Calvinism, both
outside Geneva and subsequent to its initial phases of development, that the decisive case for its being " the real

main force of Protestantism " in the present [124] must be made. Powerful and profound transmutations set in in the process of this extension — changes and adaptations that immeasurably increased Calvinism's significance at the level of historic and cultural effect. In this framework the delineation of ascetic Protestantism and the clarification of its importance comes into view as the real *terminus ad quem* of the broad chapter on Protestantism.

Troeltsch ordered his discussion of *Neo-Calvinism,* as he now began to refer to it, in terms of " two momentous inferences, which more or less logically proceed out of [Calvinism's] essence." [125] These were " the Free Churches " and " Puritanism or Pietism within the Church *(der inner-kirchliche Puritanismus oder Pietismus)* ." [126] The discussion of each of these two points is heavily dependent on his understanding of the development through which Calvinism passed in England, though it is not restricted to this.[127] In the former instance, brief sketches of the work of Robert Browne and Henry Barrowe, and treatments of Congregationalism and of the English Independents provide the context in which he strove to formulate the penetration of the Free Church principle into genuine Calvinism, with attention to the rise of religious tolerance in this whole development, as well as its liberal character and its basis in natural law. In the latter instance his understanding of English Puritanism set the stage for his observations of what he regarded to be similar developments in the Netherlands, the area of the lower Rhine, and Switzerland. Coming out of this discussion Troeltsch stated the heart of his conception of ascetic Protestantism. Obviously he regarded this as the clue to the real significance of Calvinism for the history of Christian social thought.

Hence follows, for the first time, Calvinism's full contemporary world importance, and its social significance for culture. Calvinism and the Sects of the Baptists, the Methodists, and the Salvation Army go together into a great religious unity, which at the same time presents itself as a great sociological collective type of the Christian idea.[128]

That he was talking about something deeper than organic combinations is already clear. It was a common ethos, rather than a new ecclesiastical institution, that he sought to depict. This common ethos, unwieldy though its description must always be, represents a momentous fusion (*Verschmelzung*) [129] of originally disparate ideas. As we have seen, with its emphasis upon the holy community Calvinism stood close to the basic sectarian concern. Within the context of developments in England, and in a process hastened by the collapse of Cromwell's experiment, a conception of the Free Church with distinctly Calvinistic coloration came to fore. The striking thing is that many of the decisive characteristics of the church type now began to take shape in terms of voluntarism, a defining characteristic of the sect type.

This [the rise of the Free Churches] signifies the transfer of the formal decision of Church membership into the will of the individual, and it signifies the conception of the Church, at least outwardly and legally, as an association, even if dogmatically the community thus brought about can be considered as a churchly, holy institution (*kirchliche Heilsanstalt*) as much as before. . . . It is clear that with this a new development of Calvinism set in, one going beyond all its hitherto existing bases, and above all that with this a formal-legal analogy with the Sect arose, even if the concept of the Church itself, with all its dogmatic-ethical consequences, is maintained.[130]

To be sure, the involvement of Calvinism in all this was reluctant. Certainly Calvin himself would have shuddered to think that a structure based on his thought would one day emerge with all the marks of " a formal-legal analogy with the Sect." Neo-Calvinism did not take readily to the circumstances in which it found itself. The passion of the " Presbyterian party " in England for an establishment of itself as over against the Anglicans is a case in point. The " principle of theocracy " would always be its real choice.[131] Troeltsch underlined this reluctance.

> In cases where it was compelled into coexistence (*Nebeneinanderbestehen*) with free confessions, Calvinism considered these as only temporary and forced.[132]

One is tempted to hazard the judgment that this very reluctance informed the decisive contribution from the side of Calvinism to the strange fusion with the sects into which it was unwillingly drawn. For Calvinism never relinquished its " objective conception of itself as a churchly institution (*Kirchenanstalt*), in spite of all the formal [appearances] of a voluntary Church (*trotz aller formellen Vereinskirchlichkeit*) ."[133] Accordingly, Calvinism never gave up its " positive affirmation of the world."[134] For Troeltsch these were two ways of saying the same thing. They manifested the limit of Calvinism's appropriation of the " Sect-motif."[135] More than that, they suggest the really far-reaching point: Calvinism taught the sects what it means for a Free Church to be a *church*.

On the other hand, the sects were also undergoing deep transmutations, and these made them susceptible to this influence from the Calvinistic side. Inexorably, growth and the emergence of favorable conditions of existence ameliorated their hostility toward the world and their propensity to withdraw from it.

With their extension and settlement under tolerant relations with the state, [the sects] became broad congregations of the masses, and thereby gave up, or at least considerably limited, their political and economic opposition to the world as well as the seclusion of the holy community.[136]

However, precisely in this close proximity between Neo-Calvinism and the sects the latter too had something to contribute. For the thrust of the whole conception of the Free Church is clearly in the direction of " the dissolution of the medieval and classical Protestant idea of a uniform totality of life ordered by the state and the Church, and of an undivided authority infallibly ruling the whole culture." [137] Here Calvinism came into contact with and shared in the development of a movement that was intrinsically " revolutionary as over against the basic concepts of the prevailing society." [138] Accordingly, elements of subjectivism and relativism, which always accompany voluntarism, came to be subtle parts of its outlook too. Voluntarism was nothing new to the sects. Their birthright was forged in terms of it. But it was surely new to Calvinism. The sects taught Calvinism what it means for a Free Church to be *free*.

As we have seen, Troeltsch was convinced that the relationship between Christianity in any of its forms and the rise of the modern world was extremely tenuous. He never relinquished this view. Accordingly, the point before us must be read with care. At this juncture Troeltsch was attempting to deal primarily with the effect upon Calvinism of its involvement in the context of profound social and political change. The process we have before us put it in contact with decisive elements in the vast complex of factors that would lead to the rise of the modern world. By

virtue of its involvement in the Free Church development
it became " open " to " democratic ideas," and in the
" amalgamation of the Free Church system and democ-
racy " it found its " relationship to political individualism." [139] In this connection its attitude would be identical
with that of the sects sharing affinity with it. More than
that, however, is the fact that in this context one of its most
characteristic modern features took shape. If Troeltsch was
right, Calvinism's claim to relevance in the midst of the
modern world owes as much, if not more, to its unfolding
relationship with the sects as it does to Calvin himself.

> Thus Calvinism stands today, together with the Sects,
> flatly and diametrically opposed to the Lutheran state
> church system, and it enthusiastically characterizes itself
> as the only form of Christianity which is appropriate to
> the essence of the modern world (*die dem modernen
> Wesen allein entsprechende Form des Christentums*).[140]

We now have enough before us to grasp what Troeltsch
meant by *ascetic Protestantism*. To be sure, there is more
to his concept than simply the issue of Calvinism's developing affinity with the sects in terms of the rise of the Free
Church. This factor is decisive, however, and may well
serve as the paradigm of his point as a whole. Two key
summarizing formulations indicate both the fluidity and
the complexity — as well as the crucial evaluation — which
the facts yielding the concept demanded as far as Troeltsch
was concerned.

> Thus out of the Puritan and Free Church development
> of Calvinism, on the one hand, and, on the other hand,
> out of the adaptation of the Baptist movements to town
> life and the adjustment of the pietistic Sects to churchly
> existence, there follows a *collective-group* of Protestant-
> ism, which . . . has been designated as " *ascetic Protes-*

tantism " in distinction from Lutheranism and Catholicism.[141]

Ascetic Protestantism, then, is shorthand for an unwieldy cluster of originally disparate elements. One's choice is either to avoid it because of its complexity, or to deal with it in spite of its awkward and elusive character. Troeltsch insisted on the latter alternative. He was driven to do so simply because there comes to the fore with this strange combination a momentous and unavoidable factor in the history of Christian social thought.

> Today this ascetic Protestantism, seen with reference to [its] historical effect and extent, is the main force of Protestantism. Next to medieval Catholicism it signifies the second great main type of Christian social doctrine, behind which, in historical effect, the more subtle but weaker designs of social doctrine in the Mystics, in Spiritualism, and in philosophical Neo-Protestantism stand far to the rear.[142]

We have yet to deal with Troeltsch's third type — that of mysticism — but even so the yield of his appropriation of Weber's concept of ideal type analysis is before us to a large extent. As applied to the broad sweep of the history of Christian social thought this procedure enabled him to approach the problem of the present far more cogently than we found him capable of doing under our heading of " The Two Protestantisms." The problem of Christianity on this side of the disappearance of Christendom received illuminating clarification in *The Social Teachings.* Protestantism's coming to terms with the world was in fact a variation on the theme that medieval Catholicism had composed. The Protestant version, then, no less than Catholicism's, is in serious jeopardy as the result of the

arrival of the new context of the modern world. Troeltsch
could now state this forcefully:

> We have now seen that there are only two . . . great
> main types [of Christian social thought] which have at-
> tained far-reaching historical significance and power. The
> one is the . . . social philosophy of medieval Catholi-
> cism. . . . The other is the social philosophy of ascetic
> Protestantism. . . . But in spite of great achievements
> continuing to the present day, both of the former power-
> ful types have exhausted themselves.[143]

Given this, he could state with precision the problem of
the present, and in so doing he set out the heart of the conclusion of *The Social Teachings:*

> Under these circumstances insight into the problemat-
> ical situation of all Christian social work is the result of
> our investigation. It is problematical generally because
> the capability of thought for the mastering of brutal re-
> ality always remains a vague and difficult thing. It is
> problematical in particular, because today the main his-
> torical forms of the Christian doctrine and shape of so-
> ciety are failing, for various reasons, in the face of persist-
> ing tasks.[144]

If this had been all that Troeltsch saw, the results of his
labors in the writing of *The Social Teachings* would be
memorable enough. To understand in this way the question that the modern context thrusts before Christianity
in all its forms is to approach this question in the full recognition of both its complexity and its intractability. This
is surely a step forward. But just how intractable is the
question that Troeltsch discerned? If one were to leave
the matter where we have it now, one could, and probably
would, assume that for him the problem will be ultimately
resolved. A new Christian social theory, applicable to and

potentially victorious within the modern context, will surely emerge. The solution is implicit in the recognition of the problem. That such a view was present in Troeltsch's own mind as he worked out the massive argument of *The Social Teachings* is true beyond a doubt. But, as we have seen, so was the increasing awareness of a problem that ultimately he could not resolve — the problem of historical relativism. One can see a controllable question emerging from *The Social Teachings* only at the expense of ignoring this. For this reason we must turn now to the remarkable element of Troeltsch's argument that unfolds in connection with the *third type*.[145] The problem of the present is difficult enough when seen in terms of the distinction between church and sect. When it is formulated with all three types in mind it denotes a real impasse.

3. THE PRESENT IMPASSE

Central though it was for the argument of *The Social Teachings,* the distinction between church and sect did not exhaust the data of the history of Christian social thought. Accordingly, Troeltsch ranged a third type alongside these two. We have already noted this in his summarizing juxtaposition of the three types, which occurs in the conclusion of the work. He delineated the third type, it should be recalled, as follows:

> Mysticism is the intensification and the making immediate of the world of ideas solidified in cult and doctrine into a purely personal and inner possession of the heart (*Gemütsbesitz*), whereby only fluid and completely personal limited group formations can assemble, [and] in which the remaining cult, dogma and connection with history tend to become so fluid that they disappear.[146]

We have alluded to this third type as being at once the most elusive and portentous of the three.[147] That it is elusive is self-evident in the diverse subject matter to which it points. That it is portentous is clear in the fact that the closer Troeltsch came to the modern situation the more he was driven to say about it. This is due, in the first place, to the fact that the rise of Protestantism liberated the propensities to which this third type refers. It is due, in the second place, to the fact that Troeltsch was haunted by the nagging awareness of an affinity between modern Christian sophistication and a growing restiveness with the structures of either the church or the sectarian communities. That religious individualism can generate social thought is a contradiction in terms. Troeltsch knew this very well. His treatment of the matter, therefore, foreshadows an ominous insight.

The third type is introduced in the concluding paragraphs of the chapter on medieval Catholicism. Troeltsch mentioned it here for the sake of systematic wholeness and for the purpose of forecasting subsequent developments. He then tabled the question, noting that its full exploration must await the discussion of " the later Protestant dissenters and their coalescence with Humanism " in terms of which the third type achieved its " universal historical significance." [148] At the very outset of his treatment of the matter at hand Troeltsch insisted that mysticism must not be confused with the sects. Its matrix was " the growth of an independent lay culture in the cities," [149] and it entailed the development of " a sociological type of the Christian idea which is no longer identical with the Sects, but signifies a new type, the radical religious individualism of Mysticism." [150]

Troeltsch's argument in this connection was carefully

constructed. Mysticism in general was not the child of Protestantism. Mysticism as an *independent sociological type* was. It was the latter that he sought to clarify.

> [Catholic] Mysticism still concealed itself under the shelter of the Church, or it discovered contact with the Orders. At no time did it stand alone. Protestant Mysticism, on the contrary, learned to consider itself as the consequence of the priesthood of all believers and of the personal religion of conviction, and thereby stood on its own feet.[151]

Furthermore, the upheaval within Christendom that the rise of Protestantism generated gave mysticism the opportunity to unfold positively and in its own right. The circumstances provided both the occasion and the catalyst for this to happen. The result was that mysticism on a Protestant ground was able to accomplish what had never emerged within the confines of medieval Catholicism — a self-understanding informed by more than simply reaction against the rigidities of ecclesiastical civilization.

> The spiritualized concept of the Church in Protestantism, and the initial instability in the accomplishment of the new Church order, gave it room for independent development and establishment. . . . Under these circumstances a Protestant mysticism unfolded which, unlike Catholic mysticism, was not a compensation for ecclesiastical formality, but felt itself to be and worked as an independent principle of religious knowledge, inwardness, and ethics.[152]

In this light Troeltsch proceeded to survey such figures as Thomas Münzer, Karlstadt, Schwenkfeld, Sebastian Franck, and Coornhert, and such movements as the Quakers, the Methodists, and the Moravians (the latter two of which had also been treated in connection with the Protestant sects). Throughout this discussion he was doing far more than simply treating those who did not fit comfortably under the heading of either church or sect. Rather, he was attempting to set out the meaning of his contention that the religious individualism of mysticism represents an authentic type in itself, which must be understood in distinction from the other two.

The case was difficult to make, for it was shot full of an ambivalence that is both hard to formulate and yet impossible to deny. The heart of this elusive point lies in the fact that insofar as mysticism has any sociological import at all this is always *derivative* in character. In its passion to internalize as profoundly as possible the religious content of which its tradition always speaks it both presupposes and rejects this tradition itself.

> Mysticism in the widest sense of the word is nothing other than the pressing toward the direct, inner, and present [character] of religious experience. It presupposes the objectivizing of the religious life in cults, rites, myths or dogmas, and it is either a reaction against this objectivizing, which it seeks to take back anew into the living process, or it is a completion (*Ergänzung*) of the traditional cult by means of the stimulation of the personal and the vital. It is thus always something secondary and something intentionally reflective.[153]

The ambivalence of the sociological significance of the third type is before us in this formulation. To the extent that mysticism consists simply of reaction against the forms of the received tradition that significance will be negative and destructive. To the extent that these forms in fact receive a completion in the development of radical religious individualism that significance will include a positive dimension. (As we shall see presently, the idea of "completion" is decisive for Troeltsch's formulation of the final outcome of *The Social Teachings*. Its import is not confined to the point at hand here.) In either case, however, the fluidity and individualism to which Troeltsch pointed in the summarizing formulation noted above [154] remain the defining characteristics. Moreover, in either case a *derivative* social significance is all that can be discerned. The third type is completely parasitic. It is "secondary to" a structure that it must presuppose in one way or another. With this in mind the difference between Catholic and Protestant mysticism, to which Troeltsch correctly and trenchantly called attention, is narrower than his formulations might seem to imply. In the broad sense it is a difference of degree, not of kind.

On the one hand, then, the sociological significance of the third type was negative and destructive. This influence is characteristically *indirect,* since the thrust of mysticism is contemplative and personal. Unlike either the church or the sect, its relationship with the concrete circumstances in the midst of which it unfolds is vague and difficult to discern. Furthermore, at the point at which its social effect is most observable it is clearly destructive. For inexorably the radical religious individualism of the third type undermines the forceful comprehensiveness of the church.

> Thus of itself it has no social effect on the general public. Its intimate circles do not penetrate into the mass, and its purely contemplative thought does not take hold in the common life, but works in a purely personal fashion or hovers in a literary manner over the whole. . . . It accompanies social conditions, but does not proceed out of them, and does not influence them directly. Of course, then, indirectly the deteriorating of the power and inclusiveness of the Church by means of it is a very important social consequence.[155]

On the other hand, Troeltsch could be just as emphatic in stating the opposite side of the ambiguous social significance of the third type. Being " a radical religious individualism," mysticism " does not press toward a relationship of man to man, but toward a relationship to God." [156] Accordingly, " it turns all the historical, the authoritative, and the cultic into merely means of religious stimulation, which it can do without if need be." [157] However, this does not mean that it has " generally no positive sociological character." Indeed, to draw such a conclusion " would not be correct." [158] For to see only the absence of sociological form as the essence of mysticism would be to overlook its specifically Christian character. This is the implication of Troeltsch's way of putting the matter:

> It is after all Christian spiritualism. This means not only that the Spirit is fully incarnate and evident in Christ, thereby gathering the faithful into an historically defined unity, but also that the ethical character of the will, [so much a part] of the Christian-prophetic conception of God, also forces upon it the tendency toward acting love and the communication of one's self to the brethren.[159]

Thus, even the third type is not capable of removing all traces of social concern, despite its decisively individualistic nature.

Clearly, it is the negative rather than the positive element that dominates the sociological ambivalence of the third type. From the standpoint of the history of Christian social thought the best that can be said is that on occasion mysticism will take shape in such a way that the positive note is at least potentially included. But this will only be " on occasion." It will obviously depend on which mystic is under consideration, and it will obviously be confined

to the question of potentiality. The only generalization
that can be defended is that the third type lacks the "or-
ganizational impulse." [160] Predictably, its significance for
the ongoing development of Christian social thought is
minimal at best.

> Resignation, a deliberate preference for the aristocratic,
> pessimism, quietism, and optimistic hope here alternate.
> There follows . . . a complete indifference or helpless-
> ness in the face of extra-religious social problems.[161]

In this light the arresting thing about Troeltsch's treatment of the third type is that throughout this discussion he
could not avoid drawing the implications of this development for the modern predicament of Christianity. The obvious point is that the radical religious individualism of
mysticism has its counterpart in the equally radical religious individualism that Troeltsch had to regard as a dominant factor in the contemporary context. This must be
emphasized. The affinity is phenomenological rather than
substantive; it has to do with religious individualism rather
than mysticism per se. Even so, what was and is true regarding mysticism as an independent sociological type is
also implied in the case of modern religious individualism,
whether it be authentic mysticism or not. The same sociological ambivalence is to be anticipated, as is the same
predictable impotence in the face of the social problematic.
Consequently, a note of real poignancy sets in when
Troeltsch finds this self-evidently unnerving implication
irresistibly emerging from his argument.

This point is explicit from the outset, and it hovers continually over Troeltsch's reflection on "the infinitely difficult situation of Christian social doctrine in the modern
world." [162] In the conclusion of the chapter on medieval
Catholicism, and closely connected with the initial intro-

duction of the question of mysticism, Troeltsch related this " infinitely difficult situation " not only to the fragmentation of Christendom in general but also to the rise of the third type in particular. The modern referrent of his descriptive formulation is obvious.

> Neither Church nor Sect, [the third type] has neither the concrete holiness of the institution nor the radical connection with the Bible. Combining Christian ideas with a rich set of modern views, [and] deriving the orders of society not from the fall of man but from natural developments, it does not have [either] the constant limit of all concessions [or] the social power which the Church type does, nor the radicalism and united coherence with which the Sect type can set aside the state, the economy, art, and science. . . . In the case of the educated world the predominance of the third type has gradually appeared. Here, then, there are only free associations of conviction, which are equally far removed from Church and Sect.[163]

This set the mood for the entire presentation of the mystic type. Moreover, it conditions far more profoundly than might be gathered at first glance the conclusion toward which the entire argument of *The Social Teachings* moves. To this matter Troeltsch returned late in the chapter on Protestantism, on the verge of proceeding first into the summation of the chapter and then the conclusion of the work as a whole. Here he adds the decisive note: Even in its modern form the third type cannot exist by itself. For no less than had been the case with the mysticism that emerged in the initial context of the Protestant Reformation the religious individualism of the present is also of a *derivative* nature. It too presupposes the continuum established and maintained by the other two types.

The modern educated class . . . understands in general only the Spiritualism [of the third type]. This is at the same time a reflection of the radical, atomizing individualism of modern culture generally, an individualism which, in the non-religious spheres of life, already begins to become soft and change into its opposite. Along with the sublimation of community, cult, history, and social ethics, [and] in spite of all the depth and inwardness of its thought, it is also a weakening of the religious life. It must be upheld by Church and Sect in its concrete fullness of life, in order to spiritualize a wholly individual Mysticism at all. Thus, and one may not conceal it, this style of Christianity, alone open to the modern educated classes, presupposes next to itself the continuation of other and more concrete Christian formations of life, and it can never be for all.[164]

Only if one is clear regarding Troeltsch's use of the third type can one grasp the full import of the central finding of *The Social Teachings*. It is not enough to hear him say that the only two main types of Christian social thought so far to emerge have now exhausted themselves.[165] This is drastically intensified when one ponders also the inexorable movement toward the third type, which sets in in the cultured world with the arrival of the modern era. In the face of this development it is not enough to wonder about the reordering of the church or the revitalizing of the fusion of church and sect. Troeltsch was not being rhetorical, nor did he seek simply dramatic effect, when he observed that " in our culture the days of the pure church type are numbered." [166] The passion that informs this remark is double-edged:

That which is self-evident for the modern view of life no longer coincides with that which is self-evident for the Church. Compulsion is no longer a protection of the whole from individual disturbances, but an assault on the real movements of life.[167]

Though true, the first half of this statement can hardly be final. Even Troeltsch's portrayal of medieval Christendom depicts a vast panorama in which such an exact coincidence was always as much a dream as a reality. Both St. Thomas and the Reformers had room for eschatology! Be that as it may, one can hardly debate the second half of the formulation. Whatever may or may not have been the case in the past, the church type is hopelessly out of touch with the dynamic of the modern world. It can maintain itself only by ignoring it or by seeking to dominate it, and neither is possible. The only real option is a new development — a new structure:

> In the reciprocal penetration of the three basic sociological forms and their combination into a structure reconciling all these motifs lie [the] future tasks, tasks of a sociological-organizational nature which are more urgent than all the tasks of dogmatics.[168]

It takes little imagination to see that to put the matter this way runs the risk of an impasse. Such will always be the case when a genuinely new problem is honestly faced. Though basically antithetical, church and sect had been effectively fused in the case of ascetic Protestantism. Deep though this antithesis is, however, and profound though the transmutations were which this fusion necessarily entailed, the distance between church and sect is small when compared with the chasm between church and sect, on the one hand, and radical religious individualism, on the other. And what transmutations would a fusion of all three involve? Indeed, is a conflation of church, sect, *and* radical religious individualism possible? Though the prototypical patterns have always presupposed the dependence of the latter on the former two, what Troeltsch was daring to envision was a genuine "reciprocal penetration" of the three. The question is, What in the world can this mean? Seeing that the concrete structural question is one that has no precedents, the problem of the *possibility* of a fusion of church, sect, and radical religious individualism emerges as an open question. Can it be that the very continuum on which the third type has always been dependent must now itself become parasitic? Is it possible that to the third type the destiny of the other two has now been entrusted? For Troeltsch this was the growing edge of a new problem. It still is.

> If there should be a Christian-social mastering of the situation, then here new thoughts will be necessary which have not yet been thought, and which correspond to this situation as the older forms have corresponded to older situations. These must be forced out of the inner motivating power of the Christian idea and its living and present reorganization, and not solely out of the New Testament, just as both of the other great main forms were gotten not out of the New Testament but out of the actual movement of the religious idea in their own " present time."[169]

The problem, of course, defies solution on the ground on which it takes its rise. Even so, Troeltsch demonstrated the fact that the Christian ethic, if the term " ethic " is taken seriously, does not take shape on Biblical bases alone. This is the singularly unforgettable lesson of *The Social Teachings*. Both theological work and sociological knowledgeability must be combined if the problem to which this work points is to be confronted with any hope of success. However, if this is to be grasped in its fullest import neither Troeltsch nor much of the theology since his day can be accepted uncritically. If the movement of theology since Troeltsch's day is not to be ignored, then one cannot concede that the new tasks " of a sociological-organizational nature " are in fact "more urgent than all the tasks of dogmatics." [170] But if Troeltsch's presentation of the astonishing perspective of the history of Christian social thought is not to be ignored, then it must be seen that the real urgency of the tasks of dogmatics will only be recognized when it is related to the irresistible claims of the present context.

Those claims are the claims of *the post-Christendom era.* They condition the basic problem absolutely. The two vast precedents for Christian social thought in the modern world — medieval Catholicism and ascetic Protestantism — are both premodern in origin and applicability. Accordingly, the question that must be faced by simultaneous theological labor and sociological knowledgeability is not simply a problem of up-dating, but a problem of new creation. To follow Troeltsch's most penetrating way of formulating it, this is the question of the " new completion ":

> The problem of the transworldly (*Das Problem der Ueberweltlichkeit*) and its inevitable result, asceticism, in either the metaphysical-dualistic or the rigorously disciplined sense, is . . . still the basic problem of the Christian ethos today, which at the same time is not simply a denial of the world or of the self. On the other side is its second basic problem, the completion (*Ergänzung*) of this religious one-sidedness by means of an ethic of culture reconcilable with it. . . . Today . . . , in the midst of a completely new cultural situation, the old completions have become impossible. A new completion is thus necessary. The Christian ethos cannot live for itself alone and be sufficient in a continuing world. The question now is, How can this completion be shaped today? Here lies the task of a new Christian ethic.[171]

What is the content of a theology that knows that " the fundamental historicizing of all our thought about man, his culture and his values " can be clarified but not contained? So we asked at the end of our analysis of *Der Historismus*.[172] Ten years before *Der Historismus* was written, Troeltsch already knew in part the answer to this question. Christianity in the post-Christendom era must move far beyond anything it has yet produced. It may be illuminated and challenged by its former accomplishments. But reduplications of these efforts will not suffice, even though they be drastic and robust. Old completions have been rendered invalid. A new one must be found. The problem of the new completion — the task of a new Christian ethic — may not be the central problem of a theology of involvement, but it will certainly condition whatever is.

Was Troeltsch able to go any farther than this? To answer this question we must turn now to a straightforward analysis of his theology. But this is the story of a collapse. Consequently it will yield only ambiguous answers. That is the nature of Pyrrhic victories.

6 The Collapse of Troeltsch's Theology

◈ ◈

The yield of Troeltsch's formal theology is incisive but thin. His preoccupation with the problem of the context within which Christianity now finds itself was inexhaustible and self-perpetuating. It was also terribly demanding. When he attempted to write in the framework of systematic theology, which by comparison with the matters we have had before us was not often, this preoccupation was always forcefully and formatively present. This indicates the elusive route along which we must travel if his *theological* reflections are to be penetrated. The collapse of Troeltsch's theology was due to the severity of his own questions. Therefore, his theological reflections must be seen in intimate connection with these questions themselves. This is absolutely pivotal for the appraisal of his lasting contributions to the discipline in which he held a chair in Heidelberg for twenty-one years, and which he did not regard himself as having deserted completely despite his leaving both Heidelberg and the discipline for Berlin in 1915.[1]

The purpose of all Troeltsch's labors, it will be recalled, included " the solution of the systematic task." As he put it in 1912, the systematic task is " to think through and formulate independently the Christian world of ideas and life with unreserved involvement in the modern world." [2]

By now we can state succinctly what the contextual side of this entailed. It entailed involvement in the post-Christendom era, in which the problem of historical relativism can be clarified but not contained. Our task now is to come to terms, insofar as we can, with the other side of the matter. What went on in Troeltsch's struggles when the business of thinking through and formulating specifically Christian doctrine was explicitly before him? Here one encounters the real problem of his theology. It is impossible to deal with it along classical lines. It is a theology driven to the task of breaking new paths. Moreover, precisely because of the overriding preoccupation with the attempt to clarify the context in which theology must now be pursued, it is thoroughly fragmentary. The critical dominated the constructive in the theology of Troeltsch. Though he died before these reflections could know anything like a final statement, it is doubtful that this would have ever changed.

Troeltsch's specifically theological pieces form a relatively small segment of his writings. This can be and has been misleading. In the broader context of the whole of his writings these monographs indicate the direction of his reflections concerning the meaning of the Christian faith, but they do so only if this broader context has been mastered. Furthermore, even when this has been done, they must be handled with care. This is particularly true in the case of his *Glaubenslehre* (The Doctrine of Faith). Heavy dependence on this work as a decisive indication of his theological position is out of the question. This work, based on the notes of one of his students, *was not brought out by Troeltsch himself.*[3] The lectures it reflects were given during the years 1911 and 1912. These were the years that saw the completion of *The Social Teachings.*

They were also years in which Troeltsch himself wrote and published some of his most significant theological monographs and articles. Valuable though it is, the *Glaubenslehre* provides only corroborative evidence for the partial illumination of positions definitively taken elsewhere.

Soon after finishing *The Social Teachings* and shortly before leaving Heidelberg for Berlin, Troeltsch worked out a careful and systematic statement of his conception of the form of dogmatics. This is to be found in an article he wrote for *The American Journal of Theology*, published in 1913 under the title *The Dogmatics of the " religionsgeschichtliche Schule."* [4] As Troeltsch himself put it, he wrote this article in response to the request of the editors of the journal that in that he was regarded as the systematic theologian of the *religionsgeschichtliche* [5] school he state " the meaning dogmatics can have under the presuppositions and in the understanding of this school." [6] This article is invaluable for our task of setting out the rise and fall of Troeltsch's theology. Before dealing with it, however, we must first ponder two striking ideas that are operative in the broader range of Troeltsch's writings. The first of these is his concept of *compromise*. The second is his concept of the *religious a priori*. The juxtaposition of these two ideas crystallizes the manner in which historical analysis conditions so drastically everything he attempted by way of spelling out his understanding of the form and content of dogmatics.

1. " COMPROMISE " AND " THE RELIGIOUS A PRIORI "

One cannot read Troeltsch's works without noticing his recurrent use of the term " compromise " (*Kompromiss*). We have purposely delayed considering it until now, for the point to his use of the term is intelligible only in the light of his thought as a whole, and the full import of his suggestion can be stated only in close connection with the demise of his theology. The idea pervades his writings. It is present in the conclusion of his first book. It plays an illuminating role — decisively so — in *The Social Teachings*. It is present in one of his last discussions (one of the five lectures prepared late in 1922 or early in 1923, to be delivered in England in March of 1923), where interestingly enough he first gave it direct attention. And it is to be found in a host of other essays and articles.

The term " compromise " is characteristically present in Troeltsch's attempts to understand Christianity in its relationship to its context. It is colored by the empirical data of the history of Christianity, especially when this is focused around the history of Christian social thought. He used the term in anything but a negative sense. Why, then, did he use it at all? Why did he deliberately select such a debatable word with such a predominantly negative meaning to refer to a process that was for him always fascinating and intensely positive in character? He did so because whenever the history of Christianity is pondered with reference to its relationship to its context — and for him, as we have seen at length, this is the only way to ponder it — the *mutually reciprocal character* of this relationship cannot be avoided.[7] He noticed that wherever and whenever Christianity in any of its forms has had a real effect on its context something of the context has become a part of newfound strength and newfound insight within the faith itself. The involvement of the church in the world is reversible. This is what Troeltsch sought to communicate with the term " compromise."

Now there is nothing novel in the observation that the

involvement of the church in the world is reversible. There well may be nothing unprecedented in noting that compromise is the characteristic feature of this relationship. What is new is the insistence that at their deepest levels and in terms of their broadest implications the compromises of the church with the world are profoundly positive in significance. This is precisely the import of Troeltsch's use of the term. It can be said that for him the history of Christianity is the history of the compromises of the church with the world. It *must* be said that for him the critical character of the involvement of Christianity in the modern world is most sharply drawn when one sees that the compromises on which medieval Christendom was built, in both its Catholic and Protestant forms, have been shattered. The implication of putting the matter this way is obvious. The problem now is to develop the new compromise. This is another way — and a more comprehensive way — of formulating what we have already seen him refer to as the problem of the " new completion." [8]

Troeltsch employed this positive idea of compromise long before the publication of *The Social Teachings* in its definitive form in 1912. Most notable in this connection are two works, both of which have already been before us. The first of these is *Die wissenschaftliche Lage und ihre Anforderungen an die Theologie* (The Scientific Situation and Its Claims on Theology), written in 1900; the second, the extensive " Protestantisches Christentum und Kirche in der Neuzeit " (Protestant Christianity and Church in Modern Times), the first edition of which was published in 1906.[9] The basic implications of his concept of compromise are evident in his use of the term in these two discussions.

In the first of these Troeltsch used the term with reference to the manner in which the Christianity of antiquity came to terms with the culture of the Roman Empire. He spoke of " the compromise of both powers " that lay at the base of " the consolidation of the Christian world of ideas into a divine means of instruction dependent upon the Holy Scriptures " and thus yielded " a scientific Christian literature." [10] At two specific points, both of which he understood as compromises, the results of what Troeltsch called the " basic settlement " [11] between the Christianity of antiquity and its context took shape. These were the logos Christology and the doctrine of the Trinity, on the one hand, and the Christian appropriation of the conception of natural law, on the other. As he put it, what took place in the first instance was " a compromise of the ecclesiastical doctrine of a supernatural revelation of God in the bearer of the Kingdom of God with the ancient philosophical doctrine of the divine logos, effective in all wisdom and philosophy." In the second instance there occurred " in a perfectly analogous fashion " the uniting of " a principal ecclesiastical concept, the concept of the new law of Christ, with a principal concept of ancient philosophy, the concept of the natural law, the *lex naturae.*" [12]

Criticism can hardly be restrained in the face of formulations such as these. If this is what Troeltsch meant by " compromise," then the process has been going on from the beginning and its traces stand out all over the pages of the New Testament itself, as even a rudimentary knowledge of where New Testament scholarship has been since Troeltsch's day makes abundantly clear. At the same time, one cannot reject too quickly the insight he was attempting to formulate, for he was groping his way toward the secret of the creativity of Christian thought. These were not compromises worked out with apologies. They were not the sacrificing of principles for the sake of survival. At these moments *gains not losses* were at stake. Though the origins of that creativity unquestionably go back farther than Troeltsch's formulation implies, his use of the term "compromise" is incisive. Christian thought was aggressively on the move, claiming more and more territory as its necessary right. What occurred were compromises in the sense that Christian thought came to utilize insights not originally its own — insights that in fact had been initially alien to it, but that were useful in terms of its deep inner compulsion to sweep everything before it.

We have already seen that the second work noted above is of major significance. In the process of probing the distinction between classical and modern Protestantism Troeltsch found the concept of compromise to be extremely helpful. In "Protestantisches Christentum und Kirche in der Neuzeit" (Protestant Christianity and Church in Modern Times) he put it to work extensively for the first time.[13] Moreover, as might be expected from the title, the work contains his first explicit designation of the problem of the present as the problem of the new compromise.

> The old compromise of the Christian ethic with the *Lex naturae* has disintegrated, and nothing remains of the Christian ethic other than either a retreat into pietistic circles, or a seeking for a new, very much more comprehensive compromise, which combines this worldly cultural goods as independent ethical values with the highest religious good, and which hurls overboard the old doctrine of the radical, sinful corruption of all that is natural and all that is extra-Christian.[14]

With this formulation Troeltsch took the crucial step in the development of his concept of compromise. We may put it this way: *Compromise is the phenomenology of involvement.* It is the necessary risk that must be taken if the gospel is to have concrete, historic effect. When the church has regarded the world positively enough to take the world's problems seriously and attempt to solve them, there it has become involved — there it has compromised — and there it has been extended by new insights and new relevance. Conversely, where compromise is either absent or rejected, there withdrawal and the lack of involvement are inevitable, and so, accordingly, is the lack of new insight and new relevance. Far from being the mark of deterioration, then, compromise in Troeltsch's sense of the term is the characteristic of authentic involvement in the world. The compromises of the past have been shattered by the arrival of a new context within which the achievements of yesterday's involvements in yesterday's world are no longer cogent or productive. If, then, authentic Christian involvement is to unfold in the present, the task of forging the new compromise is of the first magnitude.

In *The Social Teachings,* the concept of compromise played a major role. Here Troeltsch utilized it on the broad canvas of the history of Christian social thought at large, and in the process he delineated it in an unmistakable way along exactly the lines we have just formulated. We have already noted it in passing in connection with the distinction between church and sect.[15] It is in this connection that the concept receives its central use and clarification. The positive relationship to the world distinguishes the church type. This is the relationship of compromise. In Troeltsch's way of seeing it, the protesting of just this fact explains the perennial rise of the sects.

Troeltsch could and did express the difference between medieval and ancient Christianity in terms of compromise.

This was one of his ways of setting out the vast " distance " that medieval Catholicism had moved from " the sociological idea of the gospel." He is surely to be challenged regarding the latter. Whatever else may be said about the radical ethic of love in the New Testament one thing is clear — it may not be phrased simply in terms of " absolute religious individualism." Be that as it may, the formulation is memorable and it typifies the use to which he put the concept of compromise in *The Social Teachings.*

> The winged horse of absolute religious individualism and the radical ethic of love had been harnessed to the plough of the order of society. . . . The new humanity of the religious personality and the love-community in God had sealed its compromise with the old humanity of the struggle for existence, of law, of coercion, of war and of power, with [that is] the natural basis of existence.[16]

When it came time to introduce the ideal type distinction between church and sect into the argument of *The Social Teachings,* Troeltsch formulated the matter initially in terms of compromise. The " radical, second tendency " implicit in Christianity from the beginning and latent until the development of medieval Catholicism must be placed alongside the " compromise of the Church." [17]

> Against the relativizing and compromise of the moral law of Jesus with the orders of the world arose the strong radicalism of the ethic of the gospel, completely regulated with reference to the sanctification of the self and brotherly love.[18]

Indeed, Troeltsch's most succinct differentiation between the two types turns on the concept:

> Development and compromise, on the one side; literal adherence and radicalism on the other.[19]

This close tie between "development" and "compromise" was for Troeltsch the heart of the matter. We have learned from him that the emergence of medieval Christendom can be construed as the realization of a third possibility lying far beyond the radical and conservative tendencies that marked the far horizon for the Christianity of antiquity. This, it will be recalled, would be the successful attempt " to shape the social orders positively, as the foundations (*Unterlagen*) and prior forms (*Vorformen*) of the attainment of the highest religious-ethical goal." [20] Compromise in Troeltsch's sense was the instrument for the realization of this possibility. The ingenious arrangement of a graded relationship between the natural and the supernatural was the rich yield of this compromise, and it was given its finest articulation by Thomas Aquinas. But for this to happen a necessary intermediary step had to have been taken first, namely, the positive evaluation of the world and at least some of its values. Development and compromise thus move hand in hand. The pre-Reformation sects protested this compromise. So did the Reformers. But the sectarian protest was against the *fact* of compromise. The Reformer's protest was against its *content*. Thus the Reformers, and the main stream of the development of Protestantism, assumed the compromise of medieval Catholicism in order to develop their own new variations on an old theme. Inexorably, then, they were subject to sectarian rejection themselves. For what they worked out was a new compromise, not a questioning of the process. They, too, produced a " compromise of the purely religious morality with the demands of the life of the world ": [21]

> The deep inner tensions of the Christian ethic, which have till now come to the fore in any undertaking to give a Christian shape to the life of the continuing world, have

also remained upheld in the reformation ethic. This is also a compromise, a double morality, above all in the basic comprehension of Luther. Only the antitheses (*Gegensätze*) are not distributed in grades, but are pushed into each other, into [that is] a doubleness (*Duplizität*) of the place in life of every individual.[22]

With the rise of Protestantism the fragmentation of medieval Christendom was well under way. It was intensified by the proliferation of the sects. The graded relationship between the natural and the supernatural was ruled out by the Reformers, but if put in terms of the concept of compromise the issue admits only one concise summation: " The compromise undertaken by Catholicism . . . is only transferred to another point [and] led into the inner depths, but it remains a compromise." [23] This accounts for the intensity and the wide spectrum of the sectarian developments that accompanied the Reformation. But far more significantly, it points incisively and relentlessly toward the inevitably temporary character of the sects. We have seen Troeltsch labor the point that the sect is " an independent sociological type of the Christian idea." [24] Even so, the fact is that with continuity, compromise in his sense is inexorable. The continued existence of the sect thus entails its dissolution as a sect. As he put it, " The enduring and suffering Sect is only provisionally possible." The point at which it ceases to await " the divine revelation of the Kingdom " coincides with the point at which " it involves itself in the continuing orders of the world." It, too, must then " relativize its standard and contract its compromise." [25] The transmutation of a sect into a church may thus be observed in the progressive involvement of the sect in the process of compromise. This is precisely what was happening to those sects which were caught up in the unfolding of ascetic Protestantism. To say as we have that the sectarians learned from the Calvinists what it means for a Free Church to be a church [26] is to say that the Calvinists taught the sectarians the necessity and the art of compromise.

In this light, *The Social Teachings* as a whole can be summed up most concisely in terms of the concept before us.

> The ethos of the gospel . . . is an ideal which demands for its full realization a new world. Accordingly, Jesus had proclaimed the Kingdom of God. But it is an ideal which is not realizable in a continuing earthly world without compromise. Therefore the history of the Christian ethos becomes the history of an always new search for this compromise, and an always new opposition to the compromise way of thinking.[27]

This passage leads directly through brief summations to the formulation that we noted at the conclusion of the preceding chapter regarding the task of the " new completion " being the task of " a new Christian ethic." [28] The task of the new completion is the task of finding the new compromise.

It is imperative that these two ideas be understood together. " Compromise " says more than " completion." The latter connotes a one-way movement; the former brings to mind an oscillation — a moving back and forth. As we have seen, Troeltsch had countless ways of saying that the history of Christian thought must be understood explicitly in terms of the contexts within which it has taken shape. His use of the concept of compromise is one of the most incisive of these. The idea summons the vision that Christian thought is not only to take something from the context but also is to contribute something to it. Compromise

thus has manifold dimensions, which conspire to circum-
scribe the locus of new insight and new relevance. The
issue is not simply a matter of Christian reaction to unavoidable external stimuli. Rather, the issue is constructive, for compromise in Troeltsch's sense implies deliberate
initiative. That the present is problematical in the extreme
yields only terror if one lacks the courage to attempt new
constructions. Given the courage it yields not terror but
fascination and hope — the fascination and hope of new
possibilities. The idea of compromise reached the full proportions of a leading concept in the pages of *The Social
Teachings*.[29] The struggle with the problem of historical
relativism that dominated Troeltsch's labors from that
point forward was rooted in his willingness to take up his
own challenge. In the broadest sense, then, and in the light
of our knowledge of where that struggle took him in the
writing of *Der Historismus*, the new compromise can be
found only in terms of that historical relativism which can
be clarified but not contained.

This preoccupation did not constitute a desertion of
theological concerns, as we have shown in the conclusion
of our analysis of *Der Historismus*.[30] It must, rather, be
construed as the attempt to clarify the context in which the
new compromise must be forged. The concept itself, then,
plays no part in this explication, because its use would be
indicated only where the attempt to deal in a constructive
theological way with the new situation commenced on a
broad scale. As we have seen, Troeltsch hoped to return
to this task after completing the projected second volume
of *Der Historismus*.[31] What we have is only the bare beginning of this enterprise, and that beginning is both fragmentary and catastrophic. Significantly enough, however,
it includes the use of the concept of compromise with all

the overtones we have been noting.[32] Moreover, it contains Troeltsch's first explicit statement of its implications. Though this is only a fleeting glimpse, it may well indicate that he would have soon put it to the constructive use that we have been considering.

Politics, Patriotism, Religion was one of the five lectures that Troeltsch was to have given in England in March of 1923. Toward the end of this lecture he touched on what he called the " way of practical compromise," [33] and around this issue he formulated his conclusion. He noted that particularly in Germany the term was worthy only of the highest contempt. " One demands the radicalism of the either-or." However, he continued, " one may twist and turn the fact as one will. All radicalisms lead into the impossible and ruin." At precisely this point he argued that " the History of Christianity is infinitely instructive. It is in its entirety an enormous and always new compromise of the Kingdom of God with the real and continuing life, and the gospel itself, with good instinct, counted on an early end of the world." [34] With this as his clue he was willing to broaden the point: " If the essence of the whole of history is compromise the thinker will not be able to avoid it." [35]

The brief paragraphs with which the English text of the lecture concludes grow directly out of these points.[36] In that these are the only lines we have from Troeltsch that set out the concept itself, we must note them in full. (He led into them by briefly noting why his English audience could be expected to look on the concept with more receptivity than his own countrymen.)

It is thus easier for me to confess my adhesion to the principle of compromise here than in my own country. I know of no other principle and I am unaware of any practical thinker who does. It is true, however, that in the use of compromise we have to guard against all precipitate capitulation to the course which presents itself as momentarily expedient, or as the easiest way out of a difficulty, but which may be thus expedient and easy only for the moment, and, once more, we have to guard against any fundamental abandonment of the ideal. Indeed, it is only by keeping this ideal ever before our eyes that we can continue to hope and to strive for a better future in the midst of a cold and sinister world.

I should not like to bring these matter-of-fact reflections to a close without giving utterance to this belief and this hope. Only through faith, hope and love, can the *bellum omnium contra omnes,* to which nature and egoism incline us, be overcome. That is the inmost meaning of the Christian Gospel, although this same Gospel has always known well enough that the task, thus set to us poor little men, is far more difficult than any merely rationalistic optimism is ever willing to admit.[37]

A note of melancholy? Certainly. But also a note of poignant conviction. A note of nostalgia? Perhaps. But not the nostalgia of the yearning backward look, only the nostalgia of the admiration of a past magnificence now gone and now somehow to be embodied in a new form. The Troeltsch who wrote these lines — and they are among the last to come from his pen — had already experienced the pathos of also writing out the decline and fall of the theology he had presupposed. The concept of compromise, however, was the child of historical analysis, not rational abstraction. It had sprung out of the raw data of the history of Christianity. It thrived in the face of what Troeltsch had learned about the modern context. It remained as the signpost to the future.

Such was not the case with another of Troeltsch's key ideas, the much better known concept of the *religious a priori*. Indeed, the striking thing about this concept is the twofold fact of its early formulation and its disappearance from his thought. In both respects it differs from the concept of compromise, which is present throughout the whole of Troeltsch's writings and does not receive explicit formulation until the very end of his life.

The concept of the religious a priori flourished during the earlier period of Troeltsch's thought. It focused one of his most lasting convictions, the conviction that without religion, culture is impossible. The conviction remained throughout his life. The passage we have just had before us is ample proof of this.[38] During the Heidelberg days this conviction was rooted in certainty, the certainty of what Troeltsch regarded to be an unshakable argument, namely, that religion is an a priori necessity for the culture of man.

The concept was finely etched in an article written in 1909 under the title *Zur Frage des religiösen Apriori* (Concerning the Question of the Religious Apriori). This was written in direct response to a critique that had been advanced by Paul Spiess in the columns of *Religion und Geisteskultur* and was published originally in this same journal.[39] The discussion consisted largely of a point for point response to Spiess. These remarks were introduced by a more general consideration of the idea itself.

Troeltsch began by noting the basic affinity between himself and Dilthey. He then proceeded immediately to clarify the intrinsic nature of his own work. He asserted that this had been characterized from the beginning by historical and systematic interests. The first of these derived from his sensitivity to the fact that all human events are interwoven — religious and nonreligious, Christian and non-Christian alike. On the other hand, and this is where his systematic interests came into play, Troeltsch argued the impossibility of surrendering this whole sphere to merely causal analysis and dealing with psychic development solely in terms of its environment. He contended that " the religious feeling " protests against this, as does " reason's entire view of itself, with all its ideal values." For these values stand or fall with religion itself. That is, " they stand or fall with the certainty of an absolute and rational ground of all things." [40]

In this light Troeltsch moved to a precise formulation of the central problem with which he was concerned. He emphasized that what he had in mind was the problem of " the general spiritual (geistigen) situation of the present." The present has experienced the triumph of its knowledge in the " historicizing, psychologizing, and relativizing of all reality." This has in turn cut it off from any approach to " the normative " and " the objective," and has in fact given rise to an " increasing yearning after the absolute," that is, " after religion." It was this and this alone which concerned him — " the general living question of the present." [41]

So construed, this " general living question of the present " evoked the concept of the religious a priori. As Troeltsch conceived it the concept would have a twofold significance. In the first place, simply because of its a priori character it would assure " the independence of reason " and offer " a formula for the dualism between the rationally necessary and the merely factually given (eine Formel für den Dualismus zwischen Vernünftig-Notwendige und bloss Gegeben-Tatsächlichem) ." Beyond this it would suggest a means by which cultural values could become scientifically intelligible. This would happen because here a general principle emerges that can penetrate the particular cases contained within it by means of the a priori it entails. In this fashion one would move beyond the merely psychologically comprehensible layers of relativity in the direction of the " generally necessary." [42]

Thus Troeltsch was convinced that the only way to do justice to the central role of cultural values was by means of the development of a religious a priori. One must proceed to the investigation of cultural phenomena at large with a previously thought through general principle in terms of which the cultural values themselves become scientifically intelligible. He was perfectly clear as to the goal he had in mind. It was nothing less than the clarification of " a system of objective values," as this system unfolds out of history itself. For Troeltsch the religious a priori represented the means whereby one can discern the ethic that history itself generates, for he was convinced that history contains its own " impulse toward the valid and the obligatory." [43]

So the matter stood in 1909. What Troeltsch regarded to be the road to the future at that point was clear. History contains its own impulse toward the ethical itself, in the highest, religious sense of the term. If one is to read history with insight, then, one must take this into account. Hence the religious a priori. However, the concept could not live long in this form, given Troeltsch's devotion to the precision that any intellectually responsible treatment of history demands. Accordingly, the qualifications were soon to come. The ultimate disappearance of the concept itself from his thought was already foreshadowed three years later in an article that he wrote in memory of William James. The article was originally written for the *Harvard Theological Review;* the German text was included in the second volume of his collected writings under the arresting title, *Empirismus und Platonismus in der Religionsphi-*

losophie (Empiricism and Platonism in the Philosophy of Religion).

Troeltsch sought to achieve two goals in this discussion: the delineation of the contrast between James's pragmatic thought and the continental approach to the philosophy of religion, and the appraisal of the significance of James's work for this latter enterprise. The discussion contains a comprehensive survey of the issues that emerge from this juxtaposition in the light of which Troeltsch sought to clarify his own position. He found that he would continue to decide for " apriori-transcendental philosophy " on the grounds that logically he could see no other way. However, he was not hesitant to give James his due, though he could not know yet that he was taking the first step in the direction of the inexorable result of the long struggle in *Der Historismus*.

> The transcendental method works out from an initially purely psychological analysis, in order to find the point where the apriori element of consciousness asserts itself. Such an analysis, however, must be made without any metaphysical or epistemological presupposition. It must proceed purely positivistically and empirically, and can therefore work very well, provisionally, with the basic assumptions of Empiricism and Pragmatism. However, this is solely a purely provisional phenomenology.[44]

It would not remain " purely provisional." One can hardly fail to observe that this was the same year that saw the completion of *The Social Teachings*. There was nothing " purely provisional " about the phenomenological dimension of that study!

What happened to the religious a priori in the face of the argument of *Der Historismus*? It disappeared. The problem is how to account for this. All the ingredients of the concept are present in this discussion. As we have seen, Troeltsch labored to clarify the a priori character of the synthesis of culture so necessary for historical reflection. This is how he sought to deal objectively with the spontaneous and the novel in all historical creativity.[45] Moreover, we have also considered the reference to the religious dimension, and in that sense the theological element, which cannot be ignored if *Der Historismus* as a whole is to be taken seriously.[46] These two elements are separated in *Der Historismus;* this is the striking thing. The former is a logical necessity for the attempt to deal constructively with historical relativism. However, that necessity could now be formulated without any reference to the religious dimension. The references to the religious overtones of *Der Historismus,* which most certainly are present, now serve only one purpose, namely, the statement — one could almost say, the confession — of conviction.

Why are these two factors, which were so decisively wedded in the discussion of 1909, so clearly though tacitly divorced in the massive work of 1922? Were it not for the fact that they had been so intimately combined in earlier days this question could be disposed of with dispatch. We could conclude as we did in the case of the concept of compromise: Since the constructive theological task was deliberately tabled in *Der Historismus,* and in the research leading to it, the concept of the *religious* a priori would be inadmissible and is therefore absent, awaiting some future development and application.[47] This, however, would be a premature conclusion, for *Der Historismus* was not Troeltsch's final product.

The movement *from* religion *to* history, with the apologetically ordered task of developing an intelligible interpretation of history in the light of religion — this may well be the animating principle of the early articulation of the concept of the religious a priori. The witness of Troeltsch's thought as a whole, however, is that he did not always move in this singular direction; he insisted, rather, on moving back and forth between the two. And each visitation of the empirically discernible, factual realm brought more trauma to the interpretative apparatus with which he began. It may be that when he left Heidelberg for Berlin he had already decided not to pack the concept of the religious a priori for the trip. One thing, however, is clear. This concept, unlike the concept of compromise, was not the child of historical analysis, but of rational abstraction. Before the analysis of the problem of historical relativism it withered and died. It did so for reasons that become clear in the specifically theological writings that Troeltsch produced and that include his final efforts.

2. THE STRUCTURE AND CONTENT OF A
" RELIGIONSGESCHICHTLICHE " DOGMATIC

The theology of Troeltsch can be appraised significantly only if it is carefully assembled. In general, this is relatively easy to do in the light of what we know about the basic contours of his thought as a whole. In particular, it is simplified by the host of explicit clues that he left those who might wish to pursue the matter. The most significant of these is the article written in 1913 under the title *The Dogmatics of the " religionsgeschichtliche Schule."* [48] Here he worked out in detail his conception of the structure theological reflection must have in the light of the scientifically ordered, historical investigation of religion in all its forms. Moreover, in this attempt to set out the form of dogmatics in the light of the history of religions he pointed to the key monographs in which, up to that point, he had already begun the task of giving substance to this form. Careful attention must be paid to these monographs.

Early in this discussion we hear Troeltsch say what is meant in general by the term " dogmatics." It is the " exposition of a normative Christian-religious view of totality (*Gesamtanschauung*) ." [49] Troeltsch was convinced that it was now possible and necessary to order this in terms of the basic method of the history of religions. He was also convinced that this had not yet been done. Precursors of the attempt there were, to be sure. Schleiermacher, on the one hand, and Hegel and the Tübingen school, on the other, would qualify in this respect. However, on two counts the historical and critical investigations of religion have moved far beyond the ground presupposed by both. In the first place, the investigations of the origins of Christianity have yielded a picture " wholly other " than that each had assumed. In the second place, the views of the universal and historical development of religion in general found at the heart of both Schleiermacher's and Hegel's systems have been drastically superseded. Troeltsch characterized these views as " completely obsolete and thin imagination," and he asserted that the whole idea of construing any historical religion as " final, completed, and overcoming all others " is both " questionable and doubtful." [50]

In the face of these developments, one could run either of two ways: either to the conclusion that dogmatics is impossible, or to the assumption that it must be worked out with no reference to the historical development of religion and thus be only an abstract formulation of " the common content of all religion." Neither the skepticism of the former nor the ahistorical character of the latter were tenable for Troeltsch. The price of this rejection was the necessity of dealing with history, and attempting to construct on the basis of it " a normative religious world of ideas for us." [51]

Such an attempt would entail *four* tasks. The *first* of these is " to show on the basis of the historical-philosophical comparison of religions [that] Christianity [has], fundamentally and generally, the highest value for our culture and sphere of life." [52] This first task leads immediately to the *second*, for it raises anew the basic question. " But what does ' Christianity ' mean? This is the second main question, and in its answering stands the *second* task and foundation of dogmatics." [53]

The intimate and irreversible relationship between these two tasks is crucial. The first task decisively conditions the second. To deal with the historical and philosophical understanding of the supreme value of Christianity in the context of Western civilization is to reflect on " the whole historical living complex of Christianity." To move *from* this reflection *to* the meaning of Christianity itself is to recognize that the " Christianity " to be interpreted is not simply identical with " the thought world and ethic of the New Testament." As Troeltsch put it, " A simple Biblicism is impossible." [54] It is impossible because the question that shapes the second task cannot be answered authentically apart from the fulfillment of the first. That is, the issue is not simply what was originally stated Biblically, but how this has asserted itself in the manifold expressions that the history of Christianity has produced. We may focus the matter in Troeltsch's terminology this way. The *first* task has to do with the *absoluteness* of Christianity; the *second* task, with its *essence*.

Only in the light of these first two steps does the traditional subject matter of theology come into view. The *third* task may be simply stated as being the task of " the expo-

sition of this ' essence.' " [55] As the direct result of the first
two steps, however, this exposition must be characterized
by a deliberate separation of the *historical* and the *conceptual* sides of the undertaking. These are intertwined,
of course, and the third task cannot be fulfilled in any
sense of the term without an equal weighting of both elements of the procedure. Be that as it may, the separation
is thorough and complete for Troeltsch, as is clear in his
formulation of the "characteristic sketch of the dogmatics
of a *religionsgeschichtliche* school " as including the following:

> I. Historical-religious theses, in which is presented the
> religious significance of the historical foundations — the
> prophets, Jesus, and the unfolding of the Christian spirit
> in history — and where in particular the person of Jesus
> in its significance for both individual and collective piety
> stands in the foreground; II. Metaphysical-religious
> theses, in which are presented the concepts of God, the
> world, and the soul [contained within] Christian thought;
> then the reciprocal relationship of these in the Christian
> concept of redemption; and finally the result of the latter
> in the Christian idea of community and of the last
> things.[56]

To these three tasks Troeltsch added a " fourth point."
He hesitated to call it a task, since he had in mind a quality
that must pervade the entire enterprise. The reflection
entailed in connection with the first three tasks " presupposes scientific knowledge and methods, but is itself not
a science. It is a confession and an analysis of this confession by way of the guidance of preaching and instruction." [57] His reluctance to refer to this as literally the
fourth task is understandable if one recalls the increasing
perplexity that the writing of *The Social Teachings*
had already caused him by the time this article was pro-

duced. Precisely the *practical* question was the focal point of that perplexity. Even so, he could speak of dogmatics as he understood it as being, along with ethics, " a part — indeed, the most important part — of practical theology." [58] With this in mind, and in spite of his demur, we may refer to the practical question as the question shaping the *fourth* task of dogmatics as he proposed to structure it.

We may, then, summarize Troeltsch's proposal as follows: The formulation of the *absoluteness,* the *essence,* the *exposition,* and the *application* of Christianity — in that order, and that order alone — constitutes dogmatics in the light of the history of religions.

In connection with this fourth point there is a decisive formulation that may serve as the real indication of the direction and ultimate result of Troeltsch's specifically theological efforts. This is especially the case in the light of the fact that with this fourth point he sought to express a dimension that must be discernible in all phases of dogmatics.

> The decisive affirmation of the Christian world of life is a personal taking of a position *(Stellungnahme)* . The determination of the essence of Christianity having value for the present is no less a matter of personal intuition.[59]

Recalling in general where he came out with the argument of *The Social Teachings,* and remembering specifically what we saw in connection with his threefold ideal type analysis,[60] we must observe that at best Troeltsch was conceiving a theology for the third type. This is already clear with only his understanding of the structure of dogmatics before us. The implication is, then, that a theology that takes its lead from the history of religions will unfold as a theology of radical religious individualism.

To deal with the substance of Troeltsch's theology one

has only to turn to the discussions he himself designates in the notes which accompany the article we have just examined, and to those treatments of a similar nature which suggest themselves. The accomplishment of the *first task,* accordingly, centers in the pivotal treatment entitled *Die Absolutheit des Christentums und die Religionsgeschichte* (The Absoluteness of Christianity and the History of Religions). This work had two precursors,[61] and it went through two editions, the first in 1902 and the second in 1912. It also has a successor, *The Place of Christianity Among the World Religions* (*Die Stellung des Christentums unter den Weltreligionen*).[62]

It is the last of these discussions that we must consider at some length. Of the five lectures that Troeltsch prepared for the trip to England that he did not live to make, this clearly meant the most to him. Professor Clement C. J. Webb, through whom the invitation to lecture at Oxford had come, had requested him to lecture on this theme.[63] The lecture contains Troeltsch's own careful summation of the argument of *Die Absolutheit,* and it culminates with his critical reconsideration of this argument in the light of his subsequent reflections — in the light, that is, of his long study of historical relativism.

As Troeltsch looked back on and understood his own book, the meaning of *Die Absolutheit* was rooted in his " deep feeling " for the clash between historical thought and the attempt to fix truth and value in a normative way.[64] The point to the entire discussion had been the investigation of " the means with which theology can defend itself against these difficulties." [65] In the initial phases of the discussion he rejected both the argument from miracle and the argument from the view that Christianity is the culmination of the historical development of religion in general as worthless for this purpose. This brought him to the crucial step. The real issue regarding the absoluteness of Christianity is not that concerning its general significance or its comprehensiveness. The decisive problem has to do with its *validity* (*Gültigkeit*).[66]

Reflecting on this question, Troeltsch noted, " It is quite possible that there is an element of validity in every religion." This element of validity, however, will always be mixed in with "a thousand individual and temporary peculiarities." It is, in fact, a matter of " insight," which " can be affirmed only personally by inner experience and pure conscientiousness," and cannot in any event " be proved." [67] Now, to leave the matter there is to base the claim to validity on the " needle's point " of personal conviction. The question is, can the need for a broader, more tangible foundation be met? He believed that such a factual foundation could be discerned in the manner in which the general validity of Christianity is " instinctively and directly expressed " in the particular kind of " faith in revelation " and " claim to truth " it possesses.[68]

Here Troeltsch found what he considered to be the real basis of a penetrating comparison of the great religions of the world — one in terms of which the absoluteness of Christianity could be articulated. As he put it, the " belief in revelation " and the " claim to universality " in the other great religions is " wholly other than that of Christianity." [69]

All the great universal religions — he mentioned Judaism, Islam, Parsiism (Zoroastrianism), Buddhism, Christianity, and Confucianism — claim absoluteness, but they do so in completely different ways. The fulcrum of Troeltsch's argument is at hand. He contended that these differences will be disclosed only by giving close attention to the *naïveté* of each individual claim. That is, what is to be compared are "naïve, not apologetically constructed absolutenesses." To compare these religions in this way is to discover the differences between them at the level of "their inner structure." Troeltsch stated flatly that this is "the most important point" in the whole comparison of religions, involving as it does "the most intimate testing of the dogmatic contents to be compared." [70]

Considered with reference to the *naïve* claims to absoluteness, the difference between Christianity and the other great religions is striking. Judaism, Parsiism, and Islam, in one way or another, know the limitations of a basically national outlook, limited to specific cultural situations. Buddhism and Confucianism are in essence more philosophical than religious in character. " As over against these, in every case, the naïve absoluteness of Christianity is wholly different." [71] In the first place, any national limitation is excluded on principle, and this very exclusion reflects " the purely humane character of its religious idea." The basic religious idea of Christianity " turns on the most simple, general, inner, and personal needs of men." Furthermore, Christianity's claim to absoluteness does not depend in any way on human reflection and " the difficult labor of thought." It rather depends on " the manifestation of God in the great prophets and their inner lives. It is thus life and not thought, power and not a social order." This led Troeltsch to his central formulation:

> To God's making himself accessible in the core of conscience and not to the correctness of its thoughts and proofs it owes its universal validity. Thus the naïve absoluteness of Christianity is as unique as its idea of God itself.[72]

For Troeltsch, then, the case for the absoluteness of Christianity turned on the question of its universal validity. This could be established by comparing it with the other great religions of the world. To Christianity, of all the religions, belongs the most intrinsically universal validity since its naïve claim to absoluteness is rooted in " the essence of God and man." Both the question of the degree of validity in other religions and that of the wider development of religion in general may be dismissed. For Christianity itself is a developing religion. Consequently it suffices that to it belongs " the highest validity in the entire circle " we can survey.[73]

Such then was the central thrust of *Die Absolutheit* as Troeltsch himself outlined it twenty years after its first appearance and ten years after its definitive second edition. This argument was presupposed when he worked out his conception of the structure of dogmatics in the light of the history of religions. By the time he prepared this epitomization of it for his audience at Oxford he had reached radical second thoughts about it. Before considering these, however, we may turn to the other three tasks of a *religionsgeschichtliche* dogmatic and ask how he had proposed to accomplish each of these.

By 1913, Troeltsch was just as clear on what must be done to deal with the *second task* of theology as he was regarding the first. Indeed, there lay behind the formulation of this second task in the essay on the structure of theology a decisive challenge that, ten years before, he had leveled at his contemporary, the renowned historian of doctrine, Adolf von Harnack. It was more than a challenge, it was a scathing critique. This critique had been evoked by Harnack's celebrated little volume on " The Essence of Christianity " (*Das Wesen des Christentums,* translated under the title *What Is Christianity?*), which had appeared in 1900.[74] In 1903, Troeltsch replied to Harnack's discussion in an extensive treatment of the question "What Does 'Essence of Christianity' Mean?" (*Was heisst "Wesen des Christentums"?*)[75]

For Troeltsch the central problems raised by this book were not alone those regarding the validity of Harnack's position. They were, rather, those concerning the nature of his attempt: What does the phrase "essence of Christianity" mean? What are the presuppositions of the attempt to discern it? What are to be considered the means serving self-evidently as the solution of these problems? Is the meaning and goal of this task generally a matter of "the simple and the obvious"? Wherein stands the task, if it must be faced and is solvable? To what extent is it really a purely historical problem? If it is not a purely historical problem, what is the significance of the most important element of Harnack's attempt, namely, its historically inductive beginning point?[76]

The answering of these questions formed the necessary antecedent, in Troeltsch's opinion, for the evaluation of Harnack's, or anyone's, attempt to achieve his goal. The essay was devoted to a detailed consideration of them. Regarding the question of presuppositions, he insisted that the attempt to delineate the essence of Christianity is purely and distinctively modern, founded as it is on historical-critical thought, and necessarily involves a process of abstraction.[77] He noted that this search for the essence of Christianity is inevitably a critique, both in the sense that the phenomena of history are appraised with reference to their success or failure in fulfilling their implicit ideal, and in the sense that one distinguishes within the whole panorama of the past those phenomena which are "essential " from those which are not.[78] Furthermore, such a process of historical criticism turns on a concept of development without which the critique in question would be impossible.[79] This led directly to the view that any concept of the essence of Christianity is an " ideal concept," and that such a treatment of the history of Christianity necessarily involves one's view of how Christianity ought to move from the present into the future.[80] This in turn brought him to the problem of subjectivity and objectivity involved in the procedure as a whole.[81]

Such was the argument that Troeltsch epitomized in setting out the second task of a *religionsgeschichtliche* dogmatic in the essay in 1913. Here he cited and dismissed three previous attempts to formulate the essence of Christianity. Schleiermacher, he noted, understood this as " faith in a redemption accomplished through Jesus," a redemption in terms of " ethical and religious power " leading to the Kingdom of God, which would consist of " a religious humanity." Hegel and the Tübingen school in general found the essence of Christianity in " the idea of the Trinity or the Incarnation." Harnack defined it in terms of " Jesus' preaching of the Kingdom of God." [82] In effect, Troeltsch argued that each of these attempts suffers from the curse of the partial picture. In the first instance " a humanization of the ecclesiastical and pietistic idea of redemption " has taken place. The second amounted to " a speculative interpretation . . . of the Trinity and the Incarnation." The third, Harnack's, is nothing but " a Kantian-ethical interpretation of the preaching of the Kingdom of God." [83]

From Troeltsch's point of view all three of these attempts must be regarded as *ahistorical*. This is so because each has overlooked the relationship between the formulation of the essence of Christianity and the historical continuum that Christianity is. To use his phrase, "the real unity of all its historical results" is not present in any of these attempts. The only defensible conception of the essence of Christianity is one that seeks to describe the dynamic of Christianity as a whole, as this is to be discerned in its widely varied manifestations.

> Thus the "essence" can only be understood as the productive new interpretations and new adaptations of the historical Christian power, corresponding to any total situation at any given time. The essence is different for each epoch, resulting from the totality of its influence.[84]

The implication of this formulation is far-reaching indeed. For Troeltsch had in fact proscribed in principle any form of reductionism. One may not *define* the essence of Christianity simply in terms of one's own propensities and preferences. Indeed, one may not define it at all, one may only *describe* it. In so doing one is under the heavy burden of having to account for both one's own understanding of Christianity and all other possibilities, both past and present. A *definition* of the essence of Christianity is bound to be ahistorical. A *description* of that essence may be authentic. In this light it is astonishing to watch Troeltsch take up his own challenge and attempt a delineation of the essence of Christianity that would satisfy his own conditions:

> The Christian religious faith is faith in the regeneration and fulfillment (*Wieder- und Höhergeburt*) of the creature who is estranged in the world from God — [which takes place] through the knowledge of God in Christ, [and which results] in his union with God, leading to the Kingdom of God.[85]

The exposition of the essence of Christianity so described would constitute the *third task* of theology in Troeltsch's schema. The Christocentric character of the delineation is obvious. What, though, did he mean by " the knowledge of God in Christ "? Here, too, he had reached settled conclusions by the time he set out the structure of theology in the light of the history of religions. These were formulated in a lecture given in 1911 under the title, *Die Bedeutung der Geschichtlichkeit Jesu für den Glauben* (The Significance of the Historicity of Jesus for Faith). The inexorable result of Troeltsch's contention that this third task entails a separation of the *historical* and the *conceptual* sides of theological reflection [86] receives an unmistakable demonstration in this discussion. The lecture is in fact a paradigm of his version of the traditional subject matter of theology.

In this discussion Troeltsch sought to work out " the effect of historical criticism on faith in Christ." [87] The direction of his argument is evident from the outset. He asserted that if Christianity is understood in traditional terms the question is meaningless, since everything " stands or falls with the conviction of the reality of the historical person of Christ." The question is cogent only for a Christianity that understands itself as primarily " a living faith in God which is new in each moment," and which understands " redemption as an always new work of God in the soul by means of the operation of faith in God." That is, the question itself presupposes " that Christianity is a distinct faith in God, an exclusive knowledge of God with its appropriate practical standard of life." The question presupposes that Christianity is " a religious idea " or " a religious principle." [88]

Troeltsch's entire discussion turns on this initial point.

This must be emphasized. The problem of the effect of historical criticism on faith in Christ is significant only if it is an open question. This is not the case for traditional Christianity. It is the case for that view which sees Christianity as a religious idea or principle. Furthermore, it must be underlined that this view takes its rise on the assumption that the absoluteness of Christianity is capable of an empirical demonstration. Accordingly, it is evident that Troeltsch regarded the religious idea that is Christianity to be unique.

What, then, in the light of these considerations, is the relationship between the Christian faith in God and the person, Jesus? Is this relationship accidental? Is it simply a matter of historical occurrence, which is, from the standpoint of pedagogy and symbolism, virtually indispensable, but which is actually not demanded by the central idea of Christianity itself? Or is this relationship " irrevocably and eternally included within the essence of the Christian idea "? With these as the alternatives the issue could be put simply. If the relationship between the Christian faith in God and the person Jesus is accidental, then " we are essentially independent of the historical critique." If, on the other hand, one must come down with the second alternative, then this critique is unavoidable.[89]

Troeltsch argued unequivocally that the second alternative is the only real option. He did so on the ground of " the clearest result of the history and psychology of religions." This is that " the essential note (*das Wesentliche*) in every religion is not dogma and idea, but cult and community." [90] To use the phraseology noted above, the relationship between Christian faith and Jesus is " irrevocably and eternally included within the essence of the Christian idea " because of the way in which the Christian community took shape. Precisely the lack of a sense of cult and community, he asserted, is " the particular disease of modern Christianity and modern religiosity generally." [91]

It was, then, on the basis of the question of *cult and community* that Troeltsch worked out his understanding of the significance of the historicity of Jesus for faith. Whatever the primitive form of the Christian community has become, its " original motive " is clear. It had no other means of fulfilling its need for community and cult than the " gathering around the communion with Christ as the revelation of God." The dogma of the Christ that arose out of this " Christ cult " ought to be construed as that which made " perceivable (*anschaubar*) and accessible (*zugänglich*) the one and eternal God in Christ." [92]

Standing now, as it did at the time of its origin, Christianity must still be Christocentric. For in the movement of Christianity from its original to its present form there is in operation a discernible " social-psychological law." Individuals cannot exist side by side without " mutual effect and correlation." This yields the general circle of community with its thousandfold connections and its pattern of dominance and subordination, all of which need a " concrete center." This law is as valid for " the religious life "as elsewhere.[93]

Being convinced that there can be " no powerful reality of the Christian idea without cult and community," Troeltsch regarded as incontrovertible the necessity of the Christocentric character of Christianity in any of its forms. Any sense of cult that would be enlightened by " the Christian idea " must continually have as its center " the gathering of the community about its head." This involves the " nourishing and the strengthening of the community through its becoming absorbed in the revelation of God contained in the picture of Christ (*Christusbilde*)." So long as there is a Christianity in any sense " it will be linked with the cultically central place of Christ. It will be only so, or not at all." [94]

Troeltsch now proceeded to set out the two decisive implications of this position, the first with reference to the past, and the second with reference to the future. In the first place, then, whereas it is true that he regarded Jesus as " the symbol of the Christian faith," he nevertheless asserted that this symbol must be rooted in *fact*. It is impossible, he contended, for one who belongs to " the Christian sphere of life " to hold that " the center and head of the community, the point of reference of the cult and the view of God " is merely " a myth." For such a one it is of genuine significance that " a real man thus lived, struggled, believed and triumphed " and that " a stream of strength and certainty flows to him from this real life." [95] In short, " a gathering around Jesus must have its origin in a real life if it is to have inner power and truthfulness." [96]

In the second place, however, this view of the centrality of Christ as a social-psychological necessity for the Christian community led Troeltsch to argue that the future of this connection itself is an open question. There is a difference between the *basis* of the centrality of Christ for the Christian community and *the question of its future*. If, argued Troeltsch, one establishes the central place of Jesus with the miracle of a strength and certainty that overcomes all the weakness and capability faith entailed in original sin, then the religion of humanity must always be Christianity, and through all eternity the ultimate religious community must revolve about the center that is the person Jesus. On this basis one can stand with Schleiermacher in reasserting that Christ was the second Adam, or with

Ritschl in referring to Christ and his community as " the essential goal of God which is identical with the goal of the world." In either case it is a relatively simple matter " to build a bridge to the old Christology of Nicaea and Chalcedon." [97] If, however, one establishes the central place of Jesus on the fact of social-psychological necessity, one faces a severe limitation. One can only say this:

> As long as Christian-prophetic piety, carrying with it as it does Stoicism, Platonism, as well as many other elements, continues, every possibility of a community and a cult, and thus every real power and propagation of believing, will be bound up with the central place of Christ in faith.[98]

Here, then, one must face the fact that the future of Christianity, given its cultural moorings, is an open question. As long as European culture lasts, " it is hardly probable that a new religion will arise which is comparable to Christianity in versatility, depth and greatness." But no one can say whether this culture will last forever or whether it will ultimately embrace the world as a whole. Accordingly, " one can neither affirm nor deny " the possibility of an " eternal duration of Christianity and the binding of community and cult to the historical personality of Jesus." [99]

This led Troeltsch to the decisive formulation of his understanding of the phrase, " God in Christ ":

> " God in Christ " can mean for us only that we worship in Jesus the highest revelation of God open to us and that we make the picture of Jesus (*das Bild Jesu*) the gathering point of all self-declarations of God which are found within our sphere of life.[100]

The necessary corollary of such a view is the categorical renunciation of traditional Christology — that is, the

" Christological dogma of Nicaea and Chalcedon." As he put it, " The people who can be happy in their own particular faith only if it is binding for the millenniums to come know nothing of the intrinsic freedom and greatness of faith." [101]

These two implications, then, yielded the conclusion of Troeltsch's attempt to formulate the effect of historical criticism on faith in Christ. The recognition of the fact that the future of Christianity is an open question was for him the crucial factor in shaping " the religious work of the present." For this work " an interest in the historicity of Jesus " is central, but it must take an entirely new turn — in the direction, namely, of that which pertains to " cult and community." This new focus evokes " only austere historical science," out of which a " kernel of fact " emerges, on which " our common interpretation and estimate of Jesus as the embodiment of faith can be based." Nothing more than this is needed if we are concerned not with " the ecclesiastical dogma of Christ," but with " the redeeming truth of the Christian knowledge of God, and with the gathering of a community on the basis of which this truth will be propagated and made effective." [102]

This lecture epitomizes how Troeltsch moved on the third task of theology. There are, to be sure, other indications. For example, he wrote fifteen articles for the first edition of *Die Religion in Geschichte und Gegenwart,* serving as the systematic theologian for the impressive and celebrated enterprise of producing this encyclopedia. Each of these manifests the same kind of theological reflection we have just observed. Likewise, of course, the posthumously published *Glaubenslehre* demonstrates on a broader scale his operations on the front of the third task.[103] Were there a point to constructing his theology in its broadest possible extent, which there is not, these would be the sources of the undertaking. This hardly demands attention, however, since both the considerable strength and the devastating weaknesses of this whole procedure are already before us.

The strong points are clear enough. His passion for concreteness was rooted in the demand that the historical nature of Christianity be taken seriously. Obviously, the insistence that cult and community are central and basic both for the origin and the development of Christian thought is cut from the same piece of cloth as *The Social Teachings.* Nor may it be dismissed! For Troeltsch, however, this meant that a radical separation between the historical dimension of theological reflection and the specific effort to formulate the significance and meaning of that dimension must be rigorously maintained. In the present instance, then, we have an impressive and unforgettable argument for the Christocentric character of the Christian community and its thought. In no sense, however, may this be called a Christology. This would be to say what Troeltsch could not say, namely, that there is a *substantive* connection between the Christian faith in God and the person Jesus. Troeltsch's lecture is a memorable manifestation of the cardinal theological fact that Christocentricity and Christology are not at all the same things.

The possibility of a new way of formulating the relationship substantively was rejected on principle by Troeltsch. That a reformulation of traditional Christology could emerge which would also assume that the older apologetic is gone once and for all [104] lay completely beyond his horizon. Any such attempt must always be suspect from a point of view such as his. Consequently, and in spite of his express argument to the contrary, there *was* something " accidental " about the relationship between the Christian belief in God and the person Jesus. For beyond doubt, the relationship itself was only one among many elements " irrevocably and eternally included within the essence of the Christian idea." [105]

What, then, of the *fourth task?* What is the application of a theology that demonstrates the absoluteness of Christianity, describes its essence, and works out the exposition of this essence along the lines we have observed? The test case here is Troeltsch's understanding of the missionary undertaking that forms such an intrinsic part of the Christian outlook. In the light of all that we have seen it is obvious that for him the missionary enterprise as a whole was exceedingly problematical. This was due, of course, to the fact that his understanding of Christianity was informed by the view that it both has been and continues to be wedded to its context. He could find no way around the disturbing fact that the missionary enterprise must necessarily involve more than simply the propogation of the faith, since this cannot take place without cultural overtones.

The issue was formulated with trenchant and relentless clarity in *Die Mission in der modernen Welt* (Mission in the Modern World) in 1906. The statement first appeared in the columns of *Die christliche Welt;* it was revised for inclusion in the second volume of the collected writings in 1913, and this revision included Troeltsch's response to the criticism of its first appearance.[106]

Four factors conspire to make the question of missions in the modern world problematical. First, there is the " religious individualism " so basic to the modern temperament, which is epitomized by the phrase, " religion is a private and personal affair." Why, asked Troeltsch, ought we invade " a foreign sphere of faith " and force upon others a new faith which they do not want in the slightest sense of the term, and which at the same time must bring with it the "burdens and needs of European civilization"? [107]

Secondly, there is the impact of "our contemporary comprehension of the non-Christian religions." This has called radically into question the traditional motivation at the heart of the missionary movement. Troeltsch argued that according to this traditional view nothing was ever said by way of differentiating the masses of the non-Christian world. These were all equally lost and condemned. "Today, for historically trained men, this is impossible." Accordingly, "the most simple and urgent motivation of the mission, the duty of sympathy and rescue" has fallen away. For such men, "it is not a question of rescue, but of an uplifting to something higher; not conversion, but elevation." [108]

Given these two points, the third and fourth factors follow directly. On the one hand there is the question of whether one has the right to interfere by means of missionary activity in the religious life of others. On the other hand there is the question of possibility: Is Christianity transferable, seeing that the process of transference must include "all the degrees of the development of civilization" of which it is a part? [109]

Against these four factors Troeltsch ranged three positive points which were equally cogent for him. In the first place, the "missionary obligation" is necessary for "the religious man." It is implicit in his faith. Indeed, "faith would no longer be faith if it did not have the courage for expansion and propaganda." [110] Secondly, it is clear that without the missionary obligation atrophy is the inexorable result. "Struggle and expansion are necessary for our own inner development and forward movement. What no longer grows, dies." [111] Thirdly, he spoke of the propensity within contemporary life of what he called the " community of all civilized nations." He argued that this cannot unfold simply on the basis of " commerce and technology " since it primarily depends on the spiritual life and must therefore be rooted in the " community of religion." His sense of urgency in connection with the problem of mission in the modern world receives its sharpest focus at this point. " Only the ethical religion of humanity can conquer the differences of races. . . . Mission is indispensable for this. . . . It concerns, then, the future of the world." [112]

Troeltsch could combine his understanding of the problematical condition of the missionary obligation in the modern world with his recognition of the irrepressible drive toward mission that authentic religion has, but he could do so only by ruthlessly transmuting and limiting the concept of mission itself. Both the transmutation and the limitation are more than simply the implications of the opening phases of this present discussion. They are the direct products of the entire understanding of dogmatics in the light of the history of religions.

> The mission of the present is something other than the mission of ancient Christianity. . . . It is something other than the mission of the middle ages. . . . Finally, it is also something other than the Pietistic mission. . . . The contemporary mission is the extension of the world of religious ideas of Europe and America in close connection with the extension of the European sphere of influence.[113]

Such a mission is no longer a matter of " rescue and conversion," but of " elevation and development." The only exception would be those cases where " religion and morality are in a state of deepest deterioration," and this is in no sense the general situation " in the pagan sphere." [114]

The severe limitation of the concept of mission grows directly out of this deep transmutation. One can no longer operate with " the barren concept of paganism as an undifferentiated and darkened mass." One must rather be informed by the history of religions, and its view of " the heterogeneity of the height and purity of religious formations." [115] In this light Troeltsch categorically rejected the validity of any missionary activity on the part of Christianity as over against Islam, Judaism, or Brahmanism.[116] He was particularly bothered by the chasm between the Christian outlook as a whole and that of the world of Islam. He regarded any mission to it as both " hopeless and purposeless." [117]

If all this is the case, why, we may well ask, did Troeltsch attempt to formulate anew the concept of mission in the modern world? Once again, as was the case in our analysis of how he would accomplish the third task,[118] we must recall that the entire argument presupposes the empirical case for the absoluteness of Christianity. Given the demonstrable supreme validity of Christianity, the ruthless transmutation and the severe limitation of the concept of mission is both necessary and possible. It is necessary because the supreme validity of Christianity must be shared. It is possible because the question of its unique contribution is already assured. Thus, Troeltsch could conclude his discussion with clear conviction. " Neither fanaticism nor sympathy " informs our mission. It is informed, rather, by " the certainty in which we remain," namely, " that the Christian religion, tied as it is to the European and ancient heritage of civilization, is the highest form and power of spiritual life, in spite of all the defects, contradictions, and impurities of our civilization." [119]

Such, then, was the theology of Ernst Troeltsch, spelled out in terms of his own conception of the structure of a *religionsgeschichtliche* dogmatic. In assembling it we have examined discussions that were presupposed when he articulated this structure in 1913. The devastating consequence which his long struggle with the problem of historical relativism would have for this entire enterprise was already on the horizon with the completion of *The Social Teachings* the year before. Even so, he did not know until he had worked through *Der Historismus* that the struggle with historical relativism would leave this structure in ruins.

3. The Failure of Troeltsch's Theology

The careful summation of the argument for the absoluteness of Christianity that Troeltsch formulated for his Oxford audience is already before us.[120] This summation prepared the way for his own critical reconsideration of it. In the light of our analysis of *Der Historismus,* there is little mystery to what bothered him. As we have seen, in *Der Historismus* the concept of individuality ultimately controlled completely the concept of development.[121] This concept of individuality is incompatible with the concept of the supreme validity of Christianity, on which the argument for its absoluteness depends. On this note Troeltsch commenced the reconsideration of the most fundamental element which his entire theology presupposed.

My hesitations lie in this, that the conflict between the concept of individuality, whose significance for history (*Historie*) has become ever clearer and more important for me, and that of supreme validity may not be so easily reconciled after all.[122]

In saying this, Troeltsch pointed immediately to *The Social Teachings,* in which he had seen " how thoroughly individual historic Christianity is," and he pointed also to *Der Historismus,* in which he had seen this same problem to be decisive for all spheres, not just that of religion alone.[123] The result was inexorable:

> The idea of the individuality of European civilization and of the Christianity which is intimately connected with it now comes to the fore more vigorously, and the idea of validity and of supreme validity, which after all was always somewhat rationalistic, considerably recedes.[124]

The dismissal of the concept of the supreme validity of Christianity — for that is precisely what has here occurred — was the death blow for Troeltsch's theology. It was not the end of his conviction, but from this point on, if not long before, this was a conviction which lacked the certainty it once could claim. The conviction remained, marked by a noble integrity in the consistency with which he asserted only that which seemed indicated by the facts, and the persistent lack of hesitation in stating the implications as he now saw them.

For one thing, even the tenuous case for missions which he had been willing to champion a decade earlier was now gone completely. It was quite meaningful to insist on the cultural moorings of Christianity when one could assume its supreme validity. It was quite another matter to see the case for this relativism increase while at the same time the argument from supreme validity evaporated. Thus we hear him say that his understanding of the non-Christian religions had led him to see that they too had their own genuine " naïve absoluteness." [125] Under the impact of what he had learned about historical individuality he could only conclude:

> The great religions appear to be just the crystallizations of the great racial spirits (*Rassengeister*) , as similarly the races themselves are the crystallizations of biological-anthropological forms. Between them there is not conversion and transformation, but agreement and understanding.[126]

For another thing, the unpredictability of the future of Christianity was now drastically intensified. Christianity is caught up in " a new period in the history of the world." Accordingly, " its development is incalculable," for it is capable of " always new individualizations." [127] Behind this remark lies the outcome of the argument of *Der Historismus*. It was moving enough to hear Troeltsch say in the conclusion of *The Social Teachings* that " if there should be a Christian-social mastering of the situation, then here new thoughts will be necessary which have not yet been thought." [128] When these lines were written the case for the absoluteness of Christianity was still intact. Difficulties of an excruciating kind could be assumed to lie ahead, but so could an ultimate resolution. What he planned now to say to his Oxford audience could no longer assume the supreme validity of Christianity. Consequently, though the words sound similar they now connoted for Troeltsch the complete unknown:

> All that is clear is that it [Christianity] stands in a critical hour of its development and that here very basic and daring innovations are necessary, which go beyond all hitherto existing denominations.[129]

Finally, and perhaps even more significantly, the collapse of Troeltsch's theology can be seen in what we must recognize as his unwilling pilgrimage toward radical religious individualism.[130] In the light of *The Social Teachings*, this must be seen as an *unwilling* movement. Troeltsch knew — empirically! — that the third type must be impotent in the face of the problem of the new compromise. As we have seen, the concept of the religious a priori disappears from his thought under the impact of *Der Historismus*.[131] This disappearance was accompanied by the relegation to the inferior " rationalistic " rank of the concept of Christianity's supreme validity. The basis of his entire theological structure, then, was gone, and with it went the tools he would need to do anything more than articulate conviction for conviction's sake.

> Christianity could not be the religion of a so highly developed section of mankind if it did not have a mighty inner power and truth, if it did not actually contain something of the divine life itself. In this, as in any other theory, there is fundamentally the always equal evidence of a deep inner experience. On this experience is its validity undoubtedly to be established, but it is quite certainly, for all that, only its validity for us.[132]

For Troeltsch the facts were relentlessly unavoidable, and so the conclusion could not be denied:

> As far as the human eye can penetrate into the future, the great revelations of the different spheres of culture will remain separated, in spite of any shifting on the borders, and the diversity of their values may never be objectively ascertained. For the presuppositions of every line of argument must indeed be connected with the fixed characteristics of the respective spheres of culture themselves.[133]

The concept of the supreme validity of Christianity had been his safeguard against basing all insight on what he called the "needle's point" of personal conviction.[134] Clearly, this was all that was left, despite his hope that his voice would not now be heard as the voice of a "spirit of skepticism and uncertainty." [135] The moving proclamation with which the lecture for Oxford culminates is noble and unforgettable, but the theology behind it was gone.

> A truth which is primarily truth for us is thereby, for all that, truth and life. . . . The divine life is, in our earthly experience, not one, but many. To anticipate the one in the many, however, is the very essence of love.[136]

There is much to learn from the collapse of Troeltsch's theology. It stands as the most memorable demonstration of a lesson we must never forget. To seek a ground for Christianity in the discussion of religion — and the attempt at a theology in the light of the history of religions is the logical result of all such efforts — is to move inexorably toward a Christianity of radical religious individualism. Can such be anything but impotent in the face of the imperative need for the new compromise? Can it ever produce a theology of involvement?

There is, however, more to be found in the ruins of Troeltsch's theology than simply this negative lesson, invaluable though it is. This stern warning is part of the legacy he left us. But ennobling inheritances consist of more than warnings. Troeltsch's own faltering, failing steps toward a theology of involvement point to the necessary risks such efforts to think new thoughts must run. The record of these steps is the outline of a ruin. In that ruin, there also resides the incentive for an urgent search for new possibilities, awaiting its own latter day. This is our real legacy from him.

7 New Possibilities

❖ ❖

In the four decades since Troeltsch's death theological reflection has moved beyond his far horizons a distance that can be reckoned only in light years. However, the question of Christianity in the post-Christendom era, which crushed his theology, still remains in all its relentless fury. What he isolated as the problem of the new compromise has yet to be solved. His failure to answer his own question needs no further demonstration. It has all the noble overtones of the authentically tragic.

What, however, of theology since his day — what of it, that is, in the light of the question he so unforgettably posed? The best that can be said is that we are ready to take it up again. In so doing, the reduplication of the failure of his theology need not be a threat. To know where and why he failed is decisive in this regard. More than that, the advances made by the gigantic theologians who triggered the theological revolution of the 1920's and have been busy consolidating new positions ever since may now be presupposed. In the light of their work the reduplication of Troeltsch's errors would be unpardonably stupid. The ignoring of the findings he reached in the process of that failure, however, would be worse.

The terrain that looms up before us is as inexhaustible

as the purview of the question of the new compromise itself. Even so, there are lines of inquiry now evident that demand attention if the yield of Troeltsch's thought is to be put to work in the present theological enterprise.

1. THE YIELD OF TROELTSCH'S THOUGHT

The most decisive point to be seen in any attempt to appraise the positive significance of the thought of Ernst Troeltsch is the fact that the failure of his theology was an *internal* matter. It was due not to external polemics but to the weight of his own question that his theology collapsed. Thus, the question remains intact.

Outside the confines of Troeltsch's thought the most significant point to be observed, accordingly, is not the self-evident overwhelming devastation of his theological position by the polemical thrusts of a rising new theology. It is, rather, the reassertion, within that new theological milieu, of Troeltsch's own question. Precisely that new theological temperament which broke entirely with any attempt to move *from* religion in general *to* Christianity in particular, and not the already fatigued and dying outlook of the nineteenth century, generated Dietrich Bonhoeffer's celebrated question of the come-of-age world.[1]

Bonhoeffer's image of the come-of-age world is essentially a poetic and germinal idea. In some fashion it must be translated into an analytical conceptualization before it can be put to work. All too often this is done by referring to the present as the *post-Christian* era. This is perfectly possible, but it is completely wrong. Such a translation of the idea of the come-of-age world overlooks the fact that the same mind which yielded this profoundly germinal image also insisted that what we must move beyond is " thinking in terms of two spheres ":

Since the beginnings of Christian ethics after the times of the New Testament the main underlying conception in ethical thought, and the one which consciously or unconsciously has determined its whole course, has been the conception of a juxtaposition and conflict of two spheres, the one divine, holy, supernatural and Christian, and the other worldly, profane, natural and un-Christian.[2]

For Bonhoeffer the resulting dilemma has become increasingly unbearable in the modern world. Nothing less than the abandoning of reality is at stake. For in the persisting two-spheres thinking, man " seeks Christ without the world, or he seeks the world without Christ. In either case he is deceiving himself." [3] Furthermore, there was a positive thrust to Bonhoeffer's point:

When Christianity is employed as a polemical weapon against the secular, this must be done in the name of a better secularity and above all it must not lead back to a static predominance of the spiritual sphere as an end in itself.[4]

A case can be made for the contention that Bonhoeffer's insistence that we must move beyond " thinking in terms of two spheres " conditions decisively his idea of the come-of-age world. Like all such arguments, however, this will deteriorate into a discussion of what Bonhoeffer " really " meant, and since we will never know, the elaboration of such a case is quite pointless. The important issue is, rather, what one does with the germinal ideas he has left us. Surely the *ethical* character of his concerns needs no massive demonstration. It was not at the level of outworn ideas, but at the level of the entire structural and concrete involvement of Christianity in the modern world that his sensitivity to the crisis of the present age for Christianity in any of its forms reached memorable and creative expression.

At this point, insights drawn from Troeltsch assert themselves. It hardly needs to be said that the issue is not that Bonhoeffer was thinking Troeltsch's thoughts after him. Indeed, there does not seem to be any line of direct development between the two. What can and must be claimed, however, is that the nature of Bonhoeffer's struggle stands out all the more clearly in the light of what Troeltsch had seen before him. The problem of Christianity in the modern world, and the vexatious question of its future, is far deeper than simply a matter for resolution at the level of the history of ideas. It is the very context which yielded the theological patterns and insights of the past that has disappeared. *Christendom* is gone. The problem of the present is acute because of *this* fact. According, it is extremely misleading to think of the present as the *post-Christian* era. This reduces the history of Christianity to an undifferentiated lump. If ours is the post-Christian era then everyone from Paul through Augustine was *pre-Christian,* and that is patently absurd.

Troeltsch's problem of the new compromise and Bonhoeffer's question about Christianity in the come-of-age world are, *mutatis mutandis,* identical. Troeltsch could not answer his question; Bonhoeffer, by virtue of his martyrdom, did not answer his. Over both, however, there brooded the same foreboding issue. It is the most disturbing question before contemporary theology: Whither Christianity in the midst of the modern world?

There are two broad and crucial contributions that reward the close study of the thought of Ernst Troeltsch. Our brief remarks regarding the unforgettable thrusts of Bonhoeffer's culminating reflections typify the first of these.

One may feel deeply, quite deeply, the impact of modern life on the ancient heritage of the Christian faith without ever having heard of Troeltsch. But once one has studied him and been disciplined by the integrity of his inquiry and the pathos of his failure, the *urgency* of the question of Christianity in the modern world increases a thousand-fold. We may no longer presuppose Christendom. All know this, in one way or another. We can never expect its return. How many really admit this?

The clarification of the goal toward which a theology of involvement must move is the first basic contribution of Ernst Troeltsch to the ongoing theological enterprise. It was a clarification that unfolded at the hands of a sociologically sensitive and theologically knowledgeable man. It more than justifies the juxtaposition between his own approach to the history of Christianity and that of his contemporary, Adolf von Harnack.[5] The *sociological, realistic,* and *ethical* understanding of this history far exceeds anything its *ideological* and *dogmatic* presentation can possibly disclose. The problem of the new compromise is not the problem of the new idea, it is the problem of the new involvement.

This carries with it a suggestion that only subsequent reflection can refine and clarify. Troeltsch's theology failed because it was conditioned by the history of religions. As a result of this fatal move it ultimately fell. This masked the real point he had been making all along. Theology is not conditioned by the history of religions, it is conditioned by history itself, as becomes clear when *both* it *and* the history of which it is a part are sociologically, realistically, and ethically understood. So understood it can only rejoice at the insight that Troeltsch could never assimilate into his own theological apparatus. " The fundamental historicizing of all our thought about man, his culture and his values " [6] should cause Christian thought no trauma in the light of its gospel and its Lord. Troeltsch's findings would seem to assert, however, that only a sociological, realistic, and ethical theology per se is in order for this, or any other, time. The marks of such a theology can be seen only in direct contradistinction to an *ideological* and *dogmatic* theology. This must now be pondered at its deepest levels.

There is a second contribution to be drawn from Troeltsch. It concerns the way *not* to go in the search for the new compromise. Here we do not refer to the demise of his theology. We refer, rather, to his insight into what might be called the *essence* maneuver. The issue was that which he debated as over against Harnack, and which we saw to be the basic point of what he called the second task of theology.[7] It is of the utmost significance to recall it now, since powerful and highly respected voices urge this option on us once again. If, as we have claimed, Troeltsch's rejection of Harnack's point carries, then the essence of Christianity may not be *defined,* it may only be *described,* and what one must describe is the creative power of Christianity throughout the ages.[8] This affirms as positively as possible a *pluralism* of theological expression, clearly evident in the history of Christianity, and yearning for full and explicit recognition now.[9] A sociological, realistic, and ethical theology thrives on this recognition. An ideological and dogmatic theology must deny it, at the expense of its own cogency and relevance.

In the light of both of these contributions drawn from the thought of Ernst Troeltsch there are two striking indications of new possibilities in the current theological conversations. The first of these is the contrast between

Paul Lehmann and Gerhard Ebeling. The second of these is the relatively recent emergence of what we may call, borrowing a term from Lehmann, the " contextual theologians."

2. THE CONTRAST BETWEEN PAUL LEHMANN AND GERHARD EBELING

Behind the contrast between Paul Lehmann and Gerhard Ebeling lies the long debate between Karl Barth and Rudolf Bultmann. This debate symbolizes, though it does not exhaust, the frontier reached by Protestant theology since Troeltsch's day. The significance of the juxtaposition of Lehmann and Ebeling emerges in the light of the work of Troeltsch because it manifests an important development in the contemporary discussion of theological ethics.

Lehmann's *Ethics in a Christian Context* (1963) is an attempt to carry forward Barth's insistence that dogmatics and ethics are inseparable. His version of this relationship is forcefully stated:

> Every ethical problem is in the last analysis a religious problem, and therefore every religious problem is in the last analysis an ethical problem. The first is the case because every authentic ethical problem raises the human question, the question who man really is, with the kind of insistence and integrity which makes the question about who God is inescapable. And the second is the case because every authentic religious problem is deeply rooted in the human problem of the wholeness or the nothingness, the greatness or the wretchedness of man.[10]

The extensive discussion of " the contextual character of Christian ethics," [11] which is what this book is, drives Lehmann to an exhaustive consideration of the theological bases this must entail and a prolonged effort to clarify the border line between theological and philosophical ethics. The argument culminates with a new and penetrating analysis of " The Question of Conscience " [12] as " the crux of the problem of freedom and obedience." [13] It is, however, restricted to a methodological treatment, as he explicitly indicates,[14] to be followed by a second volume which " will deal with questions of the content and implementation of a Christian ethic and will include a critical consideration of natural law." [15]

The mere prospect of such a second volume — a consideration of natural law on a Barthian basis, of all things — is enough to warm the heart of one who has learned from Troeltsch that the problem of the new compromise entails the development of a " new completion." [16] That this is precisely what is in the offing is already clear in the volume that we do have. For throughout this volume there is a growing preoccupation with the question of " humanization " that portends a vast expansion of the implications already seen:

> It is just possible that the special force of humanism has made explicit what has been implicit in philosophical ethics from the first, namely, the exclusion of religion, Christianity in particular, from the humanization of man. The issue of humanization is the decisive ethical issue, and a Christian ethic that understands its proper task will not seek to have it otherwise. On the contrary, the fact that philosophical ethics must reject Christian ethics serves as a cogent reminder that only a Christian ethic that focuses upon the issue of humanization is on the right path.[17]

This is the decisive indication of the way Lehmann proposes to go. Accordingly, his proposal to explore fully what it means to understand that " Conscience is the focal instance of theonomous behavior" must be construed as an assault on what we have learned from Troeltsch to call the problem of the new compromise.

On the other hand, there is the compelling epitomization of the thought of Gerhard Ebeling, his lectures in 1958–1959 for "students of all faculties" [18] at the University of Zürich, published under the title *Das Wesen des christlichen Glaubens* (translated under the title *The Nature of Faith*). Considered against the background of his collected essays (*Wort und Glaube,* 1960; English translation, *Word and Faith,* 1963), this suggests the route along which Ebeling proposes to move beyond Bultmann. Here one notes explicit appropriation of the very maneuver that Harnack championed, and that was severely questioned by Troeltsch.

> The decisive thing in Christianity is faith. In line with the famous lectures by Adolf von Harnack at the turn of the century, I could indeed have formulated the theme as "The Essence of Christianity." But I thought I might try to be more precise. If we ask about the essence of Christianity, then we must ask about the essence of Christian faith.[19]

Though the shift here indicated is far more drastic than might seem at first glance, the question that bothered Troeltsch about Harnack's attempt still remains. It remains in a haunting fashion that corroborates Troeltsch's basic insight into all such maneuvers.[20] For one who moves this way will invariably resist the full impact of the problem of Christianity as a historical continuum. That is, one who moves this way will resist the problem of the new compromise.

That such an appraisal of Ebeling is not too drastic is clear in the light of the following passage:

Justification by faith alone, according to Reformed teaching, is not one doctrine beside many others, but constitutes the whole of Christian faith. . . . Justification by faith alone is not an object of faith, but the very reality of faith. It defines faith itself, not a partial aspect of it. If faith alone justifies, then no completion of Reformed doctrine is possible. If completion and correction are thought necessary, then Reformed teaching is in effect abolished.[21]

No *completion* necessary? (His word is *Ergänzung*.) [22] None of any kind? If Troeltsch was even remotely correct, then to put the matter this way runs perilously close to outright rejection of the very Reformed teaching Ebeling seeks to further. For the fact is that this teaching did achieve a completion, and this is why it had such a monumental effect in the history of Christian social thought. More significantly than that, to put the matter this way is to come perilously close to an a priori rejection of the whole problem of the new compromise.

This makes it all the more striking that Ebeling comes out where Lehmann does, with a deep concern for the problem of conscience. In one of the terminal essays of *Word and Faith*, entitled *Theological Reflexions on Conscience*, we hear him assert his own compelling articulation of the centrality of conscience as " the very concept in whose light the connexion between dogmatics and ethics should be thought through." [23] This is hardly a peripheral matter for Ebeling. It is at the heart of the basic hermeneutical problem, as the following passage from his *Discussion Theses for a Course of Introductory Lectures on the Study of Theology*, in *Word and Faith*, makes abundantly clear:

The text of holy scripture can open up to very different ways of approach. No angle is *a limine* forbidden, although considering the nature of the text questions from certain angles forbid themselves. And not every possible approach is really appropriate to the character of the text as a linguistic event. The question which is ultimately appropriate to the biblical text is, how it affects the conscience. The hermeneutic principle of proper exegesis of holy scripture is therefore man as conscience.[24]

The question that irresistibly suggests itself is this: Which account of the problem of conscience is correct, Lehmann's or Ebeling's? Which moves us *toward* a theology of involvement, the one that accepts the problem of the new compromise or the one that rejects it a priori? These questions must not be answered too quickly. In the light of all that we have learned from Troeltsch, there is a self-evident affirmation of Lehmann and a self-evident questioning of Ebeling that cannot be denied. But the affirmation of Lehmann is restrained by the fact that it depends on a promise that has yet to be fulfilled. And the questioning of Ebeling is restrained by the possibility that any penetrating probing of the problem of conscience cannot rest forever within the comfortable assumption that the world may be left within the realm of *law* while faith and its meaning can be plumbed completely under the heading of *gospel*. What *is* clear in both cases is this. We are in the presence of new possibilities, which point the way beyond the present confines of theological exchange. For in neither case will merely a new articulation of the inner connection between dogmatics and ethics suffice. However incisive and however illuminating such articulations might be, they cannot forever beg the question, What *in the world* does this mean?

3. THE CONTEXTUAL THEOLOGIANS

We could think of Troeltsch as the first real *contextual* theologian. By this we mean that he deliberately attempted to combine theological knowledge with sociological knowledgeability seeking to sharpen the former by means of the latter.[25] Moreover the term "sociological" here refers to that broad spectrum of the sociological, realistic, and ethical dimensions that were always inseparable for him. His efforts were abortive, but this was due to the incapacity of his theological generation to move beyond attempts to ground Christianity in particular in religion in general. In spite of this he was prophetic. Bonhoeffer would be a second contextual theologian in our sense. Writing in the midst of chaos he nevertheless was the first to apply the new theology, on this side of the revolution of the 1920's, to the effort to combine theological knowledge and sociological knowledgeability. Lehmann and Ebeling? The former clearly, the latter at best potentially, move beyond the germinal insights of Bonhoeffer in this fashion.

One would have to be terribly insensitive not to have noted the rising surge in our present days of discussion that fits this motif and that has seized a great hearing. Prime examples of such discussion are the works of three figures in particular: Martin Marty, Peter Berger, and Harvey Cox.

Recognition of the fact that this is the *post-Christendom era is* the decisive element in the writings of Martin Marty. His " call for a culture ethic for American Protestantism," in *The New Shape of American Religion* (1959) was actually a " preliminary study " as he himself indicated.[26] It prepared the way for the compelling and incisive *Second Chance for American Protestants,* in 1963. The central emphasis of the book, stated at the outset, will make this clear:

> Ground-occupying Christendom, claiming a place under the sun, is a romantic vision. . . . That this place-inhabiting Christendom was an episode which is coming to an end is a main theme of this book. . . . The argument . . . calls not for further retreat from the occupied ground Christianity holds, but for a change to a different set of ground rules.[27]

One does not wait long to find out what Marty means by this " change to a different set of ground rules." Primarily, he means two things: Pluralism and its " cousin," secularity. What he means by each of these is crisply stated. " By ' pluralistic ' we mean only that many fonts of religion and values flow, many kinds of signals are free possibilities." [28] And the term secularity refers to " a way of looking at life which is nonreligious in the ordinary sense of the term." [29] This latter is memorably typified: " We consult the weatherman instead of God to learn meteorology." [30]

The decisive turning in this presentation is the causal relation that Marty sees between these two. Secularity is the result of pluralism: " The birth of the modern world and its pluralism led to the conception of this secularity." [31] Accordingly, it is primarily with reference to the fact of pluralism that he works out his points. " The basic fact of American life and religious life today is its pluralism — a displacing fact as far as any Christian empires are concerned." [32] How are we to act in the midst of it? As Marty sees it, Protestantism has three options: It can ignore pluralism; it can combat it; or, and this is obviously his choice, it can come to terms with it. " ' Protestantism in pluralism ' seeks redefinitions and a new course of action in the setting in which Protestantism will inevitably live." [33]

The crucial elements of Marty's constructive suggestions now begin to fall into line. For one thing, there is a striking appeal to the Old Testament:

> The prototype for later Christian development is God's ancient people of the old covenant. The Old Testament as appropriated in the New, in particular, points to modes of seeing the cultural possibilities of faith in the life of wanderers. . . . The Old Testament drenches us in a worldliness from which Christians can still learn. It reveals countless kinds of bonds with changing environments in wilderness and promised land. But the characteristic tests of faith were in the characteristic situations of exodus and exile.[34]

Put this perspective to work; read the New Testament in the light of it; ponder the present question of Christian culture. Can it — will it — prevail? Theologically, of course it can. There are no limits on what God can do. Sociologically, though, it will not: " Almost as assuredly as we could answer theologically that it *can,* we must answer ‘ sociologically ’ that it will not." [35] The problem, that is, is not what God can do, but what we must do, seeing that we are where God has put us. And in our situation one thing is abundantly clear: " One of the earmarks of the displacing situation is the inability of Christians who are consistent with their heavenly vision, to baptize and monopolize a culture." [36]

In this mood, Marty moves to his real question: " *Should a Christian culture prevail?* " [37] His asking this question is hardly an attempt merely to make a virtue of necessity, and answer with the expected " probably not." For he is seeking to detect what he will later call " theological potential in social change." [38] What he says at this juncture is the clue to the remainder of the book as a whole:

Somehow the Christian faith must find cultural expression, and must find it in ways consistent with its own genius, bearing the shame and the glory of the wounded and risen Christ in the middle of the world. Christians must act with disregard for the consequences which this action may bring upon their protected name.[39]

That this is also the clue to what Marty means by " theological potential in social change " in particular is clear, both in a negative and in a positive sense. Thus he constructs his own assault on the view that pluralism is in itself the highest good. It has, he insists, " its own set of problems." [40] In examining it and working in terms of it one is dealing only with " ground rules." [41] Theological sensitivity is thus in operation in Marty's caustic observation that pluralism, like secularity, " is not the unfolding of the kingdom of God. It is an assertion concerning how the cards of history are dealt, an awareness of things as they are. It can be instrument or trap." [42] In saying, however, that " disregard for the consequences" must mark the action of Christians " in the middle of the world " Marty willingly asserts the necessity of " a ' risked ' mode of life " [43] as the only real option. Significantly enough, the work culminates in a powerful analysis of preaching. It is an analysis, however, which is once and for all conditioned by the clear recognition of the context in which displaced Christianity must now labor. Is it too much to suggest that whereas the risks of conscious involvement in pluralism are staggering, the potential of such involvement is filled with the fascination of new possibilities?

Even in the displaced situation, after exposure, we do not yet know what moral life and political conduct would look like entirely apart from Christian witness. The

churches . . . are now involved in interpreting a society
and then producing for it: first, a man; then, an informed
man; then, an involved man — a sojourner and a stranger
in the City, who cares for it and is careful in it.[44]

Peter Berger, of course, does not write as a theologian
who is sociologically knowledgeable, but exactly the reverse. Writing as a sociologist who is theologically knowledgeable, he has already made an unforgettable contribution in his plea for *disestablishment* as the necessary route
along which must move the contemporary search for Christian relevance. This is the burden of his widely read *The
Noise of Solemn Assemblies* (1961). This is, however,
Berger the diagnostician at work. It is his other volume of
1961, *The Precarious Vision,* that should be given painstaking scrutiny. For here both the methodology and the
substance of his reflections find their more incisive articulation.

The subtitle of this second volume offers the important
lead. *The Precarious Vision: A Sociologist Looks at Social
Fictions and Christian Faith.* In its simplest form, Berger's
thesis is that we all live in terms of social fictions — that
is why our vision of reality is precarious. In unfolding this
technically, astute social science penetrates the layers of
fabrication in the name of reality. Berger draws on role
theory, as this has been developed from William James
through Charles Horton Cooley and George Herbert
Mead, for this purpose.[45] This he combines with the " sociology of knowledge," as pioneered by Max Scheler and
developed by Karl Mannheim.[46] Now the point to all this
is to broaden " the curious ability to look around the cor-
ners of one's own *Weltanschauung*," [47] as he puts it in one
of the host of marvelous phrases with which his writings
abound. He argues that " freedom begins with conscious-

ness." [48] He later asserts that "debunking . . . becomes a moral imperative." [49]

Sociologists often talk this way. The question is, How does this qualify as contextual theology? Only those with preconceived notions of what theology entails can read Berger and miss his theological concern:

> The natural inclinations of man lead him to take society for granted, to identify himself fully with the social roles assigned to him, and to develop ideologies which will organize and dispose of any doubts that might possibly arise. There is an instructive affinity between Christian faith and the analytic enterprise of the social sciences in that both serve to disturb this happy state of affairs. . . . The smashing of idols, with whatever hammers, is the underside of prophecy. [50]

But what is the content of that prophecy which, in Berger's sense, is equipped with sociological hammers? Is it too much to claim that for him it is an understanding of the authentically human that is profoundly Christian, both in its origin and in its import? Is it going too far to insist that the remarkable culmination of *The Precarious Vision* with a *theological* analysis of humor, sociologically applied, represents a far-reaching breakthrough of immense *theological* significance? The problem with the revolutionary, Berger argues, is that he "is almost always a thoroughly humorless type." [51] Yet, "Only God is ultimately to be taken seriously." [52] Therefore,

> At the bottom of any debunking job undertaken in a Christian spirit is not a nihilistic guffaw but a redeeming smile. The "unmasking" of society is undertaken on behalf of an affirmation of man. . . . There is always an awareness that this particular colossus staring us in the face at the moment, like all the colossi of this world, is swallowed up in Christ's victory and will be swept away

when this victory is consummated. Nothing human is ultimately dangerous, not even the most determined stupidity. Thus nothing human can ultimately keep us from the liberation of laughter.[53]

By far the most radical and most penetrating example of what we are calling contextual theology so far to appear is the very recent *The Secular City* (1965), by Harvey Cox. In this book the contemporary situation is pondered in a fashion that brooks no ameliorating qualification:

> Secularization has accomplished what fire and chain could not: It has persuaded the believer that he *could* be wrong, and persuaded the devotee that there are more important things than dying for the faith. The gods of traditional religions live on as private fetishes or the patrons of congenial groups, but they play no role whatever in the public life of the secular metropolis.[54]

This sets the mood for the book: *All* bridges to the rear are down. *Only* total involvement in the secular city may be countenanced.

Cox's effort is no mere attempt to ring violent changes on the down-with-suburbia theme. It is, rather, an attempt to deal responsibly with problems that only in our generation have begun to break on the theological horizon with gale force. His use of the Old Testament in setting out the Biblical basis for and understanding of secularization is magnificent to behold.[55] His discussion of " The Church as Cultural Exorcist " [56] represents an astonishingly new use of a long discarded concept. But above all, the assault on the notion now abroad that in the present situation the very term " God " must be expunged from the theological vocabulary represents the most creative possibility yet to appear with reference to what cannot be tabled as a cavalier question. Taking his lead from Bonhoeffer, Cox builds on the basic insight that " ' God ' is a name." [57] How does one *name* the one who has made himself known in Jesus Christ — how, that is, does one *name* him in the midst of the secular city? This is both a new question and an old one. But old answers to it, in an age when all thought has been relativized and, accordingly, theology's use of philosophy has been undermined in a radically new way, can no longer suffice.

Perhaps exploration is needed into realms we long thought to be secured beyond question.

> The Exodus marked for the Jews a turning point of such elemental power that a new divine name was needed to replace the titles that had grown out of their previous experience. Our transition today from the age of Christendom to the new era of urban secularity will be no less shaking. Rather than clinging stubbornly to antiquated appellations or anxiously synthesizing new ones, perhaps, like Moses, we must simply take up the work of liberating the captives, confident that we will be granted a new name by events of the future.[58]

Here contextual theology has penetrated to the very heart of the entire theological enterprise. Its voice cannot be stilled.

Marty, Berger, and Cox, then, also press toward new possibilities. With them, however, and the point dare not be suppressed, *new* possibilities are the *only* possibilities. The theology of involvement, toward which Troeltsch pointed, now emerges as the only road ahead. The church's mission, and accordingly theology's task, in the post-Christendom world must unfold in the context of secularization and pluralism. The task is to keep the pluralism plural. The continual rediscovering of its own identity in the midst of this involvement may well be the church's great contribution to this effort. In this continual rediscovery the church may take its part in the struggle to block the deterioration of the world into something demonic and destructive. That this is not an option but an absolute necessity lays upon it yet again the heavy burden of finding new, *positive* ways of proclaiming the ancient faith.

This involvement, however, is marked by unprecedented unpredictability. No theology has ever admitted to foreclosing the future. But today theological reflection must know that its task unfolds in the midst of uncontrollable transition. The fact is that the world has come inside the church.

This is indeed a time of a new exodus. We are " on the way " somewhere — to a destination that we ourselves will never know. We are not the first, though, to recognize that we are in the wilderness, with a land behind us that may have been the land of bondage, but that now looks preferable to what we must endure.

Endurance, however, is a strange word to apply to the pilgrimage in which we are involved. In one of the really choice moments of *The Social Teachings,* Troeltsch paused to differentiate his work from that of his friend and fellow laborer Max Weber. He referred to the contexts within which medieval Catholicism and ascetic Protestantism came into being and called each " a historical accident." He then reflected:

> But out of such accidents . . . the great historical developments arise. . . . If I speak here of accidents, this is meant merely logically, that here no immanent development may be constructed, not that these things have happened *sine Deo.*[59]

Not at the level of science but at the level of confession the history of Christian social thought discloses the providential traces of the presence of God. Ahead of us — in this present wilderness — the tracks of this same God will be found.

Notes

◇ ◇

1. Cf. the letter dated June 8, 1944, in Dietrich Bonhoeffer, *Letters and Papers from Prison* (first published as *Prisoner for God*), ed. by Eberhard Bethge, tr. by Reginald H. Fuller (The Macmillan Company, 1962), pp. 194 ff. For the original text, cf. Dietrich Bonhoeffer, *Widerstand und Ergebung*, herausgegeben von Eberhard Bethge (Munich: Chr. Kaiser Verlag, 1959), pp. 215 ff.

2. Ernst Troeltsch, *Christian Thought: Its History and Application*, ed. and with an introduction and index by Baron F. von Hügel (A Living Age Book, published by Meridian Books, Inc., 1957), p. 14.

3. *Ibid.*, p. 15.

4. *Ibid.*

5. Troeltsch first published this work in parts in the *Archiv für Sozialwissenschaft und Sozialpolitik*, Bde. 26–30, 1908–1910 (as we learn in *Gesammelte Schriften*, IV, p. 866; for the information concerning this fourth volume of Troeltsch's collected writings, see note 7, in this chapter). The final extensive sections on Calvinism, and the sect type and mysticism, did not appear until the work as a whole was published as the first volume of Troeltsch's collected writings (Ernst Troeltsch, *Gesammelte Schriften*, I, *Die Soziallehren der christlichen Kirchen und Gruppen* [Tübingen: Verlag von J. C. B. Mohr (Paul Siebeck), 1912; unveränderte Neudrucke, 1919 und 1923]; for the point just noted, cf. p. ix of this work). The

English translation is by Olive Wyon, under the title *The So-cial Teaching of the Christian Churches* (London: George Allen & Unwin, Ltd., and New York: The Macmillan Company, 1931, second impression, 1949) in two volumes. In 1960, Harper & Brothers reprinted this translation by arrangement, with an introduction by H. Richard Niebuhr (Harper Torchbooks, The Cloister Library, numbers TB 71 and TB 72). The title of the translation is inexact; it should read "The Social Teachings of the Christian Churches and Groups." Throughout this study this work will be referred to as *The Social Teachings*. References in the notes will be indicated by *G.S.* I, followed by *ET* I or II, to indicate the corresponding passage in the English translation.

6. *G.S.* I, p. viii; cf. *ET* I, p. 19. The italics are mine. The sentence in question is difficult to render into English apart from some such paraphrase, the crucial phrase being "*mit rückhaltloserem Eingehen auf die moderne Welt die christliche Ideen- und Lebenswelt zu durchdenken und zu formulieren.*" Olive Wyon's translation reads as follows: "All this research, however, was only intended to serve the purpose of solving the systematic problem, in order to think through and formulate the world of Christian thought and life in frank relation to the modern world." This is far too tame! It does not capture at all the thrust of Troeltsch's formulation.

7. The study of Troeltsch's thought will always be indebted to the work of Hans Baron, the editor of the posthumously published fourth volume of Troeltsch's collected writings. (*Gesammelte Schriften*, IV, *Aufsätze zur Geistesgeschichte und Religionssoziologie,* herausgegeben von Dr. Hans Baron [Tübingen: Verlag von J. C. B. Mohr (Paul Siebeck), 1925].) Baron included in this volume an exhaustive and chronologically arranged bibliography of Troeltsch's writings. This is indispensable for the organization and analysis of the whole range of his thought.

CHAPTER 2. THE MODERN SPIRIT AND
THE QUESTION OF METHODOLOGY

1. The essay is in *Gesammelte Schriften,* IV, pp. 3–18. The passage cited is on p. 7.

2. *G.S.* IV, pp. 338–339.

3. For those not familiar with German, it should be noted that the word "scientific" (*wissenschaftliche*) refers to the humanistic, historical, and literary sciences as well as to the natural sciences. The phrase "the scientific situation" could almost be rendered "the intellectual situation."

4. *Die wissenschaftliche Lage und ihre Anforderungen an die Theologie* (Tübingen: Verlag von J. C. B. Mohr [Paul Siebeck], 1900), pp. 4–5.

5. *Ibid.,* p. 21.

6. *Ibid.,* p. 27.

7. *Ibid.,* p. 27.

8. *Ibid.,* p. 32.

9. This essay was altered only slightly for the second edition of the symposium in 1909 and included in this form in the second volume of *Gesammelte Schriften* (pp. 452–499). Troeltsch brought out this second volume of his collected writings in 1913. (*Gesammelte Schriften,* II, *Zur religiösen Lage, Religionsphilosophie und Ethik* [Tübingen: J. C. B. Mohr (Paul Siebeck), 1913].)

10. *G.S.* II, p. 462.

11. *G.S.* II, p. 463.

12. Roland H. Bainton, "Ernst Troeltsch — Thirty Years Later," *Theology Today,* Vol. VIII, No. 1 (April, 1951), pp. 71–72.

13. *G.S.* I, p. viii; cf. *ET* I, p. 20.

14. *G.S.* I, p. viii; cf. *ET* I, p. 20.

15. *G.S.* I, p. viii; cf. *ET* I, p. 20. Here, as at many other points, the English translation is very misleading. Troeltsch's text, which my paraphrase reflects, reads: "*So kam ich auf die Frage, wie denn ein derartig neu sich bildener Begriff der christlichen Lebenswelt zu ihren alten Organisationen, den Kirchen, sich verhalte, ob sich eine solche neue Erfassung*

überhaupt auf die alten Organisationen aufpfropfen lasse, und
wenn nicht, welche Möglichkeit der Gemeinschaftsbildung
und des Anschlusses eine solche Neubildung überhaupt habe"
(my emphasis). The translation reads: "I was confronted with
this further question: What, then, would be the relation of
such a new and formative conception of the Christian attitude
to life to its own ancient organizations, the churches? Further,
could such a new conception, indeed, in any way be grafted on
to the old organizations at all and, *if this were possible, what
kind of social adhesion or relation with a fellowship would be
possible in harmony with this new view of life?*" (my italics).
The translator overlooked the fact that what Troeltsch had in
mind were opposite alternatives! Accordingly, Troeltsch's
point has been completely reversed.

16. Both in the text of his introduction and in the notes appended to it Troeltsch indicated the figures whose thought had
become decisive for him in the position he was developing.
These included: Simmel, Rickert, Kistiakowski, Max Weber,
and G. Jellinek. He was particularly dependent in this immediate context on the thought of two nineteenth-century
writers, Lorenz von Stein and Rodbertus. Cf. *G.S.* I, pp. 8–9,
nn. 4 and 5; cf. *ET* I, pp. 28–29.

17. For Troeltsch's formulation of this, cf. *G.S.* I, pp. 7–8;
cf. *ET* I, p. 28.

18. *G.S.* I, p. 9; cf. *ET* I, p. 29.

19. *G.S.* I, pp. 11–12; cf. *ET* I, p. 32.

20. *G.S.* I, p. 12; cf. *ET* I, p. 32.

21. *G.S.* I, p. 11; cf. *ET* I, p. 31.

22. *G.S.* I, p. 11; cf. *ET* I, p. 31.

23. *G.S.* I, pp. 13–14; cf. *ET* I, pp. 33–34.

24. *G.S.* I, p. 14; cf. *ET* I, p. 34.

25. *G.S.* I, pp. 14–15; cf. *ET* I, p. 34.

26. *G.S.* I, p. 15; cf. *ET* I, p. 34.

27. This is one of the most significant pieces Hans Baron
selected for the fourth volume of the *Gesammelte Schriften*
(pp. 739–752). Baron gave it the suggestive title under which
it there appears: "*Die kulturgeschichtliche Methode in der
Dogmengeschichte. — Bedeutung der lex naturae für Katholizismus und Reformation.*"

28. *G.S.* IV, p. 741.
29. *G.S.* IV, p. 741.
30. *G.S.* IV, p. 743.
31. *G.S.* IV, p. 743.
32. *G.S.* IV, p. 743.
33. Troeltsch published this study (which will be introduced and considered at length in the next two chapters) as the third volume of his collected writings. (*Gesammelte Schriften*, III, *Der Historismus und seine Probleme, Erstes Buch: Das logische Problem der Geschichtsphilosophie* [Tübingen: Verlag von J. C. B. Mohr (Paul Siebeck), 1922].) The statement is found on *G.S.* III, p. 369, n. 190. It is of such crucial significance that Troeltsch's exact formulation should be noted: "*Ich darf bei dieser Gelegenheit auch auf mein Buch 'Die Soziallehren der christlichen Kirchen und Gruppen,' 1912, hinweisen, das der grossen wesentlich ideologisch-dogmatischen Darstellung des Christentums, die Harnack gegeben hat, eine wesentlich soziologisch-realistisch-ethische, zur Seite stellt.*"

CHAPTER 3. THE NATURE OF HISTORICAL RELATIVISM

1. Cf. *supra*, p. 38.
2. R. S. Sleigh, the author of the first comprehensive treatment in English of the thought of Troeltsch dated both these articles along with three others that Troeltsch wrote for the *Encyclopedia of Religion and Ethics*, in the year 1910. (Cf. R. S. Sleigh, *The Sufficiency of Christianity: An Enquiry Concerning the Nature and the Modern Possibilities of the Christian Religion*, with special reference to the religious philosophy of Dr. Ernst Troeltsch, Introduction by William Fulton [London: James Clarke & Co., Ltd., 1923], p. 28.) For some reason Hans Baron did not include notice of these in the otherwise comprehensive bibliography at the end of *Gesammelte Schriften*, IV. "Historiography" is found in the *Encyclopedia of Religion and Ethics* (ed. by James Hastings, with the assistance of John A. Selbie and Louis H. Gray), Vol. VI, pp. 716–723; "Contingency," in Vol. IV, pp. 87–89. The Ger-

man text for the latter article, in slightly expanded form, is contained in *Gesammelte Schriften*, II, pp. 769–778.

3. *Historismus* is difficult to translate. Baron von Hügel's "The Historical Standpoint" (in his introduction to *Christian Thought: Its History and Application*, p. 15) is surely too neutral. I am convinced that H. A. Hodges is right in rendering the term "historical relativism," in connection with his studies of Dilthey (cf. H. A. Hodges, *Wilhelm Dilthey: An Introduction* [London: Kegan Paul, Trench, Trubner & Co., Ltd., 1944], p. 33). This is Troeltsch's meaning also. Throughout this study this work will be referred to as *Der Historismus*. References to it in the notes will be indicated by *G.S.* III.

4. The extent of the literary activity leading to the publication of *Der Historismus* is far greater than might be supposed. In accordance with his way of doing things, and in spite of the chaos of the First World War, Troeltsch published no less than eleven essays later incorporated in this work: one in 1916, one in 1918, two in 1919, three in 1920, one in 1921, and three in 1922. Cf. Hans Baron's bibliography at the end of *G.S.* IV.

5. The title of *G.S.* II is *Zur religiösen Lage, Religionsphilosophie und Ethik* (Concerning the Religious Situation, the Philosophy of Religion, and Ethics).

6. *G.S.* III, p. vii.

7. *G.S.* III, p. vii.

8. *G.S.* III, p. 1.

9. E.g., cf. "Historiography," *Encyclopedia of Religion and Ethics*, Vol. VI, p. 721.

10. *G.S.* III, p. 1.

11. *G.S.* III, p. 3.

12. *G.S.* III, p. 4.

13. *G.S.* III, p. 4.

14. *G.S.* III, p. 5.

15. "*Das Verhältnis durchaus ein gegenseitiges ist: eine Bedeutung der Geschichte für die Weltanschauung und der Weltanschauung für die Geschichte.*" *G.S.* III, p. 7.

16. *G.S.* III, p. 9. Troeltsch's italics.

17. *G.S.* III, p. 11.

18. *G.S.* III, pp. 11–12.

19. *G.S.* III, p. 13.

20. *G.S.* III, p. 13.

21. *G.S.* III, p. 14.

22. *G.S.* III, p. 14, my italics.

23. Cf. *infra,* Chapter 6.

24. *G.S.* III, p. 18.

25. *G.S.* III, p. 19.

26. *G.S.* III, p. 19.

27. *G.S.* III, p. 20.

28. *G.S.* III, p. 29.

29. In this connection, cf. particularly *G.S.* III, pp. 22–24.

30. For an illuminating exposition of the controversy between Dilthey and Windelband, cf. the second of H. A. Hodges' volumes on Dilthey: H. A. Hodges, *The Philosophy of Wilhelm Dilthey* (London: Routledge & Kegan Paul, Ltd., 1952).

31. *G.S.* III, pp. 32–54. The page numbers for each of the ten categories and concepts are as follows: (1) pp. 32 ff.; (2) pp. 38–39; (3) pp. 39–40; (4) pp. 40 ff.; (5) pp. 42 ff.; (6) pp. 44 ff.; (7) pp. 46 ff.; (8) pp. 48 ff.; (9) p. 50; and (10) pp. 50 ff.

32. *G.S.* III, p. 54.

33. *G.S.* III, p. 54.

34. *G.S.* III, pp. 54 ff.

35. *G.S.* III, p. 54.

36. *G.S.* III, p. 32.

37. *G.S.* III, p. 33.

38. *G.S.* III, p. 33.

39. *G.S.* III, p. 33.

40. *G.S.* III, p. 33.

41. *G.S.* III, p. 37.

42. *G.S.* III, p. 39.

43. *G.S.* III, p. 41.

44. *G.S.* III, p. 40.

45. *G.S.* III, p. 41.

46. *G.S.* III, pp. 41–42.

47. Indeed, he had *explicitly* pointed to it in the discussion of *representation.* Cf. *G.S.* III, p. 42.

48. *G.S.* III, p. 54.

49. *G.S.* III, p. 55.

50. *G.S.* III, p. 57.
51. *G.S.* III, pp. 58 ff.
52. *G.S.* III, pp. 62 ff.
53. Cf. *infra,* pp. 107 ff., for the close relationship between Weber and Troeltsch.
54. *G.S.* III, p. 66.
55. *G.S.* III, p. 67.
56. *G.S.* III, p. 67.
57. *G.S.* III, p. 67.
58. *G.S.* III, pp. 83 ff.
59. *G.S.* III, pp. 102 ff.
60. E.g., cf. the article on "Historiography," to which we have referred above on p. 43.
61. Cf. *supra,* p. 50.
62. *G.S.* III, p. 70.
63. *G.S.* III, p. 70.
64. *G.S.* III, p. 102.
65. *G.S.* III, p. 104.
66. *G.S.* III, p. 107.
67. *G.S.* III, p. 110.

CHAPTER 4. THE PROBLEMS OF HISTORICAL RELATIVISM

1. *G.S.* III, p. 111.
2. *G.S.* III, p. 111.
3. *G.S.* III, p. 112.
4. *G.S.* III, p. 112.
5. *G.S.* III, p. 113.
6. *G.S.* III, p. 113.
7. "*Das ist die einzig mögliche philosophische Bewältigung des Historismus.*" *G.S.* III, p. 113.
8. Cf. *supra,* p. 60.
9. *G.S.* III, p. 118.
10. *G.S.* III, p. 118.
11. *G.S.* III, p. 119. Troeltsch's italics.
12. *G.S.* III, pp. 119 ff.
13. *G.S.* III, pp. 120 ff.
14. *G.S.* III, p. 169.

15. *G.S.* III, p. 167.

16. *G.S.* III, p. 179.

17. *G.S.* III, p. 179. At this point Troeltsch devoted some extended remarks to the juxtaposition of his apriority, which is a "fact of life," with Kant's "transcendental deduction" (p. 179). With the latter he would have nothing to do in this connection because contemporary natural science no longer submits to it, and, furthermore, in the practical sphere Kant's point is not a deduction but an intuition. His stand against Kant is epitomized by the following remark: "The great shadow of Kant need not trouble us in these matters: an apriori derivation of the apriori is impossible, in any case the idea of the apriori itself remains important and decisive as an ingredient of the entire empirical realm" (p. 180).

18. *G.S.* III, p. 181.

19. *G.S.* III, p. 224.

20. *G.S.* III, p. 224.

21. *G.S.* III, pp. 224–225.

22. *G.S.* III, p. 226.

23. *G.S.* III, p. 227. Cf. *supra,* pp. 55–56.

24. *G.S.* III, p. 226.

25. *G.S.* III, p. 227.

26. Cf. *G.S.* III, pp. x–xi, 227–656.

27. *G.S.* III, p. 656.

28. *G.S.* III, p. 657.

29. *G.S.* III, pp. 658–659.

30. *G.S.* III, p. 659.

31. *G.S.* III, p. 663.

32. *G.S.* III, p. 102. Cf. *supra,* p. 60.

33. *G.S.* III, p. 669.

34. *G.S.* III, pp. 669–670.

35. *G.S.* III, p. 673.

36. *G.S.* III, p. 672.

37. *G.S.* III, p. 673.

38. *G.S.* III, p. 102. Cf. *supra,* pp. 60 and 73.

39. *G.S.* III, p. 692.

40. *G.S.* III, p. 110. Cf. *supra,* p. 61.

41. *G.S.* III, p. 692.

42. Cf. *supra,* pp. 43 f.

43. Cf. *G.S.* III, pp. 220–221, n. 96.
44. *G.S.* III, p. 708.
45. *G.S.* III, p. 709.
46. *G.S.* III, p. 710.
47. *G.S.* III, p. 727. My italics.
48. *G.S.* III, pp. 730 ff.
49. *G.S.* III, p. 700. Troeltsch's italics.
50. *G.S.* III, pp. 701–703.
51. *G.S.* III, p. 731.
52. *G.S.* III, p. 733.
53. *G.S.* III, pp. 748 ff.
54. *G.S.* III, p. 733.
55. *G.S.* III, p. 754.
56. *G.S.* III, p. 755.
57. *G.S.* III, p. 756.
58. *G.S.* III, p. 756.
59. *G.S.* III, p. 756.
60. *G.S.* III, p. 710. Cf. *supra,* p. 78.
61. *G.S.* III, p. 727. Cf. *supra,* p. 78.
62. *G.S.* III, p. 102. Cf. *supra,* p. 60.
63. *G.S.* III, p. 694.

64. It should be noted at least that the actual closing remarks of the chapter corroborate this point, though they add nothing substantial to it. Troeltsch terminated the volume with three theses embodying the results of his insight into " the relation of sociological and ideological elements of history" (pp. 768–772). Here he asserted (1) the relative independence of "spiritual history" *(geistige Geschichte)*, (2) the unavoidably sociological character of the present, normative task confronting historical reflection, and (3) the somewhat wistful recognition that the blending of these two so that " a new wholeness and unification is brought forth out of the crucible of historicism " (p. 771), which he now proposed to undertake, surely transcends the powers of any one person.

65. A similar though not nearly so clear-cut instance can be observed in the concluding phases of Section 4 of the second chapter ("Apriority and Objectivity of Any Such Cultural Synthesis"); cf. *G.S.* III, pp. 182–186 ff., and pp. 198–199.

66. Cf. *supra,* pp. 61 and 76.

67. *G.S.* III, pp. 692–693.

68. *G.S.* III, p. 110. Cf. *supra*, pp. 61 and 76.

69. *G.S.* IV, p. 14. Cf. *supra*, p. 20.

70. *G.S.* IV, pp. 14–15. The decisive second sentence reads as follows: "*Das ist meine erste Liebe, und auch in der von der Geschichtsphilosophie zu zeichnenden gegenwärtigen Kultursynthese bleibt des Religiöse im Zentrum*" (p. 15).

71. Cf. *supra*, pp. 78 ff.

72. *G.S.* III, p. 102. Cf. *supra*, p. 60.

CHAPTER 5. THE END OF CHRISTENDOM

1. *Protestantism and Progress*, tr. by W. Montgomery (London: Williams & Norgate, Ltd., and New York: G. P. Putnam's Sons, 1912; Boston: Beacon Paperback, Beacon Press, Inc., 1958), pp. v–vi. This is the translation of the second, and definitive, edition of *Die Bedeutung des Protestantismus für die Entstehung der modernen Welt* (1911), to which extensive reference is made below.

2. Cf. *supra*, p. 26.

3. Cf. *supra*, pp. 21 ff.

4. In so doing, we are deliberately broadening a term which, on occasion, Troeltsch used in a more restricted way. Speaking of the marked difference between Lutheranism and Calvinism, he noted the need for discussing "two Protestant-isms" in a work to which we will be giving close attention momentarily. (*Die Bedeutung des Protestantismus für die Entstehung der modernen Welt* [1911], p. 29; cf. *Protestantism and Progress*, p. 53.) One can hardly overemphasize *this* distinction, as far as Troeltsch's thought is concerned. However, for the purposes of our discussion the use of the term in the broader sense we are suggesting is irresistible, for reasons that will become apparent as the discussion proceeds.

5. In 1891 he brought out his doctoral dissertation in expanded form. For the bearing of this discussion on the point at hand, cf. *Vernunft und Offenbarung bei Johann Gerhard und Melanchthon* (Reason and Revelation in [the thought of] Johann Gerhard and Melanchthon) (Göttingen: Verlag von

Vandenhoeck und Ruprecht, 1891), pp. 95–97, where he distinguishes between the dogmatics of early Protestantism and Catholicism, on the one hand, and the dogmatics of modern Protestantism, on the other.

6. This was one of the two essays that Troeltsch contributed to the massive symposium, *Die Kultur der Gegenwart,* ed. by Paul Hinneberg. A second edition appeared in 1909, and a reprinting in 1922. (The other essay contributed to this symposium was "Wesen der Religion und der Religionswissenschaft," to which brief reference was made above, pp. 24–25.)

7. One learns from Wilhelm Pauck's introduction to the English translation of Karl Holl's *The Cultural Significance of the Reformation* that we owe this work of Troeltsch to the fact that he delivered the lecture in question as a substitute for Max Weber, who was ill. Cf. Karl Holl, *op. cit.,* tr. by Karl and Barbara Hertz and John H. Lichtblau, introduction by Wilhelm Pauck (A Living Age Book, published by Meridian Books, Inc., 1959), p. 16.

8. See note 1 in this chapter. We have only a few pieces of Troeltsch's writings in English other than the translation of *The Social Teachings.* Given the significance of the point at hand for the understanding both of that work and of Troeltsch's thought as a whole, it is fortunate that this is one of them. There are problems with this translation, however, and we shall note them on occasion. The most serious of these has to do with the unhappy and completely misleading title. "Protestantism and Progress" clearly implies that the former is the indispensable key to the latter. Nothing could be farther from the thrust of Troeltsch's argument than this, as we shall see. The distortion is almost too much to bear!

9. "Protestantisches Christentum und Kirche in der Neuzeit," in *Die Kultur der Gegenwart,* herausgegeben von Paul Hinneberg (Berlin and Leipzig: Druck und Verlag von B. G. Teubner, 1906), Teil I, Abteilung II, pp. 253–254.

10. *Ibid.,* p. 257.

11. *Ibid.,* p. 261.

12. *Ibid.,* p. 261.

13. *Ibid.,* p. 261.

14. *Ibid.,* p. 261.

15. *Ibid.,* pp. 261–262.

16. *Ibid.,* p. 262.

17. *Ibid.,* p. 266.

18. *Ibid.,* p. 265.

19. *Ibid.,* p. 268.

20. *Die Bedeutung des Protestantismus für die Entstehung der modernen Welt* (Munich and Berlin: Druck und Verlag von R. Oldenbourg, 1911), p. 32. Cf. *Protestantism and Progress,* p. 59.

21. *Protestantisches Christentum,* p. 266.

22. *Ibid.,* p. 266.

23. *Ibid.,* p. 267.

24. *Ibid.,* p. 267.

25. *Ibid.,* p. 268.

26. *Ibid.,* p. 268.

27. *Die Bedeutung des Protestantismus,* pp. 12–16; cf. *Protestantism and Progress,* pp. 17–26, though the translation is vulnerable at several points, notably its failure to use Troeltsch's key word " autonomous." (Cf. p. 12 of the original with p. 17 of the translation.) In thus characterizing the spirit of the modern world Troeltsch is entirely consistent both with his earlier and with his later attempts to formulate the matter as incisively as possible. Cf. *Die wissenschaftliche Lage und ihre Anforderungen an die Theologie (supra,* pp. 21 ff.) and, of course, *Der Historismus und seine Probleme.* References to *Die Bedeutung des Protestantismus* will henceforth be indicated by *D.B.d.P.;* references to *Protestantism and Progress,* by *P. and P.*

28. Cf. *supra,* p. 95.

29. *D.B.d.P.,* p. 26 (Troeltsch's italics); cf. *P. and P.,* pp. 46–47.

30. *D.B.d.P.,* p. 25; cf. *P. and P.,* pp. 45–46.

31. *D.B.d.P.,* p. 25; cf. *P. and P.,* pp. 45–46.

32. *D.B.d.P.,* p. 25; cf. *P. and P.,* p. 46.

33. *D.B.d.P.,* p. 45; cf. *P. and P.,* p. 87.

34. *D.B.d.P.,* p. 45; cf. *P. and P.,* p 87.

35. *D.B.d.P.,* p. 45; cf. *P. and P.,* p. 87.

36. *D.B.d.P.,* p. 45; cf. *P. and P.,* p. 87.

37. Cf. his preface to *P. and P.,* p. vi. Cf. *supra,* p. 90.

38. *D.B.d.P.*, p. 54; cf. *P. and P.*, p. 106.

39. *D.B.d.P.*, p. 63; cf. *P. and P.*, p. 126.

40. *D.B.d.P.*, pp. 86, 87; cf. *P. and P.*, pp. 174, 175.

41. *D.B.d.P.*, p. 87; cf. *P. and P.*, p. 175.

42. *D.B.d.P.*, p. 89; cf. *P. and P.*, p. 179.

43. *D.B.d.P.*, p. 92; cf. *P. and P.*, p. 184.

44. *D.B.d.P.*, p. 92; cf. *P. and P.*, p. 185.

45. *D.B.d.P.*, p. 101; cf. *P. and P.*, p. 203.

46. Cf. *supra*, Chapter 5, n. 4, and pp. 103–104.

47. Cf. *supra*, Chapter 1, n. 5.

48. Cf. *From Max Weber: Essays in Sociology*, tr. and ed., with an introduction by H. H. Gerth and C. Wright Mills (Oxford University Press, Inc., 1946), p. 11, for the following: " [Weber's] circle of friends included Georg Jellinek, Paul Hensel, Karl Neumann, the art historian, and Ernst Troeltsch, the religionist, who was to become one of Weber's greatest friends and intellectual companions, and who for a time lived in the Weber household." Roland Bainton notes that Troeltsch lived in Weber's house during the time in which he produced *The Social Teachings*. Cf. Roland H. Bainton, " Ernst Troeltsch — Thirty Years Later," *Theology Today*, Vol. VIII, No. 1 (April, 1951), p. 70.

49. This essay was first published in the *Archiv für Sozialwissenschaft und Sozialpolitik* under the title *Die " Objektivität" sozialwissenschaftlicher und sozialpolitischer Erkenntnis* on the occasion, in 1904, of the assumption of the coeditorship of this journal by Weber, Edgar Jaffé, and Werner Sombart. The essay was written by Weber, but it served the function of a statement of editorial policy, at least insofar as Part I of this two-part essay was concerned. Weber himself assumed sole responsibility for Part II, on which our analysis is based. The essay was reprinted in the posthumously published *Gesammelte Aufsätze zur Wissenschaftslehre* in 1922. It was translated under the title noted above by Edward A. Shils and Henry A. Finch for their volume *The Methodology of the Social Sciences* (The Free Press of Glencoe, 1949). We shall depend on this translation for our analysis, referring to it in the notes as *Objectivity* (and giving the corresponding passages in the German text under the designation *G.A.z.W.*). For the

notice of Weber's responsibility for Part II of the essay, cf. Max Weber, *Gesammelte Aufsätze zur Wissenschaftslehre* (Tübingen: Verlag von J. C. B. Mohr [Paul Siebeck], 1922), p. 146, n. 2, and Shils and Finch, *op. cit.*, pp. 49–50. It is interesting to observe that it was in this journal, during the years 1908–1910, that Troeltsch published the first two chapters, and part of the third, of *The Social Teachings* before bringing it out in its final and definitive form in 1912; cf. *supra*, Chapter 1, n. 5.

50. *Objectivity*, p. 67; cf. *G.A.z.W.*, p. 165.

51. *Objectivity*, p. 67; cf. *G.A.z.W.*, p. 165.

52. *Objectivity*, p. 68; cf. *G.A.z.W.*, p. 166. Weber's italics.

53. *G.A.z.W.*, p. 166.

54. *Objectivity*, p. 93; cf. *G.A.z.W.*, p. 194.

55. *Objectivity*, p. 101; cf. *G.A.z.W.*, p. 202.

56. The phraseology is taken from the following passage, which is cited here in its entirety since it remarkably illuminates Weber's concept. (However, I have departed from Shils' and Finch's translation at a pivotal point: They render Weber's " *durch gedankliche Steigerung bestimmter Elemente der Wirklichkeit* " as " by the analytical accentuation of certain elements of reality." I believe it is closer to Weber's concern to read " through the conceptual heightening of certain elements of reality," and have adopted this rendering throughout my discussion as a whole.) " We have in abstract economic theory an illustration of those synthetic constructs which have been designated as ' *ideas* ' of historical phenomena. It offers us an ideal picture of events on the commodity-market under conditions of a society organized on the principles of an exchange economy, free competition and rigorously rational conduct. This conceptual pattern brings together certain relationships and events of historical life into a complex, which is conceived as an internally consistent system. Substantively, this construct in itself is like a *utopia* which has been arrived at by the analytical accentuation of certain elements of reality. Its relationship to the empirical data consists solely in the fact that where market-conditioned relationships of the type referred to by the abstract construct are discovered or suspected to exist in reality to some extent, we can make the *characteristic* features of this relationship pragmatically *clear* and *understand-*

able by reference to an *ideal-type.*" (*Objectivity,* pp. 89–90; *G.A.z.W.,* p. 190.)

57. *Objectivity,* p. 90; cf. *G.A.z.W.,* p. 190.

58. Here too is a passage that must be cited in full, though one needs to know that earlier in the essay Weber has defined "nomological knowledge" as "the knowledge of recurrent causal sequences" (*Objectivity,* p. 79; cf. *G.A.z.W.,* p. 179): "Before going any further, we should emphasize that the idea of an ethical *imperative,* of a ' model' of what ' ought ' to exist is to be carefully distinguished from the analytical construct, which is ' ideal ' in the strictly logical sense of the term. It is a matter here of constructing relationships which our imagination accepts as plausibly motivated and hence as ' objectively possible ' and which appear as *adequate* from the nomological standpoint." (*Objectivity,* pp. 91–92; cf. *G.A.z.W.,* p. 192. Weber's italics.)

59. *Objectivity,* p. 106; cf. *G.A.z.W.,* p. 208.

60. *Objectivity,* p. 106; cf. *G.A.z.W.,* p. 208.

61. *Objectivity,* pp. 93–94; cf. *G.A.z.W.,* pp. 194–195.

62. *Objectivity,* p. 94; cf. *G.A.z.W.,* p. 195.

63. *G.S.* I, p. 364, n. 164; cf. *ET* I, p. 433, n. 164.

64. Max Weber, *Gesammelte Aufsätze zur Religionssoziologie,* Dritte photomechanisch gedruckte Auflage (Tübingen: Verlag von J. C. B. Mohr [Paul Siebeck], 1934), Bd. I, p. 207. (This source will hereafter be referred to as *G.A.z.R.,* I.) Weber says this in the context of an introductory note attached to the second essay in the collection, "The Protestant Sects and the Spirit of Capitalism " (*Die protestantischen Sekten und der Geist des Kapitalismus*). The essay had been originally published in 1906 under the title *Kirchen und Sekten,* and as such is noted by Troeltsch as the principal source of his own point in the passage we have just referred to above. For a similar statement by Weber, cf. *G.A.z.R.,* I, p. 153, n. 1, a note appended to the first essay in the collection, the celebrated *The Protestant Ethic and the Spirit of Capitalism (Die protestantische Ethik und der Geist des Kapitalismus),* which had been originally published in 1904–1905.

65. Max Weber, *The Protestant Ethic and the Spirit of Capitalism,* tr. by Talcott Parsons, with a Foreword by R. H.

Tawney (Charles Scribner's Sons, 1939), p. 144; cf. *G.A.z.R.*, I, pp. 150–151.

66. Weber, *The Protestant Ethic and the Spirit of Capitalism*, pp. 144–145; cf. *G.A.z.R.*, I, pp. 152–153.

67. For Weber's way of saying this, cf. the note in question: *The Protestant Ethic*, pp. 254–255, n. 173; cf. *G.A.z.R.*, I, p. 153, n. 1.

68. Cf. *supra*, Chapter 5, n. 56.

69. Troeltsch, *Die Kulturbedeutung des Calvinismus*, *G.S.* IV, pp. 785–786. This was an article that Troeltsch wrote in 1910 in response to Felix Rachfahl's *Calvinismus und Kapitalismus* (1909), in which both he and Weber had been under attack.

70. *G.S.* IV, pp. 786–787.

71. *G.S.* I, p. 967, my italics; cf. *ET* II, 993.

72. We have already touched on this in the analysis of the methodology informing *The Social Teachings;* cf. *supra*, p. 36.

73. *G.S.* I, pp. 15 ff.; cf. *ET* I, pp. 39 ff.

74. *G.S.* I, pp. 58 ff.; cf. *ET* I, pp. 69 ff.

75. *G.S.* I, p. 72; cf. *ET* I, p. 82.

76. The phraseology of this entire paragraph is drawn from *G.S.* I, pp. 80–81; cf. *ET* I, p. 88. The formulation itself is typical of the many complicated sentences in Troeltsch's writings which almost defy translation.

77. Cf. *supra*, pp. 25 ff.

78. *G.S.* I, p. 172; cf. *ET* I, p. 159.

79. *G.S.* I, p. 172; cf. *ET* I, p. 159.

80. *G.S.* I, p. 172; cf. *ET* I, p. 159.

81. *G.S.* I, p. 72; cf. *ET* I, pp. 82–83.

82. *G.S.* I, p. 72; cf. *ET* I, pp. 82–83.

83. Cf. *supra*, pp. 35, 117, and 95.

84. *G.S.* I, p. 182; cf. *ET* I, p. 203.

85. *G.S.* I, p. 286; cf. *ET* I, p. 280.

86. *G.S.* I, p. 182; cf. *ET* I, p. 203.

87. Cf. *supra*, pp. 116 ff.

88. *G.S.* I, p. 367; cf. *ET* I, p. 333.

89. *G.S.* I, pp. 366–367, my italics; cf. *ET* I, p. 333.

90. *G.S.* I, p. 371; cf. *ET* I, p. 338.

91. *G.S.* I, p. 371; cf. *ET* I, p. 338.

92. *G.S.* I, p. 375; cf. *ET* I, p. 341.

93. *G.S.* I, p. 376; cf. *ET* I, p. 341.

94. *G.S.* I, p. 375; cf. *ET* I, pp. 340–341.

95. *G.S.* I, p. 368; cf. *ET* I, p. 334.

96. *G.S.* I, p. 372; cf. *ET* I, pp. 338–339.

97. In the light of our long examination of *Der Historismus und seine Probleme,* to which, as we have seen, *The Social Teachings* inexorably pointed, this is no surprise.

98. *G.S.* I, p. 432, Troeltsch's italics; cf. *ET* II, p. 465.

99. *G.S.* I, p. 431; cf. *ET* II, p. 465.

100. *G.S.* I, p. 450; cf. *ET* II, p. 479.

101. *G.S.* I, p. 452; cf. *ET* II, p. 481.

102. *G.S.* I, p. 452; cf. *ET* II, p. 481.

103. *G.S.* I, pp. 457–458; cf. *ET* II, p. 484.

104. *G.S.* I, p. 458; cf. *ET* II, p. 484.

105. *G.S.* I, pp. 458–459; cf. *ET* II, p. 484.

106. *G.S.* I, p. 459; cf. *ET* II, p. 485.

107. *G.S.* I, p. 605; cf. *ET* II, p. 576.

108. *G.S.* I, p. 647; cf. *ET* II, p. 605.

109. *G.S.* I, pp. 647–648; cf. *ET* II, p. 605.

110. *G.S.* I, p. 648; cf. *ET* II, p. 605. Once again we are in the presence of the deep influence of Max Weber on Troeltsch. We have touched on the idea before (cf. *supra*, pp. 96 and 100), but this is the first time we have cited it in its fully articulated form. Both the term and its content originate with Weber. Troeltsch explicitly noted this in the first edition of *Die Bedeutung des Protestantismus für die Entstehung der modernen Welt* (Munich and Berlin: Druck and Verlag von R. Oldenbourg, 1906), p. 26, pointing out that " he [Weber] had first exhaustively discerned the special manner of reformed asceticism." In the second edition of this same work he conceded that " the concept is certainly full of contradictions, but the contradiction lies in the fact which it expresses." (*Die Bedeutung des Protestantismus* [1911], p. 42.) The problem of translation is difficult. Talcott Parsons, in his translation of Weber's *The Protestant Ethic and the Spirit of Capitalism,* uses " worldly asceticism " and in a concise note states that the phrase " means asceticism practiced within the world as contrasted with *ausserweltliche Askese,* which withdraws from the world (for

instance, into a monastery) ." (*The Protestant Ethic*, tr. by Talcott Parsons, pp. 193–194.) On the other hand, W. Montgomery, in his translation of *Die Bedeutung des Protestantismus,*
first suggested " intramundane asceticism " (*Protestantism and
Progress*, pp. 80–81, n. 1) , which is characteristically adopted
in the translation of *The Social Teachings*. Both of these suggestions I find wanting, particularly the latter, which is far too
abstract to carry the burden of Troeltsch's point.

111. Within this immediate context Troeltsch formulates
these two points in two ways. As first stated, this " *doppelten
Bedeutung* " entails " *metaphysische Weltverurteilung* " and
" *rationelle Sinnlichkeitsdisziplin* " (*G.S.* I, p. 647; cf. *ET* II,
p. 605; cf. *supra*, pp. 128–129) . As he proceeds to build on the
point in distinguishing between Lutheran and Calvinistic
asceticism, the two tendencies are formulated as " *die meta-
physisch-gefühlsmässige Entwertung der Sündenwelt und die
methodische Disziplinierung der Sinnlichkeit* " (*G.S.* I, p. 648;
cf. *ET* II, p. 606) . Clearly the latter is the more fluid, and it
is the one that informs Troeltsch's elaboration. On the one
hand, there is a depreciation of the world that is both metaphysical and emotional, both ontological and evaluative —
and this colors Lutheranism's version of this-worldly asceticism. On the other hand there is a methodical disciplining of
life — and so one must put it, since to translate literally and
read " a methodical disciplining of the sensual " is quite misleading in English. This typifies Calvinism's version of this-
worldly asceticism.

112. *G.S.* I, p. 648 (Olive Wyon, in her paraphrase, omits
this; cf. *ET* II, p. 606.)

113. *G.S.* I, p. 648; cf. *ET* II, p. 606.

114. *G.S.* I, p. 649; cf. *ET* II, p. 607.

115. *G.S.* I, p. 649; cf. *ET* II, p. 607.

116. *G.S.* I, p. 667; cf. *ET* II, p. 617. For another of
Troeltsch's ways of characterizing this, cf. *supra*, p. 121.

117. *G.S.* I, p. 667, my italics; cf. *ET* II, p. 617.

118. *G.S.* I, p. 627; cf. *ET* II, p. 593.

119. *G.S.* I, p. 625, Troeltsch's section heading; cf. *ET* II,
p. 590.

120. *G.S.* I, p. 625; cf. *ET* II, p. 591.

121. *G.S.* I, p. 625; cf. *ET* II, p. 591.

122. *G.S.* I, pp. 628–629; cf. *ET* II, p. 593.

123. Troeltsch clarified the relationship between himself and Weber in this connection in a long note attending his own delineation of *ascetic Protestantism;* cf. *G.S.* I, p. 950, n. 510; *ET* II, pp. 986–987, n. 510.

124. Cf. *supra,* p. 128.

125. *G.S.* I, p. 733; cf. *ET* II, p. 656.

126. *G.S.* I, p. 733; cf. *ET* II, p. 656.

127. *G.S.* I, pp. 733 ff.; cf. *ET* II, pp. 656 ff.

128. *G.S.* I, p. 792; cf. *ET* II, p. 689.

129. *G.S.* I, p. 793; cf. *ET* II, p. 690.

130. *G.S.* I, p. 734; cf. *ET* II, pp. 656–657.

131. *G.S.* I, p. 740; cf. *ET* II, p. 661.

132. *G.S.* I, p. 739; cf. *ET* II, p. 660.

133. *G.S.* I, p. 793; cf. *ET* II, p. 690.

134. *G.S.* I, p. 793; cf. *ET* II, p. 690.

135. *G.S.* I, p. 793; cf. *ET* II, p. 690.

136. *G.S.* I, p. 793; cf. *ET* II, p. 690.

137. *G.S.* I, p. 733; cf. *ET* II, p. 656.

138. *G.S.* I, p. 733; cf. *ET* II, p. 656.

139. *G.S.* I, p. 757; cf. *ET* II, p. 670.

140. *G.S.* I, p. 757; cf. *ET* II, p. 670.

141. *G.S.* I, pp. 948–949; cf. *ET* II, pp. 807–808. The passage is difficult to render in English with the same impact that it has in the original: " *So ergibt sich aus der puritanischen und freikirchlichen Entwicklung des Calvinismus einerseits, aus der Verbürgerlichung des Täufertums und aus der Verkirchlichung der pietistischen Sekten anderseits jene Gesamtgruppe des Protestantismus, die bereits oben als ' asketischer Protestantismus' bezeichnet worden ist, im Unterschiede vom Luthertum und vom Katholizismus."*

142. *G.S.* I, pp. 793–794; cf. *ET* II, pp. 690–691.

143. *G.S.* I, p. 984; cf. *ET* II, pp. 1011–1012.

144. *G.S.* I, p. 985; cf. *ET* II, p. 1012.

145. Cf. *supra,* pp. 116–118.

146. *G.S.* I, p. 967; cf. *ET* II, p. 993; cf. *supra,* p. 116.

147. Cf. *supra,* p. 117.

148. *G.S.* I, p. 420; cf. *ET* II, p. 377.

149. *G.S.* I, p. 418; cf. *ET* II, p. 376.

150. *G.S.* I, p. 420; cf. *ET* II, p. 377.

151. *G.S.* I, p. 797; cf. *ET* II, p. 693.

152. *G.S.* I, p. 861; cf. *ET* II, p. 740.

153. *G.S.* I, p. 850; cf. *ET* II, pp. 730–731.

154. Cf. *supra*, pp. 116–118 and 141.

155. *G.S.* I, pp. 960–961; cf. *ET* II, pp. 816–817.

156. *G.S.* I, p. 864; cf. *ET* II, p. 743.

157. *G.S.* I, p. 864; cf. *ET* II, p. 743.

158. *G.S.* I, p. 865; cf. *ET* II, p. 744.

159. *G.S.* I, p. 865; cf. *ET* II, pp. 744–745.

160. *G.S.* I, p. 940; cf. *ET* II, p. 800.

161. *G.S.* I, p. 941; cf. *ET* II, p. 801.

162. *G.S.* I, p. 424; cf. *ET* I, p. 381.

163. *G.S.* I, pp. 424–425; cf. *ET* I, p. 381.

164. *G.S.* I, pp. 938–939; cf. *ET* II, pp. 798–799.

165. Cf. *supra*, p. 140.

166. *G.S.* I, p. 981; cf. *ET* II, p. 1008.

167. *G.S.* I, p. 981; cf. *ET* II, p. 1008.

168. *G.S.* I, p. 982; cf. *ET* II, p. 1009.

169. *G.S.* I, p. 985; cf. *ET* II, pp. 1012–1013.

170. Cf. *supra*, p. 150.

171. *G.S.* I, p. 975; cf. *ET* II, pp. 1001–1002.

172. Cf. *supra*, p. 89.

Chapter 6. The Collapse of Troeltsch's Theology

1. As was clear in the conclusion of the discussion of *Der Historismus und seine Probleme,* there is a conclusive case for the view that Troeltsch never considered himself as having abandoned finally the basic concerns of theology; cf. *supra,* p. 87. This point will become even more clear as the present chapter unfolds.

2. *G.S. I,* p. viii; cf. *ET* I, p. 19; cf. *supra,* Chapter 1, n. 6.

3. *Glaubenslehre von Ernst Troeltsch,* Nach Heidelberger Vorlesungen aus den Jahren 1911 und 1912, mit einem Vorwort von Marta Troeltsch (München und Leipzig: Verlag von Duncker & Humblot, 1925). Note especially the "Vorwort"

by Marta Troeltsch, pp. v–vi, and "Vorbemerkungen" by Gertrud von le Fort, pp. ix–x.

4. The article was included in *Gesammelte Schriften,* II, pp. 500–524. The English translation was published in *The American Journal of Theology,* Vol. XVII, No. 1 (January, 1913), pp. 1–21; though a translator is not named, it seems clearly evident that this was not Troeltsch's English (cf. p. 1, n. 1, and p. 13, n. 1). Furthermore, it is likewise apparent that he extended the article somewhat for inclusion in the *Gesammelte Schriften,* even though the appearance of the journal issue and that of *G.S.* II were separated only by a matter of months (the Foreword of *G.S.* II is dated April 8, 1913). The English version does not include the last four pages of the definitive form of the article. Cf. *The American Journal of Theology,* XVII, p. 21, and *G.S.* II, pp. 519 ff.

5. Interestingly enough the translation for the journal does not indicate Troeltsch's dissatisfaction with the English term "comparative religion." Troeltsch himself, at least in *G.S.* II, p. 500, n. 35, called attention to the fact that the term "*religionsgeschichtliche*" does not exist in English. In its place "the unfortunate expression 'comparative religion' has been coined." The German term is impossible to render in English. It is an adjective derived from the noun "*Religionsgeschichte.*" The noun is readily translated "History of Religion," but one cannot put this into an English adjective apart from circumlocution which would be even more awkward than just using the German term itself. Thus the "*religionsgeschichtliche Schule*" is that school of thought which is generated by the discipline of the history of religions. A "*religionsgeschichtliche Dogmatik*" is a theology that takes its leads from this discipline. To try to suggest this by fabricated English terms such as either "religio-historical" or "historico-religious" is useless. For the purposes of our discussion, there seems to be no alternative better than simply using the term "*religionsgeschichtliche*" itself (thus concurring with the editors of *The American Journal of Theology;* cf. Vol. XVII, p. 1, editors' note).

6. *G.S.* II, p. 500; cf. *Am. Jour. of Theol.,* XVII, p. 1.

7. We have already elaborated this as one of the decisive

elements of the methodology informing *The Social Teachings;* cf. *supra,* pp. 35 ff.

8. Cf. *supra,* pp. 152–153.

9. For our prior consideration of the first of these, cf. *supra,* pp. 21 ff.; for the second, cf. *supra,* pp. 93 ff.

10. *Die wissenschaftliche Lage,* p. 15.

11. *Ibid.,* p. 22.

12. *Ibid.,* pp. 23–24.

13. "Protestantisches Christentum und Kirche in der Neuzeit," in *Die Kultur der Gegenwart,* herausgegeben von Paul Hinneberg (Berlin and Leipzig: Druck und Verlag von B. G. Teubner, 1906), pp. 273, 287, 294, 317, 334, 362, 363, 372, 373, 377, 422, 425, 427, and 449.

14. *Ibid.,* p. 372.

15. Cf. *supra,* pp. 123–124.

16. *G.S.* I, pp. 350–351; cf. *ET* I, 322. It should be noted that the concept does find occasional use in the first chapter of *The Social Teachings,* but this use is characteristically peripheral. (Cf., e.g., *G.S.* I, pp. 69, 79, 90, and 116.) The concept does not play its decisive role until the discussion of medieval Christendom begins, for the self-evident reason that only then does the positive relationship with the world begin to take shape in terms of explicit social thought. In this connection one must also note the problem generated by the English translation. There is a tendency for the conventional negative usage of the term " compromise " to be employed, with the result that the term itself occurs where Troeltsch himself does *not* use it. (For example, cf. *G.S.* I, p. 372, with *ET* I, p. 339, where Troeltsch's " *Konnivenz* " is rendered " compromise "; or *G.S.* I, p. 423, with *ET* I, p. 379, where Troeltsch's " *Konzessionen* " is rendered " compromise.") Troeltsch himself is to blame for this, since the concept is ambiguous and he never gives it direct attention until a passage in one of his last writings. Even so, given the use to which he puts the term, it should be used exclusively as he used it. As a general rule, one may assume that wherever the term has an obviously pejorative meaning in the translation, Troeltsch himself did not use the word " *Kompromiss.* " The facts of the case are similar in W. Montgomery's translation of *Die Bedeutung des Protestantismus für die Ent-*

stehung der modernen Welt (1911). Troeltsch used the term only three times in this work (cf. pp. 11, 39, and 67). In addition to these three instances, Montgomery used the term four times in the closing phases of the work (cf. *Protestantism and Progress,* pp. 157, 164, 176, and 186). Troeltsch did not use the term in any of these instances (cf. *Die Bedeutung des Protestantismus,* pp. 78, 81, 88, and 92).

17. *G.S.* I, p. 359; cf. *ET* I, p. 329.

18. *G.S.* I, p. 359; cf. *ET* I, p. 330.

19. *G.S.* I, p. 370; cf. *ET* I, p. 337.

20. Cf. *supra,* p. 120. The passage is in *G.S.* I, p. 72; cf. *ET* I, pp. 82–83.

21. *G.S.* I, p. 507; cf. *ET* II, p. 511.

22. *G.S.* I, p. 505; cf. *ET* II, p. 510.

23. *G.S.* I, p. 507; cf. *ET* II, p. 511.

24. Cf. *supra,* p. 122. The passage is in *G.S.* I, p. 371; cf. *ET* I, p. 338.

25. *G.S.* I, p. 947; cf. *ET* II, 806.

26. Cf. *supra,* p. 136.

27. *G.S.* I, p. 973; cf. *ET* II, pp. 999–1000.

28. Cf. *supra,* p. 152. The passage is in *G.S.* I, p. 975. cf. *ET* II, pp. 1001–1002.

29. For examples other than we have considered of Troeltsch's use of the concept of compromise *before* the writing of *The Social Teachings,* the following may be consulted: *Vernunft und Offenbarung bei Johann Gerhard und Melanchthon,* p. 213; *Die christliche Weltanschauung und ihre Gegenströmungen* (1894), *G.S.* II, p. 286; *Religion und Kirche* (1895), *G.S.* II, p. 181; *Grundprobleme der Ethik* (a discussion of Wilhelm Herrmann's *Ethik,* 1902), *G.S.* II, p. 663, and p. 667, n. 59; " Das Historische in Kants Religionsphilosophie," *Kantstudien. Philosophische Zeitschrift,* IX (Berlin: Verlag von Reuther und Reichard, 1904), p. 97; *Der Modernismus* (Troeltsch's reaction to Pius X's *Pascendi dominici gregis,* 1909), *G.S.* II, pp. 52, 55; *Die Zukunftsmöglichkeiten des Christentums im Verhältnis zur modernen Philosophie* (1910), *G.S.* II, pp. 839, 852, 854, 855, and 859; *Religiöser Individualismus und Kirche* (1911), *G.S.* II, pp. 126–128; and *Die Kirche im Leben der Gegenwart* (1911), *G.S.* II, p. 104.

30. Cf. *supra,* pp. 84 f.

31. Cf. *supra,* p. 87.

32. For examples of Troeltsch's use of the concept of compromise *after* the writing of *The Social Teachings,* other than the lecture to be considered in our discussion, the following may be consulted: *Logos und Mythos in Theologie und Religionsphilosophie* (1913), *G.S.* II, p. 816; *Das christliche Naturrecht* (1913), *G.S.* IV, pp. 160, 161, and 164; *Die alte Kirche* (1916–1917), *G.S.* IV, pp. 91, 106, 107, and 111; *Die Sozialphilosophie des Christentums* (Bücherlei der christlichen Welt; Gotha: Leopold Klotz Verlag, 1922 [not to be confused with another article under this title, written in 1911, and later included in *G.S.* IV under a new title, *Epochen und Typen der Sozialphilosophie des Christentums*]), pp. 9, 13, 17–19, and 28; and two of the lectures for England, *Die Personlichkeits- und Gewissensmoral,* and *Der Gemeingeist,* in *Der Historismus und seine Ueberwindung* (details given in n. 33, below), pp. 18–21, and 47.

33. *Der Historismus und seine Ueberwindung,* fünf Vorträge von Ernst Troeltsch, eingeleitet von Friedrich von Hügel-Kensington (Berlin: Pan Verlag Rolf Heise, 1924), p. 101. This source will hereafter be designated *D.H.s.U.* For the English translation, cf. *Christian Thought: Its History and Application,* ed. and with an introduction and index by Baron F. von Hügel (A Living Age Book, published by Meridian Books, Inc., 1957 [originally published, London: University of London Press, Ltd., 1923]), p. 172. This source will hereafter be designated *C.T.*

34. *D.H.s.U.,* p. 104; cf. *C.T.,* p. 177.

35. *D.H.s.U.,* p. 105; cf. *C.T.,* p. 178.

36. For some unexplained reason the German text of the lecture stops with the paragraph containing the passages noted in the three preceding notes. The final three paragraphs of the English text occur in the translation only. This may be because the words are addressed specifically to the English audience. One cannot help wondering, however, whether Baron von Hügel, the editor of both the translation (in 1923) and the German text (in 1924), had something to do with this. Notice the title for the German edition. This was not

Troeltsch's title! (Neither, for that matter, was the title of the English edition, as Baron von Hügel explains at some length in *C.T.*, p. 11.) As we know, Troeltsch never arrived at the conquest (*Ueberwindung*) of historical relativism!

37. *C.T.*, pp. 178–179.

38. We have had this point before us many times. Two of its choice expressions fix the continuity of this conviction throughout Troeltsch's thought. Cf. *supra*, p. 105, for the expression of this conviction in the closing phases of *Die Bedeutung des Protestantismus für die Entstehung der modernen Welt.* Cf. *supra*, p. 87, for its expression in 1922 in *Meine Bücher*.

39. The article was included in *Gesammelte Schriften* II, pp. 754–768. A representative early example of Troeltsch's use of the concept may be found in " Das Historische in Kants Religionsphilosophie," *Kantstudien. Philosophische Zeitschrift,* IX (Berlin: Verlag von Reuther und Reichard, 1904) , pp. 21–154, noting especially pp. 48–49. Another such example occurs in Troeltsch's *Psychologie und Erkenntnistheorie in der Religionswissenschaft* (Tübingen: Verlag von J. C. B. Mohr [Paul Siebeck], 1905) , pp. 46–55. Troeltsch himself calls attention to these in *G.S.* II, p. 756, n. 86.

40. *G.S.* II, p. 755.

41. *G.S.* II, p. 755.

42. *G.S.* II, p. 757.

43. *G.S.* II, p. 757.

44. *G.S.* II, p. 383.

45. Cf. *supra*, p. 66.

46. Cf. *supra*, pp. 84 f.

47. Cf. *supra*, p. 166.

48. The article has been noted in the introduction to this chapter; cf. *supra*, nn. 4 and 5. Throughout the following discussion, references to the German text of the article will simply be indicated by *G.S.* II; references to the English translation (in *The American Journal of Theology,* Vol. XVII, No. 1 [January, 1913], pp. 1–21) will be indicated by *Journal*.

49. *G.S.* II, p. 505; cf. *Journal*, p. 6.

50. *G.S.* II, p. 508; cf. *Journal*, p. 9.

51. *G.S.* II, p. 509; cf. *Journal*, p. 10.

52. *G.S.* II, p. 509; cf. *Journal*, p. 10.

53. *G.S.* II, p. 510; cf. *Journal,* p. 11.

54. *G.S.* II, p. 510; cf. *Journal,* p. 11.

55. *G.S.* II, p. 512; cf. *Journal,* p. 13.

56. *G.S.* II, pp. 513–514; cf. *Journal,* p. 15.

57. *G.S.* II, p. 514; cf. *Journal,* p. 16.

58. *G.S.* II, p. 515; cf. *Journal,* p. 17.

59. *G.S.* II, p. 515; cf. *Journal,* p. 16.

60. Cf. *supra,* pp. 141 ff.

61. These were " Die christliche Weltanschauung und ihre Gegenströmungen " (1893–1894), which appeared in the columns of the *Zeitschrift für Theologie und Kirche,* and was later included in *G.S.* II (pp. 227–327), and " Die Selbständigkeit der Religion " (1895–1896), which appeared in the same periodical. These are both noted in *G.S.* II, p. 227, n. 11.

62. Cf. *supra,* n. 33, for the details concerning the sources for this lecture. Especially in connection with this present discussion it is interesting to note that in his prefatory note to the English translation of the lectures for England, Baron von Hügel records that each of these lectures was read before the university groups Troeltsch would have addressed; this, in fact, is the reason why the English translation was published before the German text. Cf. *C.T.,* pp. 7–8.

63. Baron von Hügel indicates this in the introduction to the German text of the lectures (cf. *D.H.s.U.,* p. vi) ; for some reason he made no note of this in the introduction to the translation.

64. *D.H.s.U.,* p. 63; cf. *C.T.,* p. 36.

65. *D.H.s.U.,* p. 66; cf. *C.T.,* p. 40.

66. *D.H.s.U.,* pp. 70–71; cf. *C.T.,* p. 46.

67. *D.H.s.U.,* p. 71; cf. *C.T.,* p. 46.

68. *D.H.s.U.,* p. 71; cf. *C.T.,* p. 47.

69. *D.H.s.U.,* pp. 71–72; cf. *C.T.,* p. 47.

70. *D.H.s.U.,* p. 72; cf. *C.T.,* pp. 47–48.

71. *D.H.s.U.,* p. 73; cf. *C.T.,* p. 49.

72. *D.H.s.U.,* pp. 73–74; cf. *C.T.,* pp. 49–50. Once again we must question a translation. Troeltsch's phrase " *Der Selbsterschliessung Gottes im Kern des Gewissens* " has been rendered " God's revelation of himself in human hearts and lives." This both adds to and detracts from Troeltsch's formulation. *Rev-*

elation and *accessibility* are not quite the same! And " the core of conscience " is hardly accurately phrased " human hearts and lives "!

73. *D.H.s.U.*, p. 74; cf. *C.T.*, pp. 50–51.

74. Adolf von Harnack's *Das Wesen des Christentums* was published in 1900 (Leipzig: J. C. Hinrichs'sche Buchhandlung); the English translation, *What Is Christianity?* by Thomas Bailey Saunders, was published in 1901 (London: Williams & Norgate, Ltd.; New York: G. P. Putnam's Sons).

75. The essay was included in the second volume of the *Gesammelte Schriften,* pp. 386–451.

76. *G.S.* II, pp. 390–391.

77. *G.S.* II, pp. 391, 393.

78. *G.S.* II, pp. 407 ff.

79. *G.S.* II, pp. 418–422 ff.

80. *G.S.* II, pp. 426–432.

81. *G.S.* II, pp. 432 ff. In all these points we are obviously seeing in germinal form issues that would later be explored at length, and on a much broader scale, in *Der Historismus und seine Probleme.*

82. *G.S.* II, p. 511; cf. *Journal,* p. 12.

83. *G.S.* II, p. 511; cf. *Journal,* p. 12.

84. *G.S.* II, p. 511; cf. *Journal,* p. 12.

85. *G.S.* II, p. 512; cf. *Journal,* p. 13. Our distinction between the description and the definition of the essence of Christianity is not contradicted by the fact that Troeltsch speaks here of a *Wesensbestimmung;* his argument forbids a narrow translation of this term.

86. Cf. *supra,* p. 177.

87. *Die Bedeutung der Geschichtlichkeit Jesu für den Glauben* (Tübingen: Verlag von J. C. B. Mohr [Paul Siebeck], 1911) , p. 1.

88. *Ibid.,* pp. 5–6.

89. *Ibid.,* pp. 18–19.

90. *Ibid.,* p. 25.

91. *Ibid.,* p. 25. Troeltsch advanced this judgment in the context of a penetrating appraisal of Schleiermacher, Ritschl, and Herrmann.

92. *Ibid.,* pp. 26–27.

93. *Ibid.*, p. 27.

94. *Ibid.*, p. 29.

95. *Ibid.*, pp. 31–32.

96. *Ibid.*, p. 33.

97. *Ibid.*, pp. 47–48.

98. *Ibid.*, p. 48.

99. *Ibid.*, pp. 48–49.

100. *Ibid.*, p. 50.

101. *Ibid.*, pp. 50–51.

102. *Ibid.*, p. 51.

103. Cf. *supra*, pp. 155–156, for decisive qualifications of relying on this volume. For an excellent example in the present connection, cf. his idea of "progressive revelation," as this is reported in pp. 40 ff. of the *Glaubenslehre*.

104. Cf. *supra*, p. 24, for our contention that from at least 1900 on, if not earlier, Troeltsch was indeed convinced that the older apologetic is completely gone.

105. Cf. *supra*, p. 187.

106. Cf. *G.S.* II, p. 779, n. 88.

107. *G.S.* II, pp. 787–788.

108. *G.S.* II, pp. 788–789.

109. *G.S.* II, pp. 789–790.

110. *G.S.* II, p. 791.

111. *G.S.* II, pp. 791–792.

112. *G.S.* II, pp. 793–794.

113. *G.S.* II, pp. 796–797.

114. *G.S.* II, p. 797.

115. *G.S.* II, p. 797.

116. *G.S.* II, pp. 801–802.

117. *G.S.* II, p. 801.

118. Cf. *supra*, p. 187.

119. *G.S.* II, p. 804.

120. Cf. *supra*, pp. 179 f.

121. Cf. *supra*, pp. 82–83.

122. *D.H.s.U.*, p. 75; cf. *C.T.*, p. 51.

123. *D.H.s.U.*, pp. 75–76; cf. *C.T.*, pp. 51, 53.

124. *D.H.s.U.*, p. 76; cf. *C.T.*, p. 53.

125. *D.H.s.U.*, p. 75; cf. *C.T.*, p. 52.

126. *D.H.s.U.*, p. 80; cf. *C.T.*, pp. 58–59.

127. *D.H.s.U.*, p. 81; cf. *C.T.*, p. 60.

128. Cf. *supra*, p. 151. The passage is in *G.S.* I, p. 985; cf. *ET* II, p. 1012.

129. *D.H.s.U.*, p. 81; cf. *C.T.*, p. 60.

130. We began to call attention to this in reflecting briefly on the *fourth task* as articulated in the article on the structure of theology. Cf. *supra*, p. 178.

131. Cf. *supra*, pp. 172–174.

132. *D.H.s.U.*, pp. 77–78; cf. *C.T.*, p. 55.

133. *D.H.s.U.*, pp. 82–83; cf. *C.T.*, p. 62.

134. Cf. *supra*, p. 180. The passage is on *D.H.s.U.*, p. 71; cf. *C.T.*, p. 47.

135. *D.H.s.U.*, p. 83; cf. *C.T.*, p. 63.

136. *D.H.s.U.*, p. 83; cf. *C.T.*, p. 63.

CHAPTER 7. NEW POSSIBILITIES

1. Cf. *supra*, p. 14. Cf. the letter dated June 8, 1944, in Dietrich Bonhoeffer, *Letters and Papers from Prison*, ed. by Eberhard Bethge, tr. by Reginald H. Fuller (published originally as *Prisoner for God* [The Macmillan Company, 1962]), pp. 194 ff.; cf. Dietrich Bonhoeffer, *Widerstand und Ergebung*, herausgegeben von Eberhard Bethge (Munich: Chr. Kaiser Verlag, 1959), pp. 215 ff.

2. Dietrich Bonhoeffer, *Ethics*, ed. by Eberhard Bethge, tr. by Neville Horton Smith (Library of Philosophy and Theology; The Macmillan Company, 1955), p. 62; cf. Dietrich Bonhoeffer, *Ethik*, zusammengestellt und herausgegeben von Eberhard Bethge (Munich: Chr. Kaiser Verlag, 1958, Vierte Auflage [Erste Auflage, 1949]), p. 61, and *ibid.*, Sechste Auflage (1963), pp. 208–209.

3. Bonhoeffer, *Ethics*, p. 63; cf. *Ethik* (1958 [1949]), p. 62, and *Ethik* (1963), p. 210.

4. Bonhoeffer, *Ethics*, p. 65; cf. *Ethik* (1958 [1949]), p. 64, and *Ethik* (1963), p. 212.

5. Cf. *supra*, Chapter 2, n. 33. For the passage, cf. *G.S.* III, p. 369, n. 190.

6. Cf. *supra,* Chapter 3, n. 64. For the passage, cf. *G.S.* III, p. 102.

7. Cf. *supra,* pp. 182 ff.

8. Cf. *supra,* p. 185.

9. We have seen the thrust of Troeltsch's thought in this direction at many points. For two specific instances, cf. *supra,* pp. 71 and 101.

10. Paul L. Lehmann, *Ethics in a Christian Context* (New York: Harper & Row, Publishers, Inc.; London: SCM Press, Ltd. [Library of Philosophy and Theology], 1963), p. 320. To be sure, Lehmann's work unfolds against a broader background than simply the thought of Karl Barth. He explicitly indicates as decisive figures Emil Brunner, Anders Nygren, Reinhold Niebuhr, and Dietrich Bonhoeffer, along with Barth (cf. pp. 43–44). However, it is primarily in terms of moving out from Barth's thought that the argument of this work takes its rise. Cf. the entire Chapter IX, "The Insufficiency of Philosophical Ethics" (pp. 268–284), with its juxtaposition of Schleiermacher and Barth, and its memorable crystallization of Barth's contribution to theological ethics (cf. especially pp. 273–277).

11. The phrase is the title of Chapter V of the book (*Ethics in a Christian Context,* pp. 124 ff.), but we are using it to typify the work as a whole.

12. Lehmann, *Ethics in a Christian Context,* pp. 285 ff. "The Question of Conscience" is the title of the third and final part of the book.

13. *Ibid.,* pp. 287–288.

14. Cf. *ibid.,* pp. 148, 223–224, and 346.

15. *Ibid.,* p. 148, n. 1.

16. Cf. *supra,* pp. 152–153, 158, and 165.

17. Lehmann, *op. cit.,* p. 283.

18. Gerhard Ebeling, *Das Wesen des christlichen Glaubens* (Tübingen: J. C. B. Mohr [Paul Siebeck], 1959); tr. by Ronald Gregor Smith, *The Nature of Faith* (Muhlenberg Press, 1961). The quoted phrase is from the Foreword.

19. Ebeling, *The Nature of Faith,* p. 20; cf. *Das Wesen,* pp. 16–17.

20. Cf. *supra*, pp. 184–185.

21. Ebeling, *The Nature of Faith,* p. 150; cf. *Das Wesen,* p. 195.

22. Cf. Ebeling, *Das Wesen,* p. 195.

23. Ebeling, *Word and Faith,* tr. by James W. Leitch (London: SCM Press, Ltd. [The Preacher's Library]; Philadelphia: Fortress Press, 1963), p. 414; cf. *Wort und Glaube* (Tübingen: J. C. B. Mohr [Paul Siebeck], 1960), p. 437.

24. Ebeling, *Word and Faith,* p. 428; cf. *Wort und Glaube,* pp. 451–452.

25. The word "contextual" is, of course, central for Lehmann, and it is from his work that this use is derived. There is, however, a shade of difference between his use of the term and this one, for which he is not responsible.

26. Martin E. Marty, *The New Shape of American Religion* (Harper & Brothers, 1959), p. ix; cf. also p. 168.

27. Martin E. Marty, *Second Chance for American Protestants* (Harper & Row, Publishers, Inc., 1963), pp. 1, 2, and 3.

28. *Ibid.,* p. 22.

29. *Ibid.,* p. 31.

30. *Ibid.,* p. 32.

31. *Ibid.,* p. 31.

32. *Ibid.,* p. 58.

33. *Ibid.,* p. 59.

34. *Ibid.,* p. 43.

35. *Ibid.,* p. 81.

36. *Ibid.,* p. 81.

37. *Ibid.,* p. 84.

38. *Ibid.,* p. 97.

39. *Ibid.,* p. 85.

40. *Ibid.,* p. 68.

41. *Ibid.,* p. 72.

42. *Ibid.,* p. 68.

43. *Ibid.,* p. 85.

44. *Ibid.,* p. 123.

45. Peter L. Berger, *The Precarious Vision: A Sociologist Looks at Social Fictions and Christian Faith* (Doubleday & Company, Inc., 1961), pp. 48 ff.

46. *Ibid.,* pp. 54 ff.

47. *Ibid.*, p. 17.

48. *Ibid.*, p. 66.

49. *Ibid.*, p. 159.

50. *Ibid.*, p. 204.

51. *Ibid.*, p. 214.

52. *Ibid.*, p. 215.

53. *Ibid.*, p. 215.

54. Harvey Cox, *The Secular City: Secularization and Urbanization in Theological Perspective* (The Macmillan Company, 1965) , p. 2.

55. *Ibid.*, pp. 21 ff.

56. *Ibid.*, pp. 149 ff.

57. *Ibid.*, p. 241. This is Cox's translation of Bonhoeffer, *Gesammelte Schriften*, IV, p. 606.

58. *Ibid.*, p. 268. This is the closing paragraph of the book.

59. Troeltsch, *G.S.* I, p. 714, n. 388; cf. *ET II*, pp. 915–916, n. 388.

Bibliography

◆ ◆

Ernst Troeltsch

NOTE: Works that exist in English translation are designated by an asterisk (*); the details concerning each of these are given separately under the heading " Works in English Translation."

Gesammelte Schriften, I–IV. Tübingen: Verlag von J. C. B. Mohr (Paul Siebeck), 1912–1925:
  *Bd. I (1912), *Die Soziallehren der christlichen Kirchen und Gruppen.*
  Bd. II (1913), *Zur religiösen Lage, Religionsphilosophie und Ethik.*
  Bd. III (1922), *Der Historismus und seine Probleme.*
  Bd. IV (1925), herausgegeben von Hans Baron, *Aufsätze zur Geistesgeschichte und Religionssoziologie.*

Works Not Included in the Gesammelte Schriften:
  NOTE: *G.S.* IV, pp. 861–872, contains an exhaustive, chronologically arranged bibliography of Troeltsch's writings, by Hans Baron.
Die Absolutheit des Christentums und die Religionsgeschichte. Tübingen: Verlag von J. C. B. Mohr (Paul Siebeck), 1902; 2d ed., 1912.
" Adolf v. Harnack und Ferd. Christ. v. Bauer," *Festgabe von Fachgenossen und Freuden A. von Harnack, zum siebzigsten Geburtstag dargebracht.* Tübingen: Verlag von J. C. B. Mohr (Paul Siebeck), 1921. Pp. 282–291.

"Ein Apfel vom Baume Kierkegaards," *Die christliche Welt*, No. 11 (1921), cols. 186–190.

Augustin, die christliche Antike und das Mittelalter: Im Anschluss an die Schrift " De Civitate Dei." Munich and Berlin: Druck und Verlag von R. Oldenbourg, 1915.

Die Bedeutung der Geschichtlichkeit Jesu für den Glauben. Tübingen: Verlag von J. C. B. Mohr (Paul Siebeck), 1911.

*Die Bedeutung des Protestantismus für die Entstehung der modernen Welt. Munich and Berlin: Druck and Verlag von R. Oldenbourg, 1906; 2d ed., 1911.

"Geschichte und Metaphysik," *Zeitschrift für Theologie und Kirche,* VIII (1898), pp. 1–69.

Glaubenslehre von Ernst Troeltsch, Nach Heidelberger Vorlesungen aus den Jahren 1911 und 1912, mit einem Vorwort von Marta Troeltsch. Munich and Leipzig: Verlag von Duncker & Humblot, 1925.

" Das Historische in Kants Religionsphilosophie," *Kantstudien. Philosophische Zeitschrift,* IX. Berlin: Verlag von Reuther und Reichard, 1904. Pp. 21–154.

*Der Historismus und seine Ueberwindung, fünf Vorträge von Ernst Troeltsch, eingeleitet von Friedrich von Hügel-Kensington. Berlin: Pan Verlag Rolf Heise, 1924.

**" Naturrecht und Humanität in der Weltpolitik," in *Deutscher Geist und Westeuropa.* Tübingen, 1925.

Politische Ethik und Christentum. Göttingen: Vandenhoeck und Ruprecht, 1904.

" *Protestantisches Christentum und Kirche in der Neuzeit,"* in *Die Kultur der Gegenwart,* herausgegeben von Paul Hinneberg. Berlin and Leipzig: Druck und Verlag von B. G. Teubner, 1906; 2d ed., 1909. Pp. 253–458.

Psychologie und Erkenntnistheorie in der Religionswissenschaft. Tübingen: Verlag von J. C. B. Mohr (Paul Siebeck), 1905.

" Religion," in *Das Jahr 1913,* herausgegeben von D. Sarason. Leipzig and Berlin: Druck und Verlag B. G. Teubner, 1913.

" Religionsphilosophie," *Die Philosophie im Beginn des zwangzigsten Jahrhunderts: Festschrift für Kuno Fischer,* herausgegeben von W. Windelband. Zweite Auflage, Heidelberg: Carl Winters Universitätsbuchhandlung, 1907. Pp. 423 ff.

" Die Selbständigkeit der Religion," I–II, *Zeitschrift für Theologie und Kirche*, No. 5 (1895), pp. 316–436; III–IV, *Zeitschrift für Theologie und Kirche*, No. 6 (1896). Pp. 71–110 and 167–218.

Die Sozialphilosophie des Christentums. Bücherlei der christlichen Welt; Gotha: Leopold Klotz Verlag, 1922.

Die Trennung von Staat und Kirche. Tübingen: Verlag von J. C. B. Mohr (Paul Siebeck), 1907.

Vernunft und Offenbarung bei Johann Gerhard und Melanchthon: Untersuchung zur Geschichte der altprotestantischen Theologie. Göttingen: Verlag von Vandenhoeck und Ruprecht, 1891.

Die wissenschaftliche Lage und ihre Anforderungen an die Theologie. Tübingen: Verlag von J. C. B. Mohr (Paul Siebeck), 1900.

" Zur Religionsphilosophie," *Kantstudien. Philosophische Zeitschrift*, XXIII. Berlin: Verlag von Reuther und Reichard, 1919. Pp. 65–76.

Articles in *Die Religion in Geschichte und Gegenwart*, herausgegeben von F. M. Schiele und L. Zscharnack, Vols. II, III, IV, and V. Tübingen: Verlag von J. C. B. Mohr (Paul Siebeck), 1910, 1912, 1913, and 1913, respectively:

" Dogma "	Vol. II, columns 105–106
" Dokmatik "	Vol. II, columns 106–109
" Erlösung"	Vol. II, columns 481–488
" Eschatologie "	Vol. II, columns 622–632
" Gericht Gottes "	Vol. II, columns 1320–1321
" Gesetz "	Vol. II, columns 1373–1387
" Glaube "	Vol. II, columns 1437–1447
" Glaube und Geschichte "	Vol. II, columns 1447–1456
" Gnade Gottes "	Vol. II, columns 1469–1474
" Gnadenmittel "	Vol. II, columns 1475–1476
" Heilstatsachen "	Vol. II, columns 2066–2067
" Kirche: III. Dogmatisch "	
	Vol. III, columns 1147–1155

" Offenbarung "   Vol. IV, columns 918–922
" Prädestination "   Vol. IV, columns 1706–1712
" Theodizee "   Vol. V, columns 1186–1192

Works in English Translation:
Christian Thought: Its History and Application, ed. and with
    an introduction and index by Baron F. von Hügel. A
    Living Age Book, published by Meridian Books, Inc.,
    1957. (Originally published, London: University of Lon-
    don Press, Ltd., 1923.) German text: *Der Historismus und
    seine Ueberwindung.*
" The Dogmatics of the ' religionsgeschichtliche Schule,' "
    The American Journal of Theology, Vol. XVII, No. 1
    (January, 1913), pp. 1–21. German text: *Gesammelte
    Schriften* II, pp. 500–524.
" The Ideas of Natural Law and Humanity in World Politics,"
    in Otto Gierke, *Natural Law and the Theory of Society,
    1500 to 1800,* tr. and with an introduction by Ernest
    Barker. Beacon Press, Inc., 1957 (first published by Cam-
    bridge University Press, in two volumes, 1934), Appendix
    I, pp. 199–222. The German text is in *Deutscher Geist
    und Westeuropa* (Tübingen, 1925).
Protestantism and Progess, tr. by W. Montgomery. London:
    Williams & Norgate, and New York: G. P. Putnam's Sons,
    1912; Boston: Beacon Paperback, Beacon Press, Inc., 1958.
    Translation of *Die Bedeutung des Protestantismus für
    die Entstehung der modernen Welt* (1911).
The Social Teaching of the Christian Churches, tr. by Olive
    Wyon. London: George Allen & Unwin, Ltd., and New
    York: The Macmillan Company, 1931, second impression,
    1949, in two volumes; Harper & Brothers (reprinted by
    arrangement), with an introduction by H. Richard Nie-
    buhr, in two volumes (Harper Torchbook, The Cloister
    Library, Nos. TB 71 and TB 72), 1960.
Articles in the *Encyclopedia of Religion and Ethics,* ed. by
    James Hastings, Vols. IV, VI, and VII. New York: Charles
    Scribner's Sons, and Edinburgh: T. & T. Clark, 1912,
    1914, and 1915, respectively:
        " Contingency "   Vol. IV, pp. 87–89

"Free-Thought"   Vol. VI, pp. 120–123
"Historiography"   Vol. VI, pp. 716–723
"Idealism"   Vol. VII, pp. 89–95
"Kant"   Vol. VII, pp. 653–659

Secondary Sources:

Bainton, Roland H., " Ernst Troeltsch — Thirty Years Later," *Theology Today,* Vol. VIII, No. 1 (April, 1951), pp. 70–96.

" Bibliographical Focus: Ernst Troeltsch," *Journal for the Scientific Study of Religion,* Vol. I, No. 1 (October, 1961), pp. 98–124, and No. 2 (Spring, 1962), pp. 220–225. (Articles by James Luther Adams, Paul Tillich, David Little, Donald E. Miller, David Quarberg, in Vol. I, No. 1; and by Robert Johnson, and Max L. Stackhouse, in Vol. I, No. 2.)

Bodenstein, Walter, *Neige des Historismus, Ernst Troeltsch's Entwicklungsgang.* Gütersloher Verlagshaus Gerd Mohn, 1959.

Diem, Hermann, *Dogmatics,* tr. by Harold Knight (Bd. II of *Theologie als kirchliche Wissenschaft: Handreichung zur Einübung ihre Probleme,* entitled *Dogmatik: Ihr Weg zwischen Historismus und Existenzialismus;* Munich: Chr. Kaiser Verlag, 1955), The Westminster Press, 1959), pp. 4–9, section entitled " The End of Dogmatics in the Work of Ernst Troeltsch."

Ignacio Escribano Alberca, *Die Gewinnung theologischer Normen aus der Geschichte der Religion bei E. Troeltsch* (Münchener theologische Studien, herausgegeben von J. Pascher, K. Mürsdorf, H. Tüchle, II. Systematische Abteilung, 21. Band). Munich: Max Hueber Verlag, 1961.

Frei, Hans W., " The Relation of Faith and History in the Thought of Ernst Troeltsch," *Faith and Ethics: The Theology of H. Richard Niebuhr,* ed. by Paul Ramsey, pp. 53–64. Harper & Brothers, 1957.

Kasch, Wilhelm F., *Die Sozialphilosophie von Ernst Troeltsch* (Beiträge zur historischen Theologie, herausgegeben von Gerhard Ebeling, No. 34). Tübingen: J. C. B. Mohr (Paul

Siebeck) , 1963. (Note Kasch's " Literatur über Troeltsch," pp. 282–283) .

Köhler, Walther, *Ernst Troeltsch*. Tübingen: Verlag von J. C. B. Mohr (Paul Siebeck) , 1941.

Mackintosh, Hugh Ross, *Types of Modern Theology, Schleiermacher to Barth*. London: Nisbet and Co., Ltd., 1937. Chapter VI, " The Theology of Scientific Religious History: Ernst Troeltsch," pp. 181–217.

Mannheim, Karl, " Ernst Troeltsch," *Encyclopedia of the Social Sciences*, ed. by R. A. Seligman and A. Johnson, Vol. XV, pp. 106–107. The Macmillan Company, 1935.

Niebuhr, H. Richard, " Troeltsch, Ernst," *An Encyclopedia of Religion*, ed. by Vergilius Ferm, pp. 795–796. The Philosophical Library, 1945.

Sleigh, R. S., *The Sufficiency of Christianity*, An Enquiry Concerning the Nature and the Modern Possibilities of the Christian Religion, with Special Reference to the Religious Philosophy of Dr. Ernst Troeltsch, intro. by William Fulton. London: James Clarke & Co., Ltd., 1923.

Spiess, Emil, *Die Religionstheorie von Ernst Troeltsch*. Paderborn: F. Schönigh, 1927.

Vermeil, E., *La Pensée religieuse de Troeltsch*. Strasbourg: Librairie Istra, Maison d'Édition de l'Imprimerie Strasbourgeoise, 1922.

Max Weber

Gesammelte Aufsätze zur Religionssoziologie, Bd. I, Dritte, photomechanisch gedruckte Auflage. Tübingen: Verlag von J. C. B. Mohr (Paul Siebeck) , 1934.

Gesammelte Aufsätze zur Wissenschaftslehre. Tübingen: Verlag von J. C. B. Mohr (Paul Siebeck) , 1922.

From Max Weber: Essays in Sociology, tr., ed., with an intro. by H. H. Gerth and C. Wright Mills. Oxford University Press, Inc., 1946.

The Methodology of the Social Sciences, tr. and ed. by Edward A. Shils and Henry A. Finch. The Free Press of Glencoe, 1949.

The Protestant Ethic and the Spirit of Capitalism, tr. by Talcott Parsons, with a Foreword by R. H. Tawney. London: George Allen & Unwin, Ltd., 1930.

The Theory of Social and Economic Organization (Being Part I of *Wirtschaft und Gesellschaft*), tr. by A. R. Henderson and Talcott Parsons, rev. ed., with an intro. by Talcott Parsons. London: William Hodge & Co., Ltd., 1947.

Other Works

Berger, Peter L., *The Noise of Solemn Assemblies: Christian Commitment and the Religious Establishment in America*. Doubleday & Company, Inc., 1961.

―――― *The Precarious Vision: A Sociologist Looks at Social Fictions and Christian Faith*. Doubleday & Company, Inc., 1961.

Bonhoeffer, Dietrich, *Ethics,* ed. by Eberhard Bethge, tr. by Neville Horton Smith (Library of Philosophy and Theology). The Macmillan Company, 1955.

―――― *Ethik,* zusammengestellt und herausgegeben von Eberhard Bethge. Munich: Chr. Kaiser Verlag, 1958; sechste Auflage, 1963.

―――― *Letters and Papers from Prison* (published originally as *Prisoner for God*), ed. by Eberhard Bethge, tr. by Reginald H. Fuller. The Macmillan Company, 1962.

―――― *Widerstand und Ergebung,* herausgegeben von Eberhard Bethge. Munich: Chr. Kaiser Verlag, 1959 (erste Auflage, 1951).

Cox, Harvey, *The Secular City: Secularization and Urbanization in Theological Perspective*. The Macmillan Company, 1965.

Ebeling, Gerhard, *The Nature of Faith,* tr. by Ronald Gregor Smith. Muhlenberg Press, 1961.

―――― *Das Wesen des christlichen Glaubens*. Tübingen: J. C. B. Mohr (Paul Siebeck), 1959.

―――― *Word and Faith,* tr. by James W. Leitch. London: SCM Press, Ltd. (The Preacher's Library); Philadelphia: Fortress Press, 1963.

―――― *Wort und Glaube*. Tübingen: J. C. B. Mohr (Paul Siebeck), 1960.

Lehmann, Paul L., *Ethics in a Christian Context*. New York: Harper & Row, Publishers, Inc.; London: SCM Press, Ltd. (Library of Philosophy and Theology) , 1963.

Marty, Martin E., *The New Shape of American Religion*. Harper & Brothers, 1959.

—— *Second Chance for American Protestants*. Harper & Row, Publishers, Inc., 1963.

Works Cited in Passing

Harnack, Adolf von, *Das Wesen des Christentums*. Leipzig: J. C. Hinrichs'sche Buchhandlung, 1900.

—— *What Is Christianity?*, tr. by Thomas Bailey Saunders. London: Williams & Norgate, Ltd., New York: G. P. Putnam's Sons, 1901.

Hodges, H. A., *The Philosophy of Wilhelm Dilthey*. London: Routledge & Kegan Paul, Ltd., 1952.

—— *Wilhelm Dilthey: An Introduction*. London: Kegan Paul, Trench, Trubner & Co., Ltd., 1944.

Holl, Karl, *The Cultural Significance of the Reformation*, introduction by Wilhelm Pauck, tr. by Karl and Barbara Hertz and John H. Lichtblau. A Living Age Book, published by Meridian Books, Inc., 1959.